D0701444

PIONEER POLICING
IN
SOUTHERN ALBERTA

DEANE OF
THE MOUNTIES

EDITED BY

WILLIAM M. BAKER

Alberta Records Publication Board
HISTORICAL SOCIETY OF ALBERTA
General Editors: David W. Leonard
and David C. Jones

Copyright © 1993
Historical Society of Alberta
Box 4035, Station C
Calgary, AB. T2T 5M9

Printed in Canada

Canadian Cataloguing In Publication Data
  Main entry under title:
  Pioneer policing in southern Alberta

  Co-published by the Alberta Records Publication Board.
  Includes bibliographical references and index.
  ISBN 0-929123-02-6

  1. North West Mounted Police (Canada)—History.
  2. North West Mounted Police (Canada)—Biography.
  3. Deane, R. Burton, 1848-1930.   4. Police—Alberta—History.
  5. Law enforcement —Alberta—History   6. Frontier and pioneer
  life—Alberta.
  I. Deane, R. Burton, 1848-1930. II. Baker, William M. (William
  Melville), 1943- III. Historical Society of Alberta. IV. Alberta
  Records Publication Board.
  FC3216.2.P56 1993   363.2'0971   C93-091786-3
  F1078,P56 1993

Front cover photo of Deane: NAC, PA-42147
Back cover photo of Deane: RCMPM 933-11-23

Alberta Records Publication Board:
Chair and General Co-Editor, David C. Jones; Co-Editor,
David W. Leonard; Secretary, Diane Rosvold; Treasurer,
Marianne Fedori; Representative Members: Sarah Carter
(University of Calgary), Hugh Dempsey (*Alberta History*),
Raymond Huel (University of Lethbridge), Ron Robertson
(Historical Society of Alberta), Paul Voisey (University of
Alberta)

TABLE OF CONTENTS

DEDICATION

To my wife,
who has been my friend, companion, support, and love
for even more years than
Deane was a
Mounted Policeman.

Thank you, Sharon. This book is dedicated to you!

ACKNOWLEDGMENTS

A project of this magnitude could not be completed without the co-operation and assistance of a host of individuals and organizations. The archivists and assistants at the National Archives of Canada and at the Glenbow Archives deserve special commendation for smoothing the path of research. The general editors of the Alberta Historical Records Publication Board, David C. Jones and David W. Leonard, along with Hugh Dempsey, have provided valuable guidance in preparing the volume. Grants from the University of Lethbridge, the Alberta Historical Resources Foundation and the Social Sciences and Humanities Research Council of Canada have supported the research. The interest and support of my colleagues in the Department of History at the University of Lethbridge have sustained me. A special tip of the hat to Ray Huel for working out computer bugs. Finally, the enthusiastic and wide-ranging assistance of the Oordt family, the Spinks family, Brian Tyson, Helen Primrose, Sheila Daly, John M. Blatchly, Paul Whitehead and Charlene Sawatsky is gratefully acknowledged.

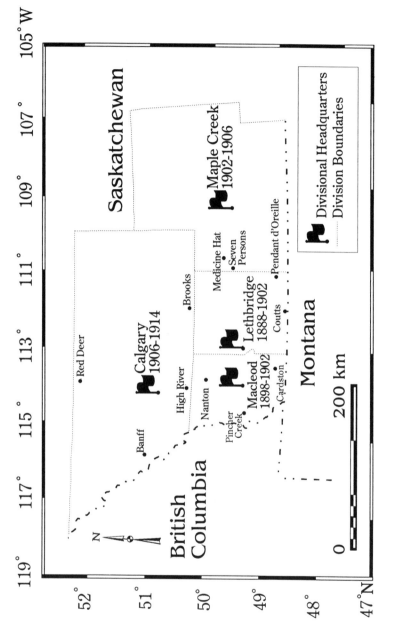

Approximate boundaries of Mounted Police divisions
while under Deane's supervision.

INTRODUCTION
Richard Burton Deane, 1848 - 1930

He even looked like a magician. Tall, fair, and spare in his younger years, with a drooping mustache and unsmiling eyes that made him seem brooding and threatening, Richard Burton Deane made an immediate impression on his contemporaries. His personality remains alive today in his writings.

Deane was a Mounted Policeman for thirty-one years from 1883 to 1914. During his tenure, the Prairies changed from the great, open, sparsely-inhabited, uncultivated, plains to the settled, farmed, increasingly-urbanized, economically-developed provinces of Alberta and Saskatchewan. In this enormous transformation of the West, the Mounted Police played an unparalleled role. All members of the force took their part, but they were not of equal significance. Bluntly stated, constables came and went, but officers seemed to be forever. Given their position of authority and given their longevity in office, it is not surprising that it was the officers who shaped the Mounted Police in the formative years between the creation of the force in 1873 and the outbreak of the First World War. What kind of men were they, these officers who created the enormously popular and highly respected force that western Canadians claimed as their own in spite of its origins as a federal body? What were their perspectives and attributes, and how did they acquire them? What, in other words, made a Mounted Police officer?

In *The NWMP and Law Enforcement 1873-1905*, R.C. Macleod analyzed the characteristics of dozens of officers and concluded that they were members of a social elite and espoused what they took to be the values of the English gentry. In fact, Macleod points out, most officers were not actually English. Most were raised in eastern Canada as members of prominent families. They usually had military training and experience, frequently had a legal background, and tended to be members of hierarchical denominations - i.e. either Anglican or Catholic. Of whatever background, however, they had the "feelings and manners of a gentleman."[1]

Deane was a typical officer in many but not all respects. He had a military background, was Anglican, was well-versed in legal matters, held the values of the elite, and served as a Mounted Police officer for three decades. But he was not Canadian-born. Indeed, he not only held gentry values, but was of a minor family of the English gentry. To a point, this was an advantage, but being English prevented his promotion to the highest positions in the Canadian police force, for these posts were reserved for Canadians. A biographical sketch reveals more of the forces that molded Deane and shaped his career.

He was born in India in 1848, the son of an Anglican chaplain of the East India Company. The family returned to England around 1851, and from about 1855 to 1870 his father was the rector of a parish on the outskirts of Ipswich in Suffolk County. Deane grew up in the arms of the Church of England and attended the elite grammar school in Ipswich where he was an adequate but not outstanding student. In fact, his great proficiency was at cricket, and as a teenager Deane often played on select teams which even contested matches with touring professional squads.[2]

The Deanes may have been of the gentry class, but they were not wealthy. R. Burton's position in the family, moreover, determined that he would not receive whatever largesse it could afford, for he was the second son. By the time the eldest male perished when Deane was fourteen, the die had long been cast; he had not been raised to carry the mantle of the family, and one of Deane's younger siblings seems to have taken that role.[3]

Deane joined the Royal Marines as a 2nd Lieutenant in 1866. As he carefully noted in his book published five decades later, this was a "non-purchase corps," meaning that one did not buy an officer's commission but had to make one's way on the basis of merit. He was promoted to 1st Lieutenant in 1867, but further advance was blocked for years because of a huge reduction in the strength of the Marines. While a Marine, Deane served on cruises to such places as Gibraltar, and he saw action in 1873-74 in the war against Ashanti tribesmen in what is now Ghana. In 1876 he became adjutant of the thirty-five hundred strong Chatham Division of the Marines. In this position, Deane found an outlet for his impressive organizational skills, but things were so bottled up that he did not achieve promotion to

Captain until 1881. He cherished the rank, and for the rest of his life was called Captain Deane with his entire approval. But he had a wife and five children and faced compulsory retirement (if merely a Captain) in less than a decade on a pension quite insufficient to maintain the social standards he wished for his family. As a consequence, he negotiated an "early retirement" pay-out and, with the encouragement of his cousin, T.C. Patteson, a prominent member of the Canadian Conservative party, took his family to Canada in 1882.

Deane canvassed a variety of opportunities in Canada for a year before he found a job that suited him. For several months, he was an aide to Governor General Lord Lorne, and this gave him some useful contacts in political circles. Eventually he was able to acquire a commission in the Mounted Police, but not before overcoming Sir John A. Macdonald's skepticism about why a relatively young Englishman would have resigned his position in the Marines. Having provided a satisfactory explanation, Deane was taken on as an inspector and reported to the newly-established administrative centre of Regina in the summer of 1883. According to one later observer, this was a mixed blessing for the force:

Atmosphere was arriving in stimulating blasts, culminating for the while in the appointment of Inspector Richard Burton Deane, the striking, the unparalleled. This gentleman, with his soldierly carriage and his scorching convictions, was to do for the Force what the picturesque Unicorn does for the shield of Great Britain. He was to lend a distinction which, like the Unicorn's, could not be called always useful. Distinction he did lend; and, curiously enough, many loved him despite his ability to slice them with a word, or to prick the hide of any conceit with his inimitably sharpened horn. To that long, long gallery of remarkable Police portraits, he was to add a new and refreshing spectacle: the bearing of a gallant, the behavior of a wasp.

Yet he was too valuable to annihilate. For fourteen years he was to bait the great Commissioner Herchmer, and yet was not destroyed. His triumph was in his nickname, "Father Deane," and in the recognition of his underlying fatherliness by the people in whose behalf he was to work so long. On that July day in 1883 when he walked across the prairie to the barracks to discover, in his phrase, that the force was but "an armed mob" he brought a stimulating if troublous accession to the Police.[4]

Deane's first task was to draft rules, regulations and standing orders for the force. He also trained recruits and studied criminal law to supplement his expert knowledge of military law. Within a year, Deane was promoted to the rank of superintendent and was made the adjutant of the Mounted Police at $1400 a year, a very healthy salary at the time. During the North-West Rebellion of 1885, he was left in charge at Regina while Commissioner Irvine was away. In the aftermath of those troubles, Deane was the jailer of the rebel prisoners including Louis Riel, who even dedicated a poem to Deane. When the Commissioner was removed in 1886, Deane understood that he was a candidate to replace Irvine, but he lost out to Lawrence Herchmer who not only had a family connection with Sir John A. but also was a good friend of Edgar Dewdney, the Lieutenant Governor of the North-West Territories. Not surprisingly, Deane and Herchmer clashed at every turn. In many ways, they were very much alike. Both were organization men, extremely able bureaucrats, but prickly individuals who wore their sense of superiority on their sleeve. Their continued presence at the same post was intolerable. Deane first was replaced as adjutant, then he was sent on a recruiting trip by the Comptroller who, during a visit to Regina, realized the impossibility of the two men working in harmony. Then, in 1888, he was placed in command of the relatively new Lethbridge division.

Deane was the Commanding Officer at Lethbridge for ten years and then became *de facto* supervisory superintendent for both Macleod and Lethbridge divisions between 1898 and 1902. In 1902 he was removed from Lethbridge at the behest of Clifford Sifton, Minister of the Interior. Sifton evidently was displeased with a nifty piece of police work Deane had done in bringing to justice some prominent and powerful cattle ranchers who had ignored the 49th parallel and the regulations of Canadian Customs. In any case, Deane languished in boredom and obscurity in the Maple Creek division from 1902 to 1906 when, with a change of minister in Ottawa, he was given the plum posting of Calgary division which he held until his retirement in 1914. The house built for him in Calgary was the best on any Mounted

Police barracks at the time and, as Deane House, has become an historic site.

Even given the exaggerated assessment of Deane, quoted above, there is no doubt that he was a controversial personality. He understood the need for military-style discipline within the force, but found it far easier to accept when he was giving the orders than when he was expected to submit, especially to those he considered unfit for their superior position. As a commanding officer of a division, however, he was largely his own boss and a very competent one at that. If he was "too valuable to annihilate," it was because of his excellence in the field. A few officers may have been as skilled as Deane in the performance of the multitudinous tasks of police command, but no one was better.

Of course, Deane was not merely a Mountie. He had a personal life as well. He was first married in 1870 when he was just twenty-two years of age. The couple had five children, all born in England, but all of whom spent their formative years in the Canadian West. Following the death of his first wife in 1906, Deane re-married in 1908. The wedding took place mere days before his sixtieth birthday so that his second wife would be eligible for a widow's pension should he predecease her. That seemed likely since she was much younger, but she died in 1914 just before they were to retire back to England. By then Deane's three remaining children were long grown up. The eldest, Reginald, was a physician who had provided medical services to the Mounties in Maple Creek before setting up permanent practice in Calgary. Deane's daughter, Lily, did not forsake the embrace of the Mounted Police, for she left her father's house to marry another superintendent, P.C.H. Primrose, later Lieutenant Governor of Alberta.

Following the death of his second wife, Deane took a long overdue leave up to his formal retirement, departing Canada for England just as the First World War was breaking out. In 1915 he was appointed by the King to the Imperial Service Order. In 1916 his book, *Mounted Police Life in Canada: A Record of Thirty-One Years' Service, 1883-1914*, was published. About 1917 he married for a third time and evidently had a quiet retirement in a tranquil English town. His house, with a beloved garden, was called Rosedene, the name a combination of his favorite flower and an alternate form of the family name. He died at what seems to have been a health resort in Italy in 1930. He left no estate, and his unfortunate widow, who was ineligible for the Mounted Police widow's pension, lingered in impoverishment into the 1960s.

Deane played many roles. He was a male whose administration had a powerful impact on women. He was a Victorian whose mid-century values continued to color his outlook and operations as a Mountie well into the twentieth century. He was a white man who had frequent dealings with non-whites throughout his career. He was an Englishman who considered himself on imperial duty but struggled with a superiority/inferiority complex when confronted with Canadian nationalist sentiment. He was a Church of England man, although that did not prevent him from marrying a Catholic in 1908. He was a military man, even while he was a policeman. He was a family man, but one who always was prepared to undertake assignments away from home. He was a bureaucrat who held many other civil servants in disdain. By manners and culture, he was a gentleman, though he was not a member of the aristocracy, nor was his treatment of others always genteel.

These characteristics also fit many other officers and do not fully capture the unique personality of Deane. Throughout his life, the range of his accomplishments and interests were considerable. He was an avid gardener; an accomplished magician, whose performances had led him to become a skilled theatrical actor, director and producer;[5] a proficient cricketer who continued to play, when opportunity allowed, until 1897; a senior member of the Masonic Lodge; a warden and occasionally a lay reader of the Church of England; a speculator in business schemes; a collector of food recipes; and a writer. He was very competitive and boasted that he had never been beaten. He bristled when opposed or criticized and was not loath to unleash a withering barrage of words to cut down anyone with the temerity to question his judgment or activity. Yet he seemed to have genuine sympathy for the downtrodden, the unfortunates, and the powerless, at times objecting to the abuse of power by those in authority. Perhaps this betrayed Deane's sense of *noblesse oblige,* but it also reflected the breadth of his understanding of human life. Not much surprised him, for there were few sides of human behavior that he did not observe during his career. From Deane's perspective, the foibles and sins of mankind did not have to be condoned, but they had to be expected and taken into consideration when performing police duties. The eradication of such things as drunkenness and prostitution, for example, was a ludicrous proposition to Deane's way of thinking.

In the final analysis, no individual is completely knowable. But Deane was more mysterious than most. He had so many personae, wore so many hats. Moreover, as he was skilled in both acting and in performing magical illusions, he was perfectly capable of covering his face with a variety of masks. Were one to meet him today, one would be both attracted and repelled by Deane. His superciliousness and competitiveness would cause offence, but his aura of mystery and the breadth of his experience and interests and competence would intrigue. He was one of those most infuriating persons: an arrogant individual with much to be arrogant about.

Whatever one makes of Deane, his personality set apart his writing from that of any other Mounted Policeman. This is apparent in his book, but even more evident in his reports. He once stated that he abhorred writing,[6] but this was a partial truth. What he disliked was the work involved in constructing prose that was lively and memorable. Perhaps the only ones who do not hate the drudgery involved in writing are those who do not care about their literary style or the very few who find writing play, not work. Deane cared deeply about his writing and worked hard at it. He also took pleasure in its recognition. He was delighted when the Montreal *Gazette* typified the Mounted Police annual report to parliament for 1884, which Deane had written on behalf of the Commissioner, as reading like a romance.[7] Even the numerous periodical reports which were required of Deane were hardly the usual bureaucratic fare. Not all were of the same calibre, but many contained humor, irony, sarcasm, allusions, lyrical descriptions, and Latin or French terms. Most employed complex sentence structure and sophisticated word usage. Deane's use of language is one of the reasons his reports fascinate today. For instance, one simply cannot imagine a police commander today beginning a monthly report the way Deane started his of December 1893: "The new criminal year ... opened gaily with an indecent assault, a robbery and a culpable homicide."[8] In short, Deane's writing makes good reading.

But stylistic merit merely enhanced the reports. The substance of Deane's accounts was both revealing and engaging in its own right. Here one sees the elite, the common folk and the underside of southern Alberta's pioneer life. His reports cover everything from political interference with the criminal justice system to technicalities of the law, from ethnic prejudice to religious persecution, from plays, concerts and parades to outbreaks of infectious diseases, from starvation on Indian reserves to labor strife, from suicide to rape, from cattle rustling to liquor smuggling, from floods to prairie fires, from rumored polygamy within the Mormon community to "promiscuous fornication" in Lethbridge, and from vagrancy to murder. Indeed, he had to deal with everything from the most serious crimes to internal Mounted Police squabbles, including the occasion when some constables threw the bedding of an unpopular N.C.O. down the latrine. Thus both the matter and manner of Deane's reports provide intriguing insights into the social history of southern Alberta from 1888 to 1914.

William M. Baker
Professor of History
University of Lethbridge
Lethbridge, Alberta

NOTES

[1] R.C. Macleod, *The NWMP and Law Enforcement 1873-1905* (Toronto: University of Toronto Press, 1976), pp.73-81.

[2] Glenbow Alberta Archives, M311, "Reminiscences of a Mounted Police Officer by Captain R. Burton Deane," pp.55-60.

[3] There were eight other siblings, seven of them male. It was Harold Arthur Deane, only eight years old at the time of the senior brother's death, who became the most prominent, eventually serving as the chief official for the British government for a huge territory in northern India and being knighted prior to his premature death at age fifty-four. See *Who Was Who, Vol.1: 1897-1915* (London: Adam and Charles Black, 1920), p.188.

[4] T.M. Longstreth, *The Silent Force: Scenes From the Life of the Mounted Police of Canada* (New York: The Century Co., 1927), pp. 126-127.

[5] W.M. Baker, "Captain R. Burton Deane and Theatre on the Prairies, 1883-1901," *Theatre Research in Canada*, 14:1 (Spring 1993):31-59.

[6] National Archives of Canada, MG28, I (The Authors' Syndicate Ltd. Papers), 259, Deane to J.W. Gilmer, 3 January, 1916.
[7] R.B. Deane, *Mounted Police Life in Canada: A Record of Thirty-One Years' Service, 1883-1914* (London: Cassell and Co., 1916; reprinted by Coles Publishing Co., Toronto, 1973), p.20.
[8] In the National Archives of Canada, RG18 (RCMP Papers), vol. 74, file 73 for 1893.

COMMENT ON SOURCES AND PUBLICATION FORMAT

Most of the documents in this volume were written by Deane. Some are excerpts taken from the annual reports made by the Mounted Police and printed in the *Sessional Papers* of the Parliament of Canada. Some were taken from unpublished manuscripts prepared by Deane. Many others were located in the massive files of the Mounted Police housed at the National Archives of Canada in Record Group 18. Each type of document has particular characteristics.

Materials in the annual reports were on the public record and were prepared with that in mind. Interest needed to be generated; prejudices unacceptable to the public could not be displayed; touchy cases had to be ignored or played down; examples of Mounted Police incompetence or discipline problems within the force needed to be whitewashed; the image of the Mounties as fearless, competent, unbiased, and admirable needed to be promoted before the political bosses and the Canadian populace. Annual reports were something of a propaganda exercise.

On the other hand, the manuscript material in the Mounted Police files was not part of the public record, although it might become so under unusual circumstances. For the most part, it was for internal consumption — the accounting of a subordinate to a superior. Such documents appear to be more frank, more unpolished. They provide much greater detail than the summaries given in annual reports. They also are more episodic and conditional, for the simple reason that while a matter was unfolding, it was not at all clear what the outcome would be. In addition, they always put the best light on the author's actions, for these more private reports also had a propaganda purpose, that of justifying oneself before one's superiors.

Finally, the unpublished manuscripts prepared by Deane towards the end of his career were certainly written with the public in mind, but also from the perspective of one who was no longer required to suppress negative opinions about the Mounties and western Canada. Some of this attitude is evident in his book, wherein he indicates his animosity to Commissioner Herchmer and Clifford Sifton, as well as his conviction that the Mounties were going downhill and would soon lose the credibility they had attained in earlier years. But Deane's unpublished manuscripts were even more contentious, since they contained material critical of the society of western Canada as a whole.

Selecting the documents to be published in this volume from amongst the thousands of pages of material required a ruthlessness worthy of the most callous military commander. Six chapters, covering roughly half a decade each and coinciding with the location and nature of Deane's commands in what has become Alberta, form the major divisions. Within each period, four or five important and intriguing topics have been selected for special emphasis, but they are not exclusive to that time and location. Liquor offences, prostitution, violent assault, theft of livestock, climatic challenges, cultural conflicts, internal difficulties within the Mounted Police — these and more were to be found in all areas under Deane's jurisdiction from beginning to end.

For the most part, the editor has avoided the temptation to provide references to secondary sources relating to particular themes, individuals, and episodes. Files on many, but by no means all, of the cases discussed in the documents, are located in the Alberta Attorney General records in the Provincial Archives of Alberta, especially accessions 79.285 (Calgary judicial district), 78.235 (Fort Macleod judicial district), and 66.166 and 67.172 (coroners and inquest files).

Explanatory information and analysis have been provided, in italics, by the editor in the introductions to the chapters and to the topics within each chapter. The editor has made few and only minor alterations to the original documents. Occasional spelling and stylistic inconsistencies, unclear punctuation, and copying errors have been rectified — merely the sort of thing that Deane himself would have done had he been preparing the material for publication. All excerpts have been given a title and have been identified along with an abbreviated location reference describing where the document is located. Examples of the two main abbreviations are as follows:

Deane, Monthly Report, September 1892 (NAC, RG18, 63, 247-92) means the report of Deane as Commanding Officer of a division to the Commissioner of the Mounted Police in Regina for the month ending September 30, 1892, which was then copied to the Comptroller in Ottawa. The report is to be found in the Royal Canadian Mounted Police Papers (Record Group 18) at the National Archives of Canada in Ottawa, volume 63, file 247 for the year 1892. The September report is simply one of the collection of the periodical reports for the Lethbridge Division for 1892 gathered together in file 247.

Deane, Annual Report, 1889 (SP 1890, No.13, pp.42-43) means the segment of the 1889 annual report of the Mounted Police to parliament specifically prepared by Deane. The report was really presented by the Commissioner, but appendices were attached from the Commanding Officer of each division. The report was then printed in the Parliamentary Sessional Papers for 1890 as number 13, and the particular excerpt designated was initially published on pages 42 and 43 of Sessional Paper number 13.

ABBREVIATIONS

GA	Glenbow Archives, Calgary
NAC	National Archives of Canada, Ottawa
PAA	Provincial Archives of Alberta, Edmonton
RCMPM	Royal Canadian Mounted Police Museum, Regina

I

"LITTLE OASIS IN A DESERT"
LETHBRIDGE DIVISION 1888 - 1892

Deane arrived in Lethbridge on his fortieth birthday, 30 April 1888, to take command of Division K. He remained there for fourteen years, the longest sojourn at one location in his life, and perhaps the best. Aside from feeling fulfilled in his role with the police, Deane derived satisfaction from his involvement in community activities ranging from theatre, to St. Augustine's Anglican Church, to cricket, to the Masons. As Deane recalled it, these days in the "little oasis in a desert," were "happy years [with] people we liked so much."[1]

Lethbridge had emerged as a headquarters for a separate police division in the aftermath of its founding as a coal-mining town in 1885. By 1888 Lethbridge had a population of about one thousand, and, under the guidance of the Galt coal company, which had become involved in building railways and acquiring large tracts of land in the territory surrounding the town, was an ambitious and progressive community.

Outside Lethbridge itself, the territory covered by Division K was truly the "great lone land."[2] On these tablelands of the plains, grasses and a few scrub bushes could be seen waving in the steady breeze, but little else was readily apparent either of natural vegetation or human life. Even the buffalo were now gone, although antelope, wolves, prairie chickens, skunks, ducks, and small animals were abundant, especially around the river bottoms, sloughs and coulees. Free-ranging cattle and horses had partly filled the gap left by the buffalo, but even by 1890 there were fewer than ten thousand head in Deane's vast territory. Beyond the community of Lethbridge, human habitation was sparse, consisting of a scattering of cowboys, non-treaty and off-reserve Indians, and small ranchers and farmers. One reason for

---

[1] Deane, *Mounted Police Life*, p. 44.

[2] This term was used as the title of an 1872 book about the North-West by William Francis Butler (London: Sampson Low, Marston, Low & Searl, 1872; reprinted by Charles E. Tuttle Co., Rutland, Vermont, 1968).

the scarcity of white settlement was that the territory was part of the drylands of the southern Canadian plains and therefore not easily farmed. The land and its weather presented an ever-present and dominant backdrop to the unfolding of the human history of the area.

The native people had lived in the territory for centuries, but by the 1880s the basis of their livelihood, the buffalo, had been destroyed. In addition, there was an incursion of white people into the territory, along with their liquor, disease, and a technological, bureaucratic, legalistic, and acquisitive culture. All these factors made for a traumatic period in the history of the Plains Indians.

While some parts of the North American plains were being settled by white farmers in the 1880s, the main economic activity

Writing-on-Stone Detachment, November 1899
GA, NA-2172-28
Many Mounted Police detachments were isolated and bleak, however necessary they were to the success of the force. Boredom, skunks, snakes, disease, lice, and fatigue were a few of the hazards encountered there. At times, the men turned on their fellows, especially against the one in charge. The crew in this detachment in the summer of 1892 even carried their dispute back to the Lethbridge barracks, as related in Document I-1 concerning Sergeant Ashe's blankets.

of whites in the Lethbridge territory, outside the town itself, was ranching. The joys and sorrows of this industry, along with the ever-changing but ever-present problems created by booze, filled many pages of Deane's reports during the first five years of his tenure at Division K.

A. Monthly Report

While Deane was the Commanding Officer of the Lethbridge Division, monthly reports were the prime means of communication with the Commissioner at Regina and the Comptroller at Ottawa. Supplemented by other materials, these reports provide a wonderful source of information about the development of the region and about the activities of the Mounted Police. They cover a huge variety of subjects ranging from weather, theft, smuggling, drunkenness, accidents, brawls, prostitution, destitution, native people, fires, livestock, settlement, and farming, to internal operations and disciplinary problems within the Mounted Police. The following monthly report provides an example of the breadth of topics covered, although mundane details such as the state of buildings and putting up hay at the outposts have been omitted.

I-1 "Down the Sergeants' Latrine"
Deane, Monthly Report, September 1892 (NAC, RG18, 63, 247-92)

In my report for August I inadvertently omitted the account of a fracas in the Hungarian quarter, which is as follows: On Sunday night the 28th August a wedding was being celebrated in the Hungarians' quarter and of course there was as usual considerable drunkenness and noise. Const Walker hearing more than usual walked over to the neighbourhood and stayed there some little time. Presently a drunken Sclav[3] came out of the house and went across the street, swearing and using filthy language, so Const Walker arrested him, a couple of Sclavs went to his rescue and Walker let him go and grabbed them. Then No 1's daughter appeared on the scene and tried to pull Walker backwards. Failing in that she hit him on the back of the head

---

[3] Deane used the Latin spelling he no doubt learned as a schoolboy.

with something she picked up on the road, as Walker says, but with her fists as she says, and Walker fell forward onto his hands and knees and his men got away from him. By this time Corpl Hare had arrived and a crowd of Sclavs. Ex-Const Potter and another civilian or two went to the help of the police and a boy rode up to Barracks saying that the two policemen were set upon by a Sclavish mob. Half a dozen men ran down at once, brought up three men charged with assault and in the course of the next day or two the original offender and his daughter were identified and brought up, all of them being fined ....[4]

A man who is popularly known as "Doc Hill" was brought in on the 6th. inst [*instant, i.e., of the current month*] as being insane. He was brought here once before for some time but was handed over to the care of a man who agreed to look after him. Since then he has had another attack, and again on the 6th. he had another, when the caretaker said he could not be responsible for him any longer. I held an exhaustive examination into the case and concluded there would be no good in asking the Lieut Governor to send the patient to Selkirk, as the asylum people would have discharged him in a week. I kept him here until the 12th. inst when he seemed to have become quite rational again and I handed him over to his former caretaker, a miner named Andrew Anderson. Hill and Anderson have recently entered into an agreement whereby Hill gives Anderson a half interest in some cattle, variously estimated from 20 to 40, and about 16 horses and mares which he possesses. In return for this Anderson agreed to feed, clothe, work for, and look after Hill for seven years ....[5]

Very heavy rain fell on the night of the 6th. inst occasioning a great deal of trouble with the hay. What with rain and high winds the contractors have had wretched luck during the month. The hay is first class, but they have lost tons of it.

---

[4] Four men and one women were fined $10 each; the original offender was fined $1.
[5] There were few options in dealing with mentally ill adults. Only if an individual were judged "insane" would the state take responsibility in the form of a committal to the asylum in Selkirk, Manitoba. Otherwise, individuals were expected to look after themselves or have family or friends take care of them. The agreement worked out in this situation seems to have been a praiseworthy *ad hoc* attempt to take care of a person who had trouble during bad times but was reasonably capable at others.

On the 6th inst Const Massena was awarded 7 days Impt. H.L. [*Imprisonment with Hard Labor*] and 14 days C B [*Confined to Barracks*] for leaving the Guard Room when in charge of prisoners and for insubordinate behaviour to the Orderly Officer. I observe that he is withdrawing his money from the Dominion Savings Bank. I hope I do not do him an injustice by expressing my belief that he will desert. He calculated the chances about 2 years ago and I am sorry that I did not give him a better chance. He is so worthless that the Force would be well rid of him.

Some celery was stolen from Insp. Casey's garden on the night of the 11th inst. Some of the tops were thrown on the roof of No. 2 stable and others were scattered about near where it was evident a person had sat and eaten. One of the 3 sentries viz: Consts Jarvis, Macfarlane, or Thorn was undoubtedly the culprit ... [*or allowed*] such matters to take place on his post without seeing it. I do not think that Thorn had anything to do with it. Nothing could be proved.

Scouts "Iron Shield" and "Dog Child" on the 12th inst arrested and brought to Barracks an Indian named "Hateful Child" who was said to be wanted on the Reserve for larceny of 3 horses from another Indian. I wrote immediately to the Agent and received a reply from Mr. Swinford, Clerk, that Col. Irvine had wanted the Indian for some time for assault & larceny but that he knew no more.

On the 15th inst as no information came and I was not justified in holding the Indian without some specified charge, I sent him under escort to Stand Off, asking the Officer Commanding the Police there, to find out whether there was or was not a charge against the man, & if so to take the necessary steps. I intimated further that I could not hold the prisoner any longer. It subsequently transpired that the prisoner was wanted at Macleod for larceny and was sent there.

On the night of the 12th inst while Sergt Ashe was on picquet [*piquet or picket or guard duty*], his blankets, sheets & rug were taken off his bed and thrown down the Sergeants' latrine. It was the act of a coward and was clearly done out of spite. When Sergt Ashe went into his room after dismounting picquet, a dog, the property of Const. Baker (who is undergoing imprisonment) ran out of the room. This struck him as strange. There were in the Post at the time 3 Constables ex-Writing on

Stone men, whom the dog would follow viz: J A Smith, Macfarlane, and Jarvis. In accordance with your orders, I sent Const J A Smith on the 19th instant to join "A" Division, via the line of outposts and on the 21st inst I assembled the Division in the messroom, and in reference to the purloining and despoliation of Sergt Ashe's bedding, informed them that in accordance with your instructions, new articles had been issued to Sergt Ashe, and that the value thereof would be charged to every Officer, Non.Com.Officer, and man present in Barracks on the night of the 12th instant unless the perpetrator should in the meanwhile confess. I added that, as a noble minded man of that sort would certainly be too modest to give us an opportunity of shaking his hand, it would be necessary for any one in the secret, to reveal his honored name, in case of any exception being taken to the afore mentioned stoppage [*fine*]. Curiously enough on the afternoon of Sunday the 18th inst Const J A Smith, being under orders to leave next day, went to the Sergt Major and told him that he suspected sundry men of suspecting him of having taken Sergt Ashe's blankets. He could not give names, or any reason for his own suspicion, but begged the Sergt Major to assure me that he was far from being that kind of man.[6]

A man named Peter Killroy was arrested here on the 14th inst for larceny. He is a tramp and sneak thief too. He was tried under the summary trials act, before Mr. Martin and myself and was awarded 3 months Impt. H.L. There is I believe a warrant out for him in Macleod.

The town fire engine has arrived and a man is on the way to test and hand it over. It will be possible soon to find out what the cost of filling a tank will be ....

On the 20th inst Sergt Ashe left this to join "D" Division, at Macleod, in accordance with your instructions ....

On the morning of the 22nd Const Loft took leave of the Division. He answered his name at Reveille and was in Barracks at 7.30 a.m. Between that time and a little before 9 a.m. he

---

[6] The conflict had originated at the Writing-on-Stone detachment and resulted in desertions. See Deane, Monthly Report, August 1892 in NAC, RG18, 63, 247-92; and H.A. Dempsey, "Writing-on-Stone and the Boundary Patrol," in *Men in Scarlet*, H.A. Dempsey, ed., (Calgary: Historical Society of Alberta/McClelland and Stewart West 1974?), pp.148-149. Information on objections to the salary deductions and related matters is located in NAC, RG18, 72, 801-92.

disappeared. It then transpired that the blankets were gone from his bed, although the rug remained, and his underclothing was missing from his kit. Some little time ago finding that imprisonment had not resulted in keeping him sober I had him brought before me and told him if he came before me again for drunkenness, I would get him dismissed from the Force. He admitted that he did not want to leave the Force and certainly would not like to be dismissed from it. This admonition worked well for a little while, but he has since been drinking a great deal, and I have sent him warning on 3 different occasions. He signed the pledge one day and broke it the next. He had become a slave to drink and could stand very little of it. He was in liquor on the morning of the 22nd inst. It appears he walked to the boundary and crossed it at 4 o'clock on the morning of the 27th inst, having walked the greater part, if not all, of the way. He was an excellent man when sober. The town and neighbourhood were thoroughly searched and a party went out to the South, but a gale of wind arose, and between the wind and the dust it was impossible to follow a trail, or even to examine the prairie, so the men returned to Barracks.

In accordance with a telegram from Supt Steele yesterday, a halfbreed named Phillip Whitford was arrested here last night for larceny. I have sent him to Kipp to-day ....

There has been very little drill this month. Escorts for prisoners have taken up all available men, seeing that the Division is a little low in strength, altho' it contains as many men as are wanted, it would certainly be in a better position if some of the useless and troublesome members could be eliminated. When the attention of two good men is taken up watching one bad one, the service is necessarily expensive. There are men in this Division whose services to the country would be dear at the price of their board. The introduction of the [*new liquor*] license system, has had a most disastrous effect upon the Division, the very opposite effect to that which is observable in the general public. The only explanation is, that a dollar will buy more whiskey than under the old system.

Const Thomson was dismissed on the 28th inst., on the expiration of his imprisonment.

About 3 p.m. to-day, two haymen came in from Milk River Ridge and reported a large prairie fire in the Ridge. I sent out a

K Division, Lethbridge, 1893
NAC, C-1899
Life in the barracks at Lethbridge, headquarters of Division K, was more orderly, disciplined, and formal than in the detachments. Nevertheless, as Document I-1 shows, drill and minor offences were frequently overlooked. Persons in the picture are not identified, but it is not believed that Deane is one of them.

party of half a dozen men, which was all I could find transport for as it happened. All the hay that will be wanted for this neighbourhood is stacked out there.

B. Land and Weather

Deane's reports provide vivid details of environmental factors. In them were described everything from blizzards causing people to become hopelessly lost and livestock to drift, to late and early frosts destroying vegetable gardens, to dry, windy conditions spreading prairie fires, to springtime rain and run-off creating swollen and dangerous streams in which people lost their lives. Deane's comments about land and weather were not balanced; he focused on the problems rather on the glories of the climate such as its wonderfully clean air and bright skies. Even his positive comments had a critical edge, as shown in his expla-

nation for the good health of the district in the 1889 Annual Report: "Wind in Lethbridge is an emblem of constancy which would have carried conviction to Juliet's heart, and germs must have a hard time of it." To Deane, almost any kind of weather had its drawbacks: a mild winter was conducive to the flu; heavy rains ruined hay; lack of snow led to prairie fires in winter; drought in summer and storms in winter caused cattle and horses to drift across the international border in search of food and shelter; and fierce winds threatened roofs, chimneys, and blew train cars off the tracks more than once during Deane's tenure at Division K.

I-2 "Double Reefer Topsail Breeze"
Deane, Monthly Report, June 1889, (NAC, RG18, 30, 130-89)

There is very little to be said in commendation of the Lethbridge climate. The prevailing feature is the rate at which the wind gambols over the prairie, dries up the soil with its hot breath and scorches the leaves of young trees, vegetables etc, like frost. I can best describe it as a "double reefer topsail breeze" and varying in intensity from that to a hurricane & never failing in constancy. I am told that 41 settlers were on their way here & were told by the conductor of the train that there was no water — half turned back at once and half stayed over one night in the place.

I-3 "Burnt Over"
Deane, Annual Report, 1889, (*SP 1890*, No.13, pp.47-48)

We have had a large and varied experience of prairie fires during the year. In the course of last winter and spring the entire country round about here was burnt over, and if these fires should be of annual recurrence, as seems more and more probable with advancing settlement, the grass will deteriorate year by year and may eventually be killed altogether. It may, therefore, be supposed that in a stock country prairie fires are an all-absorbing question. There is no doubt that locomotives are responsible for a large proportion of these fires, and nothing short of a strip 100 feet wide burnt on each side of the track will obviate danger from that source. Of the rest, I believe the majority of prairie fires are the result of criminal negligence or worse. The country is so large, distances so deceptive and the time occupied in reaching a fire so great, that it is very difficult to discover the origin and bring it home to the culprit ....

On the evening of the 4th of April Mr. Howell Harris, manager of Mr. Conrad's and I.G. Baker's ranches, asked for assistance to put out a large prairie fire, supposed to be from twelve to fifteen miles north of this, which was threatening his range. I was very short of men just then, but went myself with a party of nine. We left the barracks at 8 p.m., crossed the river near here and made straight for the fire. We rode until 3 a.m. next day, and seemed to be as far from the fire as when we started. From 3 to 4 a.m. we halted to rest and feed the horses, and then, as we were not rationed for a lengthy stay, and there was a great uncertainty about water, we retraced our steps, reaching the river at 11 a.m., and the barracks soon after noon. We had thus travelled from 8 p.m. till noon, with one hour's intermission, and must have covered fifty miles. We found afterwards that the fire was burning in an arc, and that the centre, which seemed to us to be the nearest point, was really the furthest from us.

As we neared our journey's end the wind gradually freshened and brought the aforesaid fire within the limits of practical extinguishment on the 6th April. On that evening it was creditably said to be within seven or eight miles. I started with a party at 9 a.m., and made the nearest point in about fifteen miles. We put out several miles of fire — all there was — and arrived in barracks at 5:30 a.m. on the 7th. Estimated distance travelled, thirty-seven miles.

I-4 "No Country for Farming"
Deane, Monthly Report, May 1890 (NAC, RG18, 39, 137-90)

The weather on the 29th & 30th was almost wintry. A keen frost on the night of the 29th, cut off potatoes, corn, etc. etc. There was also a sharp frost on the night of the 11th, which cut up peas pretty badly, and they are tolerably hardy. What with the cold winds, & hot winds, frost and drought, vermin, and dust, it may be accepted as a fact that this is no country for farming.

A number of trees arrived from Ottawa on the 23rd and we have been hard at work trying to get them into the ground. I am however very shorthanded and progression is slow.

Holes measuring at least two feet each way have to be dug. The ground in most places, six inches below the surface, being a hard clay, which has to be loosened with pick and crowbar, the soil to fill the holes has to be obtained elsewhere and brought to the spot, and the planting of 2 or 3 dozen trees entails upon us an amount of work which would not be supposed. In order to get in as many trees as possible, while they are yet alive, I have engaged an outsider to dig 36 holes 2 ft each way at eighteen cents each. I have already about 36 trees planted, and with the above mentioned help, I shall manage to save the most promising specimens of the consignment. I trust this expenditure will meet with your approval under the circumstances.

The evergreens are all planted and if they will not grow where they now are, they will not grow anywhere here.

I am going to tell Mr Saunders [*Director of the Canadian Experimental Farms Service*] that 40 or 50 trees at a time, are as many as I can handle.

The trees I transplanted from the river bottom last fall, are doing well — all but one, have put out, or are budding. They are watered every other day, so they should do well.

I-5 "Unfortunate Year"
Deane, Annual Report, 1892 (*SP 1893*, No.15, pp.83-93, *passim*)

It has been an unfortunate year all round ....

Two destructive fires have taken place in Lethbridge during the year — one which broke out on the 7th December, 1891, threatened at one time to leave very little of the town to welcome the new year. It originated in a furniture store where there was a quantity of hay, dried sea weed &c., and a gale of wind was blowing at the time.

Fortunately, when the fire was at its height, the wind veered a couple of points to the southward, and thus the burning fragments were discharged into the large square which forms a prominent feature of the town and where there was only grass to burn. This change of wind, slight as it was, unquestionably saved from destruction all that part of the town lying to the east of the burning buildings. A burning piece of wood was carried by the wind, before it changed, for several hundred yards, and ignited the prairie at a point just opposite our barrack gate ....

[T]here was a terrible storm on the 24th April [*1892*]. On that night it began to rain, and rained steadily all the following morning. In the afternoon it turned to snow, and snowed all the night and the next morning until noon, with a strong and bitterly cold north wind blowing. Numbers of cattle which had been thoroughly drenched and chilled by the rain succumbed to the terrible cold which followed it. The poor creatures could do nothing but drift before the storm, turning neither to the right hand nor to the left, and if any obstruction, such as a fence, barred their onward progress, they simply stood there till they died with the snow drifting over them.

Old timers agree in saying that no such blizzard has visited this country for upwards of 20 years.

I append a list of losses [*31 horses, 15 colts, and 202 cattle*] sustained by settlers in this district as given by themselves, but it is questionable whether they are aware of the full extent of their losses. The list was not completed until August, but Messrs. Conrad Brothers' manager told me the other day that they were about 500 calves short of their reasonable estimate for this year ....

I regret to have to record the death of Constable Hans Prahl, who died here on the 3rd May last from concussion of the brain. The joint application of spur and rein to a young horse that he was riding on the previous day caused the animal to lose his footing and to fall with his rider. The accident occurred in the stable yard where the ground was very muddy and slippery, after the storm of the 24th April and succeeding days ....

After this disastrous storm ensued a long period of drought. Seeds sown in May did not appear above the ground until August, consequent upon the rain which should have fallen in June. That state of things, however, is curable by irrigation, which, it is hoped, is within a measurable distance ....

Boring for an artesian well was undertaken by a local company in the spring, and a depth of 717 feet was reached, but there it was found necessary to abandon the work on account of the pressure of gas ....

Of course during the drought prairie fires were rampant ... on the 21st July a disastrous fire broke out and burnt furiously during the 22nd and 23rd over the country lying between the Little Bow and Big Bow rivers ....

Fortunately the round-up party was in the vicinity. Mr. Harris, manager of the Circle Ranche, slaughtered no less than fourteen beasts, cut them in halves and "snaked" the carcases along. He said that twenty-eight of his horses had had their feet badly burned — that the ground itself was literally on fire; it was so dry that the roots of the grass held the fire after the blade had been consumed and a breath of air would fan it into a flame, so that it was impossible to tell when the fire was out ....

I have satisfied myself that planting trees here is a waste of time and energy. The wind is fatal to them, the bark becomes discoloured, cracks and curls up, and that part of the tree is doomed. I have hardly one tree living that I planted three years ago, and it is certain that wind is the drawback, because some small ashes which were planted in the spring of 1890 on the lee side of the barrack room building have survived. The subsoil there is not so hard as in other parts of the barrack inclosure, but the main point is that the trees are sheltered from the prevailing wind ....

C. Native People

As there were no Indian reserves in Division K, the natives appearing in Deane's reports in this period were either off their reserves or non-treaty Indians. For the most part, they were Crees or members of the Blackfoot confederacy, especially that segment known as Blood or Kai'nah Indians, since their reserve, the largest in Canada, abutted the Lethbridge Division. Natives venturing onto the territory of Division K were attempting to follow aspects of a traditional way of life. Although the buffalo had disappeared a decade earlier, there was smaller game to hunt. Moreover, there were raids to carry out against hereditary enemies, and it should not be forgotten that the so-called last great Indian battle had been fought less than two decades earlier, in 1870, between Cree and Blackfoot in the valley where Lethbridge is now situated. Even just stretching out on the endless prairies under the wide open sky was part of the Indian lifestyle before the treaties of the 1870s began to hem them on reserves.

The decades of the 1880s and 1890s were difficult for all the Plains Indians. The Blood people, for example, continued to suffer grievously from disease and hunger. Their population, already hard-hit by epidemics earlier in the century, declined further: from 2,488 in 1878, to 1,776 in 1885, and to 1,111 in 1920.[7] *Indeed, in Deane's time it was half assumed that the so-called "Indian problem" would disappear because natives would simply die off.*

Deane's reports from 1888 to 1892 reveal several aspects of native life at the time. For the most part, they concentrate on the negative side of that life since Deane's official interest in natives focused on actual or potential violation of the white man's sense of law and order. Almost all agents of the government, Deane included, agreed that the simplest solution to any "Indian problem" was to restrict natives to their reserves and certainly to keep them from crossing back and forth across the 49th parallel. These measures were gradually implemented. By 1892, the space devoted to Indian matters in Deane's reports was but a fraction of what it had been five years earlier. Like most other government functionaries, Deane was not particularly hostile, cruel, or even unsympathetic towards natives. There were times when he came down on their side, such as in January 1890, when, as Justice of the Peace, he ordered a white man to pay wages owed to an Indian with the extraordinary name of "Chief Teat." And he appreciated the qualities of certain individuals such as Red Crow and even Star Child, the supposed killer of Constable Graburn. But Deane shared the attitudes, enforced the laws, implemented the practices, and encouraged the transformation that undermined the traditional way of life of the native people and turned them into displaced people in their own land. Although not so gullible as to believe all the rumors about Indians, he was not above the prejudices and stereotypes that whites held of the native people. The language and terminology he used often betrayed his assumption of the inferiority of Indians.

I-6 Well-Behaved
Deane, Annual Report, 1889 (*SP 1890*, No.13, pp.42-43 and 53)

The Indians have behaved very well during the past year. "Red Crow's" good example must count for a great deal. I am

---

[7] H.A. Dempsey, *Indian Tribes of Alberta* (Calgary: Glenbow-Alberta Institute, 1979), p. 25.

convinced that the key to the true repressive treatment of Indian delinquencies is to make plenty of what "Little Person" called a "fuss" over their misdoings, and to teach them that the law has a very long arm, which never grows weary ....

The Bloods think that they are the cream of creation, and it is time for them to begin to imbibe some modification of the idea.

We have been unsuccessful in keeping them on their reserve. A firm and persistent pressure will in time have the desired effect.

I went to the sun dance on the reserve this year, and I came away with the impression that it serves no useful purpose whatever, and might be profitably replaced by some other form of entertainment. No more than half a dozen would-be braves underwent the ordeal, and some of them were only brought to the scratch by obtrusive and derisive encouragement. The Indians could not agree among themselves as to where it should be held, and Red Crow did not appear. It has the effect of bringing out all the bad qualities of the Indians, without any compensating advantage. It feeds the naturally cruel nature of the spectators, it panders to the lust of both sexes, and unsettles the marital relations of the Indians themselves; and last, though not least, it acts as an incentive to the triumphant participant to evince a courage to which he is far from feeling in the commission of some lawless act.[8]

On the 22nd April, Scout "Star Child" reported that four days previously a party of Bloods had gone to the States on a horse-stealing expedition against the Gros Ventres. I thereupon warned Col. Otis, commanding at Fort Assiniboine, who wired to me on the 10th May that "three Bloods with stolen stock passed through Bear Paw Mountains on the 8th, and there killed an Indian." We had at this time 56 men on outpost duty, and patrols were moving night and day. On the 13th May, at about daybreak, two men from Corporal Elliott's flying patrol, saw an

---

[8] Evidently, Deane witnessed only the one Sun Dance and never wanted to see another. His recollection of it is located in his *Mounted Police Life*, pp. 83-85. In the aftermath of an attempted arrest and subsequent confrontation between Mounted Police and Indians at the 1889 Sun Dance, there were reports of natives buying up quantities of ammunition. Deane did not know whether the rumors were correct, but he warned storekeepers against selling cartridges to Indians (see Deane, Monthly Report, July 1889 in NAC, RG18, 30, 130-89).

Indian about five miles off driving some ponies towards the reserve. He soon caught sight of them and set off at full speed, heading for one of the many coulees thereabouts. He was so hard pressed, that he had to abandon his booty and "caché" himself. The patrol found first the mare which he had just ridden, with her flanks and back badly gashed by the Indian's knife, and which died from exhaustion soon after; they then found three more ponies and a yearling colt, which completed the tale. I subsequently sent these to Col. Otis, to be returned to the Gros Ventre owners ....

On the 2nd October I received a telegram from Medicine Hat that eight horses had been stolen from there on the night of the 30th September. Descriptions of the horses reached me on the afternoon of the 3rd, and the two owners, Cree Indians, arrived on the morning of the 4th October. I sent one of them with a constable to Stand-Off, and the other to Corporal Turnbull, on the Little Bow, with orders to follow the river bank until they found the trail of the horses crossing the Belly. It was, of course, a foregone conclusion that the horses were safely "cachéd" on the Blood reserve before I received notice of the theft, and the only thing to be done was, if possible, to bring the larceny home to the Bloods. Corporal Turnbull's patrol picked up the trail where it crossed the Belly River ... and followed it <u>viâ</u> Kipp to the reserve. On arrival there they heard that the horses had been given up to the Macleod police, so went there and recovered them .... I issued a warrant for the thieves .... The Crees took their horses home in great delight.

At the end of May it was reported by the Kennedy's Crossing detachment that twelve lodges of Canadian Crees were encamped about nine miles down the river on the American side. These roving bands are always likely to lead to trouble, so I wrote to Col. Otis, saying that if they were Canadian Crees, and if he would have them escorted within our reach, I would have them conducted northwards, away from the line, and out of harm's way. Some days, of course, elapsed before I could communicate with Col. Otis, but he immediately sent out a party to act in accordance with my suggestion. I fancy, however, the troops were unable to find them, as the Indians had split up into twos and threes and gone on various hunting expeditions. The troops looked for them for some time, but I never heard any more of the Indians in question.

Apropos of roving bands of Indians, I would respectfully submit that the issue of passes from the reserve to Indians, enabling them to roam about a cattle country, such as the Little Bow, is much to be deprecated. I recognize the difficulty of an Indian agent in refusing a pass to a plausible Indian; but there are two main points to be remembered: one; that the cattle must be protected; and the other, that Indians will never work on the reserve so long as they are permitted to roam the country ....

Owing to the Indians not having overrun the country, as they did last year, the antelope have had time and opportunity to increase and multiply, and if they have a similar chance next year there will be a tolerable stock of such game.

In the spring I was pointing out to the spokesmen of a band of Indians that they would not be allowed to molest the antelope in the breeding season, and said that if such slaughter were permitted the antelope would soon go where the buffalo had gone. A smile, "child-like and bland," played over the Indian's face as he replied: "Yes, but then the white men are the buffalo."

I-7 Dubious Accusations
Deane, Monthly Report, July 1888 (NAC, RG18, 21, 373-88)

On the 2nd inst Inspector Bradley who with Sergt Blake and party had gone to Grassy Lake (50 miles) to look up 50 or 60 Indians said to be near there with a large number of horses, including one stolen from the Oxley Ranche, returned and reported that there were 7 lodges of Indians under "Day Chief" who had been hunting. The horse supposed to have been stolen was one which "Day Chief" claimed to have bought two years ago at M[*acl*]eod and which was vented [*i.e. the matter was investigated*]. It had been tied to a waggon which ran away and the animal was so nearly strangled that the owner was going to shoot it and end its misery but Day Chief persuaded him to sell it for $7. The horse bears the marks of the rope to this day.

On receipt of a telegram from J. Bailey, Dunmore, that Indians were forcing the Section House Keeper's wife at Woodpecker to give them food, and had been doing so for 3 or 4 days, Inspr Bradley left by train and Sergt Blake and party by trail for Woodpecker to see the Indians. The party returned on the afternoon of the 8th having turned these Indians back to the Reserve.

There was no foundation for the report. The woman had recently come from England, and was timid about Indians but had no complaint to make against them.

On the 20th in consequence of a complaint made by Mr Harris, Rancher, and Mr McLean, manager of the Cypress Ranche, that Indians were camped on their range, and, as they had missed a number of cattle and suspected the Indians of killing them, I despatched Sergt Blake and party for Wood-pecker to look after the suspected Indians who were said to be there. Sergt Blake arrived here again on the 23rd inst and reported to the following effect — that he went to the Cypress Coy's Ranche and inquired where the Indians suspected of kill-ing the cattle were camped. The manager told him that the Indians had moved across the river; he then asked if he had any proof of their having killed his cattle. He said he had no positive proof, but still strongly believed that they did. Sergt Blake and party then crossed the river and searched the surrounding coun-try thoroughly, but failed to find any trace of Indians. He also went to the two adjoining ranches, and parties there informed him that they had seen no Indians for weeks .... No remains of dead animals were ever found.

I-8 Child Prostitution?
Deane, Monthly Report, February 1891 (NAC, RG18, 49, 192-91)

Apropos of Mr Wilberforce Wilson's letter to the Indian Com-missioner about the defilement of Indian girls of tender years, I should have added to my report of the 12th instant that Blackfoot Indians very seldom come here with their lodges. A stray buck comes now and then, but women very seldom come. Mr Wilson may hear plenty of similar stories if he lays himself out for them, and will furnish a good deal of amusement to the purveyors of the same. It may be convenient for purposes of record to insert here Mr Reed's letter and my reply thereto.

From Mr Hayter Reed to Commissioner Herchmer.
"I learn that Mr Wilberforce Wilson, (a brother of the Rev. Mr Wilson of Sault St Marie) has during his recent stay at the Blackfoot [*Blood*] Reserve been informed that youngsters of 12

to 14 years of age were brought from the Reserve to Lethbridge for immoral purposes; that the parents held them while being outraged, and that their shrieks were terrible.

"Although I do not think there is any truth in these reports, it seems that they should be investigated; but with or without foundation, I wish you would kindly instruct the Commanding Officer at Lethbridge to cause a sharp look out being kept at all times for loitering Indians and to see that Indians found without a pass be sent back to their Reserves."

From Supt Deane to the Commissioner.

"With reference to the Indian Commissioner's letter dated the 4th instant.

"I have the honour to report that unless Mr Wilberforce Wilson can and will divulge the name of his informant &c. &c. his story is not worthy of credence.

"It is doubtless another version of a story which was told me some time ago, to the effect that sundry Blood Indian children were used for immoral purposes by about eighty different men of Lethbridge and a harrowing tale it was. I begged my informant as a favour to obtain for me information which would enable me to identify even one of the children in question. He subsequently gave me a list of four, with their respective ages;

As-in-a-ke — Cree Woman — 11 - 13
Me-kot-si-a-mo-ne — Red Otter — 9 - 12
Sino-pa-ke — Kit Fox Woman — 11 perhaps
Pooks-ka — Baby Face — 12 - 14

"I found on enquiry that the first mentioned 'As-in-a-ke' had been a married woman for 5 years, and had had two Indian husbands. She swore that her age was 17.

"The second, 'Mek-ot-si-a-mo-ne' also swore that she was 17 years old, and had had an Indian husband for some years.

"The third 'Sino-pa-ke' was sold[9] some time ago to 'Heavy Runner' a Blood but left him. Joe Healy says she is 14 years old and that she has no connection with men. I have not been able to ascertain that she has.

---

[9] In all likelihood, this was a misrepresentation of Blood marriage practices which involved an exchange of gifts between the families of the couple, with the groom's side giving about double the amount it received. See H.A. Dempsey, "The Blackfoot Indians," in R. B. Morrison and C. R. Wilson, eds., *Native Peoples: The Canadian Experience* (Toronto: McClelland and Stewart, 1986), p. 423.

"The fourth, 'Pooks-ka' is according to her mother 19 years of age. She lived with Joe Healy for two years and is a dissolute woman.

"Having obtained this information, I asked my informant if his informant would consent to have a chat with me upon the subject. He promised to bring about such interview if he could, but I never was able to get nearer to the original source.

"As I have always expected some day or other to see some sensational story of the kind published in the Press, I took particular pains to get at the truth of it.

"I do not think Mr Wilson is likely to know as much about Lethbridge doings as I am, and the prostitution of Indians is a subject to which I devote special attention.

"As to sending back to the Reserve Indians who come here without a pass, I do so on every possible occasion, but seeing that the Police have no right to do anything of the kind it behoves one to be very careful so as not to have to take 'back-water'."[10]

1-9 "Truth of the Indian Stories"
Deane, Annual Report, 1890 (*SP 1891*, No.19, p.49)

Five horses are reported to have been stolen during the year; in one of these cases an Indian lost his horse and after some months saw the animal in the herd of a white man who said he had bought the mare two years previously from a half-breed whose name he did not know. He would not give up the mare which was too closely herded for the Indian to take away without causing a breach of the peace, and the Indian had not the means to replevin [*a legal mechanism for the restoration of goods taken from a person*].

Such cases as these are not uncommon, and are hard upon the Indian owners, who cannot understand why the police cannot remedy their wrongs. A suit of replevin would cost at least

---

[10] The pass system may not have been legally enforceable, and Indians ignored it when that suited their purposes, but from the mid-80s to mid-90s, at least, it was utilized as an effective source of pressure on the native people. In his *Mounted Police Life*, p. 263, Deane put it this way: "our 'bluff' was never 'called' by the Indians, who invariably did as we wanted them to do."

three times the value of the animal and could not be undertaken without the support of the Indian Department.

In this, as in other like cases which have come to my notice, I am impressed with the truth of the Indian stories.

I-10 Star Child
Deane, Monthly Report, April 1889 (NAC, RG18, 30, 130-89)

On the 12th Scout "Star-child" came upon a couple of white men with a ten gallon keg of liquor, took it from them, held it, and handed it over to Staff Sergt. Ross.

The men tried to frighten him, then to bribe him, and finally to ride him down, but he held on to what he had got in spite of all. He will now by your authority receive $25.00 instead of $15.00 a month while acting as scout. I wish I could find another like him. I engaged one "Calf Chief" recommended by Supt. Steele but found him useless and so discharged him.

The trouble is the Indians do not like duty that takes them away from home — every 3rd or 4th day they must come in to see their wives and this is sometimes inconvenient.

"Star Child" however, notwithstanding that he has an "affaire" on hand having as alleged decoyed a white man's putative wife, is more reasonable than any I have met. This is the Indian who is said to have shot Graburn [*in 1879*]; whether or not, he is a man with a great deal of character, and is better employed as a friend than an enemy.

Deane, Annual Report, 1889 (*SP 1890*, No.13, pp.41-42)

Out of several Indian scouts that I have tried none have proved to be worth their salt but "Star Child," and I am sorry to hear that he is dying of consumption [*tuberculosis*]. He did some good work for us, and I do not expect to replace him. He was a determined rascal, and the Indians generally were afraid of him. After he brought to a successful conclusion an intrigue in which he was much interested, no less than the enticing of a white man's Indian wife from him, he became less reliable and energetic, and I was at last obliged to discharge him. I should be glad to get another native scout of similar calibre.

Star Child

GA, R.N. Wilson Photograph, NA-451-1

Star Child (Kukatosi, sometimes known as Kucka-toonisah) was suspected of having killed a Mounted Policeman in 1879, but Deane employed him as a Police Scout nonetheless. As Document 1-10 demonstrates, Deane was very impressed with him for a time. Star Child is an intriguing figure whose life illustrates much of the difficult transition of the Plains Indians in the 1870s and 1880s. He died in December 1889.

I-11 Bad Indian
Deane, Monthly Report, June 1891 (NAC, RG18, 49, 192-91)

A little 4 or 5 year old child of an Indian in the river bottom was playing on the coal railway track with some other Indian children and a coal car; and the little one somehow fell under the car and had his arm badly broken in two places. The child's first impulse was to flick the wounded arm at the car four or five times and call it the while a "Son of a b___ "

The Indians came to me and I asked the Doctor if he would attend to it.

He would have done it just as readily if the Indians had gone straight to him on their own account but considering that he has done and does a very great deal of surgical and unremunerative work for the Blood Indians, it occurs to me that the Indian Department would probably be glad of an opportunity to make some graceful acknowledgement to Dr Mewburn in connection with the case of the Indian child.

The youngster's arm is making capital progress, the only difficulty being that of keeping the bandages on. For these cases, as in Police practice, the Doctor uses the most improved dressing &c which he provides himself and this alone is an item of expense out of pocket.

It may confidently be predicted that if the said child grows up and becomes a bad Indian he will be very bad.

I-12 Clearing The Border
Deane, Annual Report, 1892 (*SP 1893*, No.15, p.86)

The Indians have been particularly well-behaved this year. One horse-stealing party was made up and started from here with a view to operations in the south, but broke up before reaching the line.

Prior to that a party of five Bloods, including a blind Indian, was arrested by some Crees in the Sweet Grass Hills ....

I never heard exactly what was the result, but think that the blind Indian and a boy were allowed to go and the others were sent to Deer Lodge penitentiary [*in the U.S.A.*] for a term of years. This leads me to draw attention to the inadvisability of giving Indians passes or allowing them to hunt in the Sweet Grass Hills or their neighbourhood, or in the vicinity of the international boundary.

In the first case, an Indian who holds a pass from his agent is always accompanied by at least double the number of persons prescribed by the pass, and it is impossible for our patrols to tell who are the authorized and who are the unauthorized persons.

Secondly, the fact of their being near the frontier is a strong temptation to steal horses from the Gros Ventres or from settlers on the other side.

In the first place they provoke retaliation, and in the second the settlers may reasonably expect us to keep our Indians from annoying them ....

Again, in the event of their relations with the Gros Ventres being peaceable, any traffic between the two is to be deprecated, because it furnishes an obvious and easy method of trading off horses that may have been improperly acquired.

As a matter of fact, we have not allowed Indians to remain in the neighbourhood of the line for some time past, and the result is that there has been less trouble every year.

D. Livestock

In Deane's early years in Division K, the main economic activity outside the town of Lethbridge itself was ranching. His reports canvassed the state of the cattle, the calf crop, and problems created by weather and wolves. His yearly account provided a reckoning of the number of cattle and horses along with the names of the major ranchers. In 1892, cattle in Deane's district numbered well over twenty thousand and horses over twelve hundred.

Since their initial acquisition by the native people of the north-western plains in the eighteenth century, horses had been both a means to and symbol of power. Raids to steal horses had become a well-established practice prior to the coming of the Mounted Police, and it was not quickly or easily suppressed. But horse thieves and their victims came in all stripes: natives stole from other Indians; and whites "appropriated" horses which belonged to Indians. In July 1890, a disgruntled whisky trader, who had lost a load of his goods to the Mounted Police, even stole three horses from the Mounties. It was not unknown, of course, for white civilians to steal from each other.

Accidents, disease, and the natural elements caused injury and death to livestock. Moreover, the Canadian-American border created difficulties for man and beast alike. In the first place, there was the problem of American cattle drifting onto Canadian territory. Deane did not even attempt to enforce the artificial boundary of the 49th parallel, but did become concerned when herds crossed the Milk River and strayed onto quarantine grounds. The second major difficulty was that the border created various Customs problems involving livestock.

I-13 Horse Raid
Deane, Annual Report, 1891 (*SP 1892*, No.15, pp.70-71)

A horse stealing party recently left here for the south, they picked up at least one horse in this neighbourhood and rode him to the scene of operations; this horse is now at a cow camp across the line, whence we shall recover it in a day or two.

This party consisted of four Indians, who started from here, viz., Prairie Chicken, Bird-Singing-in-the-Morning, Tall Man and Low Man, and were joined by two more Indians from the reserve, viz., Deadman and another. They went to the Sweet Grass Hills, and on the 18th October, stole four horses from Mr. Toole's ranche, cutting through a four strand barbed wire fence to get at them.

As soon as I heard this, I advised Mr. Toole to cause enquiry to be made at the South Piegan Agency, as it was probable the horses would be taken there and cached in the first instance, and be brought over to this side of the line as time and opportunity might allow.

The agent on that reservation had recently found three of the animals, and apprehended four Blood Indians, who admit having taken them.

I hear that some of the thieves turned States' evidence, and that the others are likely to see the inside of a penitentiary. The fourth horse, stolen from Mr. Toole's ranche, the property of a man in his employ, is now here with a very sore back, recovered from the Blood Reserve, though I have not been able to discover the name of the Indian who took it thither.

I have now instructed the outposts to allow no Indians to remain in the vicinity of the Milk River.

I-14 Theft by "The Kid"
Deane, Annual Report, 1888 (*SP 1889*, No.17, p.65)

Edward Austin was brought in on the 27th November from Milk River Ridge, having been given into custody there for stealing a horse, saddle and bridle and overcoat in Lethbridge on the 4th November. Immediately he had stolen the articles, the property of different people, he rode off across the line, but was followed by the horse's owner, who found him at a ranche about thirteen or fourteen miles on the other side. The stolen horse it appears had got away from him and the ranchmen fetched his saddle, &c., from where he was thus set afoot, about ten miles from the ranche. Mr. Tom Purcel, the owner of the horse, having explained his errand, the saddle and bridle were taken charge of by the foreman, and the next morning Austin stole the saddle again and hid it, stowing himself away in a root house. Upon hearing of this audacious theft the ranchmen turned out and the culprit was soon unearthed. Asked why he stole the saddle, which could be of no use to him without a horse, he guessed that he meant to steal a horse as well. The question then arose as to whether he should be sent to Benton or whether the ranchmen should "deal with him" themselves. Neither alternative appeared to suit the prisoner, for he said he would rather come back to this side of the line, which he did with Mr. Purcel, and was given in charge of the first Police post. I now hear that Austin, popularly known as "The Kid," presumably because of his age, which cannot be more than twenty or twenty-one, came into this country on a horse which he stole at Benton and sold here — so he was doubtless right in conjecturing that his shrift would be short if he prolonged his stay on the southern side of the international boundary.[11]

---

[11] On 7 January 1889, Judge Macleod sentenced Austin, alias Edward Rodgers, to two months imprisonment (see Deane, Monthly Report, January 1889 in NAC, RG18, 30, 130-89).

I-15 Disease
Deane, Monthly Report, June 1888 (NAC, RG18, 21, 373-88)

On the 2nd Thomas Berubé was brought in from Pendant d'Oreille [*on the Milk River, south of Pakowki Lake*] with four glandered horses which were destroyed .... In this connection I submit that the Customs Department should either do its own work or be prepared to pay expenses for having it done by others. For instance — the Police had perforce to destroy the animals and dispose of their remains. I gave all the odds and ends of lumber that I could spare for burning the bodies, as the Customs' Officer could not purchase any in town, and all that I could spare proved to be insufficient. The Customs' Officer was helpless — he could do nothing himself and had no means of hiring assistance. The animals had to be buried and Thomas Berubé undertook to bury them 6 feet below the surface for $5.00 which the sub-collector was to get for him from his superiors at once. It is needless to say that nothing more has been heard of it, and the man comes to me every second day for his five dollars. If the half burnt bodies had been allowed to remain on the prairie to pollute the atmosphere, I should have been blamed — no one would have expected the Customs['] Officer to set to work himself with pick and spade. If I had men to spare the burial would have been easy enough, but I had not and have not enough to keep the Post clean. In addition to which the destruction of the horses and disposal of the remains was a dirty job. The men naturally got their clothes soiled, and I think they are entitled to be paid the reasonable sum for which I recommended them. The Customs Department could not have had the work done by outsiders for 5 times the amount.

I-16 Heads and Horns in the Snow
Deane, Monthly Report, April 1892 (NAC, RG18, 63, 247-92)

Heavy losses of cattle are reported from all sides. A man named Walwork living close to town lost 4 mares & colts, dead, and 25 head of cattle missing.

Al Whitney found six head of his cattle dead. Carscadden, an employee of the C.Y. Ranche at the Little Bow reports having seen 15 head of cattle dead in one coulee.

The railroad men on the southern road report about 75 head of cattle dead between here and Brunton, 40 miles.

They say the cattle could not be pushed off the track.

Ex-S/Sgt Ross reports about 300 head of horses & cattle dead between here and Kipp. I have not been able to verify this as yet, but there are some very large snow drifts and until the snow melts it will not be possible to estimate the loss.

A settler hard by, named Ritchie, reports having seen 7 head of horses dead in one coulee. The patrol from Kipp yesterday reports 40 head of cattle dead in one bottom about 8 miles from here.

Insp Begin reports heavy losses of calves in the Milk River District, and says that many cows and horses have been buried in snow drifts. All this has taken place since the 22nd inst, and it says a good deal for the eccentricity of the climate to read Sgt Ashe's report from Writing-on-Stone that on the 20th inst mosquitoes were observed there for the first time this year.

The land needs the moisture badly, but the stock owners are paying a heavy price for it. The snow that fell last night will have covered a good many carcasses.

About the 31st May the air on the prairie will be redolent of cow, calf, horse & sheep. Graham, Conrad Bros' butcher, says he has lost 60 head of sheep.

Steve Cleveland, late Manager of Strong's Ranche, came down from Macleod yesterday and says all he could see was nothing but heads and horns sticking out of all the snow banks.

I-17 Runaway Team
Deane, Monthly Report, December 1892 (NAC, RG18, 63, 247-92)

On the 28th Inst. about 10.20 p.m. the fire bugle rang out for a fire in the river bottom; a number of us went down but could not do anything, the building, a brewery belonging to Joseph Noel, was hopelessly gone long before we could reach the spot, and the "steady double" that we started with soon became demoralized by the crusted snow. Fortunately there was no wind and Mr. Noel's dwelling house and even a diminutive hay stack close by escaped damage. As soon as I realized what the travelling was like going down hill, I thought of what it would be like going up hill, so left an order for a team to follow, and this team met with an unfortunate accident; while driving to the fire along the bottom, where the road seemed perfectly fair, they "struck a snag" in the shape of a mound on one side and a depression on the other and the sleigh upset throwing the box & its occupants off and out. The teamster couldn't hold his horses, who pulled the reins through his fingers, and started off at a gallop with the bobs [*bobsled*]. They met Mr. Morris and two ladies, who in a cutter were returning from the fire, and the pole struck the horse fair on the right breast, making an ugly looking hole, which bled a good deal, and throwing the occupants out of the cutter. The cross bar of the cutter was split and marvellously enough that was all the harm that was done; how someone was not killed, no one is able to explain. Const. Aylsworth's horses are always quiet, and well in hand, and after they had struck the horse they stood still. Morris explains that being white horses, he did not see them on the snow covered ground or he might have got out of their way. As soon as this was reported to me, I had the occupants of the sleigh driven home, and the horse and cutter brought to Barracks. Yesterday I took the evidence of those who were present at the time and forward the board separately. The Division carpenter being with the outposts, I sent the cutter into town to be repaired, and for the present while Mr. Morris' horse is under treatment here, I will lend him a quiet, fat old horse No. 728, which we use as a slop cart horse, to do his delivering for him. He cannot borrow a horse, and cannot hire one under a dollar a day, so I hope you will think this is the best way of obviating a possible claim for damages.

I-18 Border Troubles
Deane, Monthly Report, December 1892 (NAC, RG18, 63, 247-92)

A large number of cattle belonging to Messrs Flowerree and Taylor are reported to have crossed the Milk River into the Milk River Ridge Country, and as the cattle are wild our men in trying to herd them back run too great risks of injuring Government horses ....

I hear Const. Pratt had a narrow escape at Pendant d'Or[ei]lle the other day. He was patrolling with Const Dickson and dismounted to have a shot at an antelope. There chanced to be hard by a "bold, bad" bull from the U.S. of America, who resented the proposition that Canada is for the Canadians and charged Pratt. He fired at him and hit him on the nose, and then his cartridge got jammed in his rifle, and to add to his trouble, his horse got away. Thereupon Const. Dickson "took a hand in" and shot the animal ....

The feed on the South Side has all been burnt off, and the cattle are bound to head northward if allowed to remain in that country at all. On the 16th inst. I therefore addressed to Mr. Flowerree the following letter:

D.A. Flowerree, Esq.,
Helena, Montana.

Dear Sir:

"Insp. Matthews has forwarded to me your letter of the 3rd Inst respecting your cattle which are ranging to the north of Milk River. While anxious to meet your views in every way it is quite impossible that these cattle can be allowed to remain all the winter where they are in the face of the quarantine regulations, and in the face of instructions which the Police have received to carry out these regulations. There are very many more of your cattle to the north of the Milk River than you have any idea of. The Circle Ranche employ a range rider to drive their cattle back across the Milk River. He ranges from about Coutts to Pendant d'Or[ei]lle and does good work. I think it would be to your advantage if you were similarly to employ a man to herd your cattle back from the Milk River Ridge Country.

"Why not drive them south and herd them with the Circle Ranche during the winter?

"You could easily make arrangements with the Circle Ranche to that end.

"The scheduling of Canadian cattle in the English market is a burning question just now, so that you must please understand, that in taking upon myself to make any suggestions, they are made solely with a view to your interests and to obviate the possibility of any trouble in connection with quarantine regulations."

In reply to this I received the following from Mr. Flowerree, a few days ago:

R. Burton Deane,
Sup't, "K" Division,
Lethbridge

Dear Sir:

"Your esteemed favour 16th Inst. duly to hand and in reply, wish to say that I will take immediate steps to put men upon the range to drive our cattle south of Milk River, where the feed is very much better and where we want them.

"At the commencement of the present winter, our cattle were nearly all south of Milk River and must have drifted North with the south and south-west winds.

"Thanking you kindly for courtesy in this matter and with the compliments of the season."

I am etc etc,
Yours Respectfully,
D.A.G. Flowerree

... Mr. Champness came to see me yesterday and brought me a letter as follows:

Capt. R.B. Deane,   Lethbridge, 30th Dec. 1892.
      Lethbridge

Dear Sir:

"I have about 75 head of cattle that I am holding for duties by order of the Minister of Customs who informs me that the Treasury Board have the matter under consideration.

"The A R & C Co. have been feeding the cattle and now inform me, that they will not be able to supply any more hay after the end of this week. Can you let me have some hay to feed the stock with until I am notified by the Dept. as to their decision in the matter?"

Yours truly,
Fred. Champness, Collector

I told him I could not let him have more than 5 or 6 tons of hay, upon his depositing a cheque for $20.00 per ton, but that that was all my instructions allowed me to do. As he has no hay

to replace any that we may let him have, he would like to buy a
few tons outright. The stack that we are now using is the last of
last year's stacks, which cost us at least $13.45 per ton, and we
of course cannot afford to sell it for less than we paid. I obtained
from him the following particulars of Olsen's cattle.

Olsen came into the country to settle, making his first entry
at Emerson. Then he returned to fetch his cattle of which he
owned about 40 head and bought some more bringing up his
total to 79 head. He said he was led by immigration agents to
believe that he could bring his cattle in as settler's effects, and
that everything would be made easy for him. At Emerson, becoming aware that his cattle would be liable for duty he offered
to sell the lot for $8. per head but could find no buyers. He
brought them here by rail, where duty was levied on them on the
valuation of $15. per head and $5. for calves. He had no money
to pay either duty or freight. Two of his cattle died en-route so
that 77 head arrived here, and 4 have died since their arrival,
leaving 73 to-day, with one dying, as I understand. The freight
bill is $350.00; the Custom's dues are about $300.: $417 are
owing for hay, which Mr. Champness has bought to keep the
cattle alive, and the liabilities thus amount to at least $1,067.
Five or 6 tons of hay from us at last year's contract price will
swell the total to over $1,100, and it is doubtful if the cattle will
sell at all. Instructions are pending from the Treasury Board,
but it is safe to say that if this matter is allowed to become
public property, it will do something towards stopping immigration and discrediting immigration agents.

E. Liquor

*Suppression of whisky traders who sold their illegal and often
adulterated goods to the native people from such posts as Fort
Whoop-Up, near present-day Lethbridge, had been the funda-
mental rationale for the establishment of the North-West Mounted
Police in 1873. It remained a prominent goal for the Lethbridge
Division in 1888.*

*The law at the time provided that no Indian was permitted to
have intoxicating drink in his/her possession under any circumstance and that no one else was to have such goods unless that
individual had a permit. Violators, especially those smuggling*

liquor across the border or otherwise furnishing booze to others, were subject to imprisonment or a heavy fine,[12] *of which, under the liquor law, half went to the informant who supplied the evidence. This was an incentive, but the law was so unpopular that few outside the ranks of the Mounties were willing to buck the general opinion that turning in a violator was grossly anti-social behavior. The Mounties themselves were unhappy about the state of affairs since it was impossible to enforce the law and their attempts to do so brought them little but denigration from the public. Certainly, the police made no concerted effort to eradicate drinking.*

Nevertheless, the vigilance of the Mounties in nabbing liquor dealers bringing in smuggled whisky from Montana pretty well ended that traffic by 1890. Although such suppression was successful, uncertainties of the law created annoyance for Deane. Even in preparing a case of public drunkenness, it was necessary to verify that the potions were indeed intoxicating.

But if the police were willing to overlook most minor liquor infractions perpetrated by whites, they were not so unconcerned if the inebriate were a native person. In part, this stemmed from the original mandate of the Mounted Police to end the whisky trade and its degradation of natives. But it also betrayed the sense of superiority held by most whites, Deane included. That attitude amounted to a belief that whites were responsible, free persons able to drink without becoming a threat to the order of society, whereas Indians were too far down the scale of civilization to be permitted the right to drink, for they could not hold their liquor and were capable of the most outrageous and dangerous behavior when drunk. Nevertheless, the penalties meted out to Indians for being drunk and disorderly were not very severe. In many cases, an Indian was let off with a warning, although repeat offenders could be sentenced to a few weeks hard labor; the real quarry for the Mounties were the individuals supplying the booze. In pursuit of those characters, Deane found that the desire of natives for a position as scout for the police could be very useful.

The records show that intoxicants were frequently connected to the other so-called "social evils" of gambling and prostitution.

---

[12] Deane's standard was $1 for being drunk, $50 for possession, $100 for first conviction for selling illegal booze, $200 for second offence, and $300 and/or imprisonment for up to six months for persistent dealing.

One whisky trader was even suspected of being involved in a two-way smuggling trade: liquor into Canada; opium into the United States. The records also demonstrate the prejudice of white persons who wanted to prevent Indians from drinking but to allow whites free access, without acknowledging that there were many whites who couldn't handle their liquor. Brawls, assaults, instances of child neglect and wife-beating all appear in Deane's files and usually were related to drinking. In July 1890, a cowboy drowned while crossing a river because he was so drunk he couldn't save himself after falling from his horse, and his mates were so incapacitated that they could not help him. Excessive consumption was very widespread, and some Mounties themselves had problems with inappropriate drinking.

The permit system was finally overthrown in 1892. Many of the offenses which had previously occupied the attention of the Police, such as possession of liquor, were no longer crimes — except for natives. A licensing system for bars was established, and supervision and regulation of such matters as closing hours were supposed to be enforced by liquor inspectors. Deane welcomed the change and thought it would be beneficial all-round. Two decades later, however, it was evident that problems still abounded, as reported in Document VI-16.

I-19 Smuggling
Deane, Annual Report, 1889 (*SP 1890*, No.13, p.40)

The two following are, I think, fair instances of the manner in which the non-commissioned officers and men on outpost duty keep their eyes about them. We knew that a man named Tom Purcel had a cargo of liquor in the neighbourhood of the line which he was endeavoring to bring in.

The 4th of July was a day which could hardly be kept in gala fashion without a little stimulant, and on the evening of the 2nd, becoming impatient, Purcel put his fate to the test and lost it all. On that evening at 7 o'clock Sergeant Macdonell started from his outpost at Milk River Ridge on patrol; came across a fresh waggon track, followed it up and overtook Purcel, who was conveying six 5 gallon kegs of fire-water. Sergeant Macdonell brought the outfit in here, where Purcel paid his fine [*$100 and costs*], and where his waggon, horses and harness were handed over to the Customs officer who confiscated and sold them. The liquor came in handy for killing some grass on a barrack road.

During the last week in July a party of police from here were building a bridge over a mud hole in the middle coulee on the road to Milk River Ridge. On the 29th July Corporal Elliott, of the flying patrol, came across a fresh waggon track and followed it. It led into the Middle Coulee, and on arrival there he found a noted whiskey runner named "Red McConnell" in the police camp; his waggon, which was empty, and horses, were close by. Something must have scared McConnell, for he had nothing in his waggon when he reached our working party's camp, and finding them there was a surprise to him. Constable Patrick, carrying despatches from the Nine Mile Butte, had also seen his trail, and was riding to overtake him. McConnell probably had an inkling of this and without stopping, pitched his kegs out of the waggon, so that they rolled down a bank out of sight from the trail. Corporal Elliott noticed from the wheel marks that the waggon was getting lighter, and thus had no difficulty in finding the kegs later on. He and his pack-horse patrol joined the working party's camp. After supper McConnell pulled out and drove off into the smoke of distant bush fires with which the country was at that time overspread. Elliott watched the kegs all night, and in the early morning McConnell began to carry them one by one to another and more convenient spot. Elliott stopped him with the second keg in his arms, and brought him and his outfit, including five 10 gallon kegs of whiskey, into barracks, where the liquor was destroyed and McConnell was fined [*$100 and costs*]. Luckily for him there was no proof that the whiskey had been carried in the waggon aforesaid. So McConnell saved his transport from seizure and confiscation. This is the first time that he has been caught in a long and merry life, and he has not travelled this way since.

I-20 "Prohibitive Law is Practically Inoperative"
Deane, Annual Report, 1889 (*SP 1890*, No.13, pp.39-41)

Last year hop beer was the prevailing beverage. These breweries were closed early in the year by the Inland Revenue Department, and thirsty ingenuity soon discovered that permit liquor was, after all, the safest thing to handle. From one point of view this is distinctly an advantage to mankind — the initiated can obtain a decent glass of liquor — instead of the fiery poison that used to be sold, which, I believe, would only find a market now under extreme pressure.

In my humble opinion, the statute itself (if the statute will pardon such a free application of the vulgar tongue) is responsible for the "nigger in the fence."

Section 95 of chapter 50, 49, Victoria enacts as follows:

"Every person who manufactures, &c., imports, &c., any intoxicating liquor or intoxicant, except by special permission as aforesaid, or in whose possession or whose premises such intoxicating liquor or intoxicant of any kind is or has been, shall incur a penalty," &c.

The words "such intoxicating liquor" can only mean that which is imported, &c., without the "special permission as aforesaid."

The permits are marked "not transferable," but the statute says nothing about the written "permission" being transferable or not.

It follows, therefore, that there is no reason why a person should not import liquor under a permit, and hand both permit and liquor over to any other person, and so long as the liquor in question is that comprehended by the permit the recipient is within the law.

The first section (declaratory) of the prohibitive statute provides that no intoxicating liquor or intoxicant shall be imported into, &c., &c., or had in possession in the North-West Territories, "except by special permission, in writing, of the Lieutenant-Governor," but there is no penalty provided for the enforcement of this broad enactment.

The consequence is that in these days, when lawyers must live, the prohibitive law is practically inoperative ....

While on this subject I may perhaps be permitted to say a few words on the question of police justices, now before the country.[13] For my part, I have always avoided trying any cases whenever I could possibly do so. Since I have been here I have accepted the situation because there has been no help for it. In

---

[13] Commissioned officers (inspectors, superintendents, and above) in the Mounted Police held judicial powers as Justices of the Peace.

former years it has been within my experience that local justices have refused to try liquor cases on the ground that they could not run the risk of injuring their business. On one occasion I visited an out station in connection with a liquor case — found a local justice there, who was disinclined to have anything to do with it; represented to him that it was his duty to try the case, but that if he would not do so I would. He finally consented, and convicted and fined the defendant.

Not long ago I happened to meet an acquaintance who hailed from that neighbourhood, and asked him how so-and-so was getting on. He replied that he was not doing much; he had lost caste ever since he allowed himself to try a liquor case some years ago, and the neighbours still looked shy at him. Who, I would ask, is able to predict that local justices will be more willing than they have been in the past to subject themselves to the disagreeableness almost inseparable from the enforcement of an unpopular law? I am not alone in thinking that if police magistrates are disestablished the law in some parts of the country will become a dead letter. I will gladly make anyone a present of my magisterial duties, but am quite sure that no one here would undertake them unless he were paid for it. In my opinion, nothing short of a stipendiary magistracy can efficiently supersede the present system.

I-21 "Selling Intoxicants to Indians"
Deane, Monthly Report, October 1890 (NAC, RG18, 39, 137-90)

On the 17th inst Paul Lavallé was arrested near Noel's Brewery for selling liquor to an Indian. The circumstances are as follows: On the afternoon of the above date "Iron Shields" an Indian, who having been very anxious to be taken on as a scout & who was told that he must first of all qualify for the position, reported that liquor was being sold to Indians in the river bottom. That night S/Major Jarvis [*who spoke Blackfoot*] went to the bottom with "Iron Shields" giving him marked money & watched him go into the house of one Paul Lavallé. In a few minutes the Indian came out with a bottle which he handed to the Sgt. Major who came back & reported. Under my instructions he went again to the bottom & about midnight arrested

Paul Lavallé in the act of giving the Indian a drink of whisky. Lavallé had the marked money upon him. He was not arrested on the first occasion as the Indian was to obtain a case against another seller of intoxicants to Indians but this did not happen to be practicable that night.

On the following day I was not well enough to leave the house & on Sunday was in bed with a high fever brought on I do not know how.

Paul Lavallé pleaded guilty on the 20th inst before Insp Casey & Mr Champness JPs to a charge of selling intoxicants to Indians & was fined $200 & costs. He had recently been granted a permit & this was the use he made of it ....

On the 25th I returned to duty from sick list. On the 26th I issued a warrant which soon after midnight was executed upon Thos. Farrar for selling intoxicants to Indians. In the river bottom in which Mr Galt's house stands there is a brewery owned by Joseph Noel, a Frenchman, whom we have suspected for a long time of selling intoxicants to Indians. Paul Lavallé who was convicted on the 20th was an employé of Noel's. Hop beer is brewed at this place & the customers for it are chiefly miners and Indians. Thomas Farrar was also an employé of Noel's. In the case of Paul Lavallé I directed each stage of the proceedings and nothing was done except by my express order. I was prevented by sickness from sitting on the bench at that trial.[14]

In the case of Farrar I did not as it happens, give any such special instructions, because Sgt Major Jarvis knew exactly what evidence would be required, & beyond receiving general instructions to work up another case, did not report to me until he came to lay the information.

A certain Indian woman named "Good Killer" was very anxious to get her husband taken on as Police Scout, & I told her that he must first prove his capacity & she therefore said she could buy beer etc. S/Major Jarvis gave her $5.00 & watched her & another woman into the brewery. When they came out he

[14] Having the powers of both policeman and judge (and frequently jailor) meant that Deane, along with all other senior Mounted Police officers, constantly had a structural conflict of interest, which, in this instance at least, did not trouble Deane one whit.

stopped them & took from them 9 bottles of beer, which he marked in their presence & subsequently sealed. The women went to their tepee & presently "Iron Shields" (an Indian whom I have employed as scout for one month & who acted in the Paul Lavallé business) came in & sent them for more beer. They went & bought 4 bottles early on Sunday morning. "Iron Shields" drank the beer & it made him drunk as he said in court. He was so far overcome that he was showing the effects later in the day when he came to Barracks. He was thus useless for our purposes & "Eagle Talker" another would be scout was called in. S/Major Jarvis & Sg't Rudd took note of his condition & swore that he was perfectly sober at about 2 o'cl in the afternoon. He was then given a little of the seized 9 bottles of beer & in a short time its intoxicating effects were apparent to the 2 previously mentioned NC officers.

The evidence was then complete & the case was tried before Insp Casey & myself on the 29th & 30th inst. Mr McCaul defended the prisoner & objected to everything — refusing even to plead. After a great deal of trouble including a personal quarrel between him & the Crown Prosecutor on the subject of putting leading questions to an Indian witness who was particularly obtuse, I took the examination in chief into my own hands & the evidence of S/Major Jarvis was fully corroborated in all material points. Finally Mr McCaul proposed to call Insp Casey & myself as witnesses, which ridiculous proposal was of course ruled inadmissable. He put in no defence & we convicted the prisoner & adjudged him to pay a fine of $300.00 and costs and to undergo 6 months Imp. with H.L. ....[15]

This Thos Farrar underwent 6 months Impt. H.L. rather more than 2 years ago for selling intoxicants to Indians.

The evidence in the case under discussion was unimpeached & the sentence is in accordance with the general feeling of respectable settlers with regard to selling intoxicants to Indians. I may say further that no other evidence as to the intoxicating

[15] As was made clear in his Annual Report for 1890 (*SP 1891*, No.19, p.52), Deane considered a jail sentence very important because otherwise an agent of a dealer in spirits had nothing to lose, provided the employer paid any fine. With a jail sentence, Deane argued, "they will be less willing to become the tools of an unscrupulous man."

properties of the beer would have answered the purpose. The uncorroborated evidence of Indians is worth very little.[16] Even in the case of "Eagle Talker" whom S/Major Jarvis & Sg't Rudd examined and found sober, Mr McCaul in cross-examination asked him "You were pretty full [*drunk*] weren't you when you went into Big Nose's room?" "Ugh" he grunted & Mr McCaul sat down.

I have engaged "Eagle Talker" as scout for one month on the distinct understanding that if he wants to be kept on after that time he must do some work.

There are several aspirants for the honor & I find it better not to make it too cheap.

I-22 "Assaulting and Resisting the Police"
Deane, Monthly Report, June 1888 (NAC, RG18, 21, 373-88)

On the 23rd about 9 p.m. Constable Arrowsmith reported that there was a disturbance among the Hungarians and that Sgt. Ross wanted six men sent to his assistance. These men had hardly left the Barracks when another (civilian) messenger rushed up breathless with the report that the Police were being badly beaten and that there was a serious row going on. I then sent every available man under Insptr. White Fraser, with the result that 16 prisoners were brought in to tenant 5 cells, two more being apprehended in the morning. Nearly the whole of my time during the past week has been taken up with trying the aforesaid prisoners; of whom 1 was discharged to come up for judgement when called upon — 4 were discharged with a caution — 3 convicted of being drunk and disorderly — 4 of common assault — 6 committed for trial on varying charges of assaulting and resisting the Police.

The trial of these last is fixed for the 9th Inst [*each was fined $20 and costs*]. Having obtained the assistance of Const. Minnezewsky of "A" Division as interpreter I thought it desirable to send him among the Hungarians as a detective with a

---

[16] Deane's prejudice against single native witnesses stemmed from an 1884 Fort Macleod case. See R.B. Deane, "The Story of Joe Bush," introduced and annotated by W.M. Baker, *Alberta History*, 40:4 (Autumn 1992): 2-15.

view to getting information as to the liquor they drink &c and if possible to obtain evidence to warrant a prosecution of the vendor of the liquor they drank on Sunday.

Their custom is to get into their homes a lot of beer for Sunday's use. This they pour into tubs and sit round soaking their bread in the mixture. More or less noise is always made on these occasions and as long as they were in a settlement by themselves it did not very much matter whether they damaged one anothers['] skulls or not, but now they have neighbours within a little distance and they complain very much of the noise. Last Sunday I find they imported large quantities of beer from a saloon keeper named Smith. About 9 o'c p.m. a fight began between 2 or 3 of them. Sgt Ross was in the neighbourhood and told them to desist. As they would not, he took them into custody, with the result reported in my weekly report of the last week.[17] Const Minnezewsky who met them in the saloon and heard them talk freely say that they claim to have "beaten the Police once" and "will do it again" when they get a fair show. They are treacherous and cowardly, and I would submit that at least 2 or 3 small pistols should be supplied for the use of Sgt. Ross and the man or men on town duty. Sgt. Ross certainly should not be left without some protection of the kind, as he sticks at nothing and takes all the risks, albeit he shews a good deal of judgement when in a hot corner.

Two or three evenings ago Const. Minnezewsky went into a saloon about 9 o'clock and stayed there till about 11.15 — during that time he calculated that 7 or 8 drank about 70 or 80 bottles of beer.[18] One of the miners named Martin Kirkmer was if able

---

[17] This was a wild donnybrook with Mounties being injured and civilians having to assist the police in re-establishing order. The episode was excerpted from Deane's Weekly Report, 28 June 1888, and transmitted to Sir John A. Macdonald for his information (see NAC, RG18, 23, 631-88).

[18] By the time of Deane's Annual Report for 1888 (*SP 1889*, No.17, p.67), the story had grown: "Taken in moderation, this beer is certainly harmless, and it is puzzling to know how a man can swallow enough to get drunk on. Given, however, a man of the required capacity, who deliberately sits down to consume two or three dozen bottles in an evening, it is to the interest of saloon keepers not to serve him beyond a certain point. Two or three Hungarian miners think nothing of drinking sixty or seventy bottles between them in an evening." The resultant stress on the bladder would have contributed, no doubt, to the occasional case recorded in the criminal returns for "indecent exposure of person."

to walk, undoubtedly under the influence of liquor. It happened that he and Minnezewsky went out of the house together, and got into some loud worded altercation in the street upon which Sgt. Ross and Const. Arrowsmith arrested them for being drunk and disorderly. Next morning the evidence shewed that the Constable though disorderly was not drunk (he had passed under the name of Patrick Murphy and as such was tried) so he was discharged — his companion pleaded guilty to drunkenness but denied the disorderly conduct. He was however convicted of both [*fined $1 and costs*] and as he made a statement to the effect that he went into the saloon about 9 o'clock having previously had nothing to drink that day save one bottle of beer at noon, that he took his share of the drink going on until about 11.15, when he found himself drunk, having drunk nothing but beer, a summons was issued against the saloon keeper for having intoxicating liquor illegally on his premises. This case is now sub judice, having lasted two days and being likely to last as many more.[19] The defendant charged Const. Minnezewsky with interpreting falsely, so he had to stand aside, but in the event of conviction and appeal I trust to be able to convince the judge of his integrity.

I-23 "Drinks of Whiskey Before Church Parade"
Deane, Monthly Report, April 1890 (NAC, RG18, 39, 137-90)

The following recounts a somewhat lamentable experience for the force and its credit.

On Easter Sunday Const MacLean was under the influence of liquor in the Presbyterian Church. Under strong pressure he admitted that he had had a couple of drinks of whiskey before church parade. He found Const Stibble and a bottle in a passage adjoining his room. Const Stibble also under strong injunctions to speak the truth admitted the fact and said that the liquor had been that morning bought by Const Oliver. Oliver and he went

---

[19] The saloon-keeper was Fred. E. Smith, presumably the same one who had supplied the beer for the festivities the previous Sunday. He was fined $100 and costs or four months hard labour, a conviction that was unsuccessfully appealed (see *SP 1889*, No.17, p. 201).

after morning stables to a house near, kept by Henry Howard and there bought two bottles of whiskey for $3.25. Oliver paid the money, Stibble had none. Upon this Oliver was charged and in his defence said that he was so drunk at the time that after morning stables he did not remember anything that happened until dinner time. Henry Howard was on the 9th instant convicted before me of selling intoxicants, upon Stibble's evidence and was fined $100.00 and costs. Const Oliver as witness for the defence remembered that he had bought eggs and not whiskey from Howard. His memory had partially returned since he was himself charged.[20]

I-24 The New Law
Deane, Yearly Report, 1892 (*SP 1893*, No.15, p.85)

In view of the proceedings of the Royal Commission now sitting, it would probably be superfluous for me to make any remarks upon the liquor law. I may, however, say this, that thirty-seven cases of drunk and disorderly conduct have been brought up this year, against thirty-two cases for the corresponding months of the year ending 30th November, 1891. This is explainable partly by the fact that a good deal of liquor was dr[u]nk on the introduction of the new law to celebrate the obsequies of the old obnoxious system, and partly by the fact that under the prohibition regime saloon-keepers exercised as much restraint as possible upon drunken men, in keeping them out of sight, &c., in order to avoid getting themselves into trouble.

I am of opinion that there is less drunkenness now than under the old system.

---

[20]Detailed evidence on the case is located in NAC, RG18, 1178, 200-90. The most amusing comment made in hearings before Deane was by Constable A. McIlveen who noticed nothing unusual about MacLean's behavior since he just seemed sleepy "and I think some of the rest of the congregation were the same way." Deane inflicted the following punishments: MacLean and Stibble — both fined $10 and fourteen days confined to barracks: Oliver — fined one month's pay. (Commissioner Herchmer reduced MacLean's fine to $5.) Deane's monthly report went on to relate how an attempt was made to buy off Stibble so that he would not be present to testify at the appeal hearing of Howard's case, and how Deane thwarted that endeavor by having Stibble hide out and then make a surprise appearance at the trial.

II
"THICK SKULLS" AND "SOILED DOVES"
LETHBRIDGE DIVISION 1893-1897

The beauty of Deane's reports is that they contain information on a wide range of subjects. The items that are especially notable in his reports from 1893 to 1897 relate to the circumstances of people at the lower reaches of the social order. Here one sees the struggle between labor and management, the strife and violence between and within ethnic groups, the nature of male-female relations, and the situation of unfortunates in the society. Deane's reports betray his attitudes towards various social groups, such as East European miners with their "thick ... skulls," or prostitutes, also known as "soiled doves." Because Deane was an involved, opinionated observer and not a bureaucratic automaton, his reports provide rich and fascinating insights into numerous aspects of the social history of the Lethbridge region a century ago.

A. Economic Circumstances and Labor Strife

In his 1889 Annual Report, Deane claimed that "business cannot go utterly to the bad in a place of this size ...." Stock interests did well during Deane's first decade in the district. By the mid-nineties, over five thousand head of cattle were being exported annually from the Lethbridge rail yards alone, and many of the beasts were driven to other depots outside the territory. The coal industry in the town continued, and a few agricultural settlers established themselves. But given the optimistic expectations for the area, growth was painfully slow. The town of Lethbridge, for example, had a negligible increase in population between 1888 and 1897, the exact figure at any particular time in the mid-nineties fluctuating from two to three thousand depending on the state of the economy. The real boom for the area was a decade away, but between 1888 and 1897, the promise of the recently-established coal town was substantiated, and the economic base of the community was consolidated. By 1897, with plans for irrigation and for the Crow's Nest Pass Railway in place, the future of the town seemed secure.

Even in the best of times, work posed dangers in any sector, even for Mounted Policemen. The division's sharpshooter, Corporal Dickson, nearly lost his eye when a carbine blew up in his face.[1] Constable Perry was drowned attempting to cross the Belly River on his horse during springtime run-off.[2] Other workers suffered similar accidents, while coal miners faced the constant threat of cave-ins and explosions, even though the Lethbridge colliery was not a particularly perilous mine. Lethbridge miners were not unionized at the time, but they did attempt to take collective action when their jobs were threatened. Deane's views on labor-management matters were shaped by his military and elite background and by his position as "boss" of the men in his division. Towards his subordinates, he was very judgmental, could be extremely critical, and was not loath to hand out significant penalties for their deficiencies in the performance of duty. On the other hand, he showed consideration towards his men and was not sparing in his compliments, especially to worthy officers and N.C.O.s under his jurisdiction. But Deane's sense of superiority extended to most human beings, including businessmen, and he therefore considered himself an admirable conveyor of reason and fairness for both management and labor.

II-1 Depressing Outlook
Deane, Annual Report, 1895 (SP 1896, No.15, p.89)

The business outlook has been depressing, albeit the stock interests have been in a flourishing condition. The town of Lethbridge is of course dependent on the mines. During the summer months when the miners are only working two or three days in each week, they cannot support themselves and their families, and the storekeepers necessarily suffer. Latterly the cry has been for more men and the monthly pay-roll is gradually increasing in amount. Just now the A.R. & C. Co. [*Alberta Railway and Coal Company*] have all they can do to supply the

---

[1] Deane, Monthly Report, December 1893 in NAC, RG18, 74, 73-93.

[2] Deane, Annual Report, 1889 in *SP 1890*, No.13, pp.49-50. A few years later, it was discovered that the horse ridden by Perry had a nasty trick of rolling its rider off when it got into deep water (see Deane, Monthly Report, June 1894 in NAC, RG18, 91, 148-94). Deane related the tale in his *Mounted Police Life*, pp. 262-266.

daily demand, the coal being largely in request in Montana for domestic consumption, but what is most wanted is a market during the summer.

Surface Buildings and Incline Railway, Alberta Railway and Coal Co., 1890

GA, Steele and Wing's photograph, NA-1323-10

Coal mining had been the reason for the establishment of Lethbridge and long remained its economic lifeblood. Coal was carried from the river valley up the steep slope of the coulees to the level of the plains in the heart of the town. There it was sorted and loaded into proper rail cars and shipped out. As shown in this picture, the miners often rode the little mine railway to and from the townsite. Even in the recently-established community, however, workers and owners squared off from time to time, as Document II-2 details.

II-2 Lockout of Miners
Deane, Weekly Report, 2 February 1894 (NAC, RG18, 91, 148-94)

There seems to be a sort of earthquake in the A.R. &C. Coy. The staff is being largely cut down, and the convulsion has not yet spent itself, so I am told.

Deane, Monthly Report, February 1894 (NAC, RG18, 91, 148-94)

On the 15th Inst. the mines were closed here and all the men discharged, the Company giving notice that they would in future require fewer men and that wages would be reduced. They gave the men until the 22nd Inst to subscribe to their terms.

On the 22nd Inst Mr. Galt showed me a threatening anonymous letter which had been mailed to Mr. Simpson, the new Superintendent of Mines, who has certainly incurred the dislike of the men, who blame him for the reduction in wages.

The Company lay to their souls the flattering unction that they have managed this "Lock-out" very well, but "the proof of the pudding is the eating". For myself I question the expediency of throwing a large number of men out of employment without warning. A total number of 580 men connected with the mines has been paid off .... Of these 580 men, rather less than 150 have actually left the neighbourhood, and of the remaining 430, Mr. Galt informed the men yesterday that the Company require to re-engage only about 130. All of those must be good miners, whose names must be approved by himself, who must be married men having interests in the town, and who must sign a contract to work at a certain wage. The proffered wage is a reduction of 17% on the prices formerly paid and the men will not consider it. They say there is no living to be obtained from the money and a man may as well starve while walking about, as starve while working.

The situation to-day is this: There are 300 men in town who have no hope of work; there are 130 men who dare not if they would, accept the Company's terms; one man has been already beaten in the mine and others are threatened. The Company are full of "tall" talk and the men are full of irritation, complaining of the many highly paid officials in & the mismanagement of their little concern.

At my prolonged and earnest remonstrance, Mr. Galt published on Monday last, 26th., a notice offering free passes to Great Falls for batches of not less than 50 men who may wish to go there; this offer to hold good for one week, and further offering to carry married men and their families to the same destination free during the month of March. So far no advantage has been taken of these offers. After many years' example of indecision on the part of the Company's management many of the men even now think that this is simply a "bluff" on the part of the Company, and that if they wait long enough they will be re-engaged at the old prices. The question is what will happen when they eventually find that it is no bluff, but an act imperatively necessary for self preservation. It goes without saying that there is something wrong somewhere. Other mines can be run at a profit, why not these? The miners have a good deal to say about it. I mix freely with them and they will talk to me as one of themselves, in fact the only reliable information that Mr. Galt gets is from me. It is not always palatable, but I cannot help that.

I think myself that if during the past few months a given number of men had been gradually paid off, told that there was no more work for them, and offered free passes to Great Falls, a great deal of the present difficulty would have been overcome. The men say they have been treated meanly and resent it accordingly. It was at first given out that no free passes would be given at all, although happily that has been set aside. The Company are under the impression that starvation will drive the men to accept their terms. That would be all very well if they could offer them all work, but when there are 300 men to be provided for whom no work can be obtained, the situation is likely to become strained, unless they can be persuaded to leave the neighbourhood. I have 3 Constables and 2 horses at No.3 shaft, two of the men for night duty, and 3 Constables similarly employed at No.1 shaft, looking after the engine house etc. Const. Tryhaft understands Sclavish and moves about those miners to hear what they have to say. They do not know that he understands them. I have also 4 Constables on town duty in addition.

If any trouble should ensue, it will take from 20 to 25 men at a time to watch the Company's property, but at present I cannot express an opinion as to what is likely to happen ....
6.P.M. I have just returned from a tour in town. Mr. Galt has made out a list of 130 miners whom he proposes to re-engage at his own terms, which are to be subsequently discussed. This list will be published at 10 a.m. to-morrow and it remains to be seen what the other men say to the selection. Mr. Galt is more confident of a mutually satisfactory settlement than I am, but I hope he may be right.

Deane, Monthly Report, March 1894 (NAC, RG18, 91, 148-94)

On the afternoon of the 7th inst, hearing that the miners were holding a meeting, I sent to ask if they would allow me to attend. They replied (with only one dissentient voice) that they would be very glad to see me and I went; talked to them for the space of about an hour, obtained from Mr. Galt a promise of favourable consideration of one or two small concessions and got them into first rate humour generally, so much so that I was quite sanguine of bringing about a satisfactory settlement. I became "our friend Captain Deane" and was finally asked if I would accompany a deputation to the authorities in order to see fair play, to which of course I cheerfully consented.

The morning of the 8th was consumed in a long interview with the Colliery Superintendent, who, it is no figure of speech to say, the men abhor. This committee, be it observed, had been appointed by the meeting of the proceeding evening, which had also indicated the lines upon which they were to work, such as cheaper powder, cheaper pick handles and wedges, allowances for yardage &c, &c. Powder is a great item to some of the miners, who pay $20 a month and more for it. It is to the interest of the Company to have as little powder used as possible, and good miners use very little, so that the Company put a high price on it to deter men from using it. We succeeded in getting the price lowered from $6 to $4 per 5 lb keg. Pick handles and wedges are reduced 20%, but coal at $1 per ton was promised to the married employees of the Company; satisfactory arrangements were made for the future with regard to measuring and allowing for what is called "bone coal" [*rock mixed in with the coal*] &c, &c, fortnightly payment was conceded, and the Company undertook not to employ any more men than was necessary to fill orders. In the case of the men paid by the day, the Company would not yield, except of the case of drivers in the mines, to whom, in the event of their being faithful and zealous, the Superintendent held out the hope of an increase of the schedule rate of wage.

I thought we had done an uncommonly good day[']s work, and went to the meeting in the afternoon full of hope. I read the minutes which I had taken and explained that their committee had done good work and had extorted the uttermost farthing from the Company. Unfortunately however, there was a miserable little firebrand there, who uses long words that he does not understand and cannot apply, who has the gift of the gab to a certain extent, and who has apparently the ear of a large number of the men, who won't take the trouble to think for themselves, and of others whose knees are weak when it comes to a question of upholding their inward convictions against a noisy demagogue and his unreasoning followers. He ridiculed the concessions as being no concessions at all, and hot words passed between him and the members of the committee, who called attention to the fact that they had worked on the lines indicated by the general meeting at which they had been appointed. This little firebrand was backed up [by] an old rascal with one foot in the grave, who was simply courting popularity and there were some hot heads amongst the Sclavs. The meeting became more or less a pandemonium and various motions that they would not resume work for anything less than $[.]80 a ton, and others to a similar effect were successively passed like wildfire, the noisy element having it all their own way and the others bestriding the fence waiting the chance to point out the safe side to get down.

The Company's offer was addressed to men whom they had selected and whose names were on a certain list that had been published. An attempt was then made to bring about a meeting to be confined to these men, and it was timed to take place at 3 p.m. on the 10th inst. Only one man at the meeting of the 9th had the gumption to speak up and he said to his fellows, "I've got children to support; do you think I'm going to see them starve? I won't." I hoped after this that he and a few more who were anxious to resume work, would turn up at the meeting in question. The great body of the miners was assembled in the main street, watching the Building Company's Hall across the Square to see who went in and only three men put in an appearance. I talked to them to induce them to stiffen their backs and then joined the mob on the sidewalks, when I admitted I had been to the meeting, that I was not at liberty to say any thing about it, and that men who were disposed to go to work had better apply for it before it was too late. Presently a miner lounged up and whispered that a Round Robin was being signed in a certain place, that 10 or 12 names were down before his, and that the men would go to work all right. As this got about gradually it took the heart out of the malcontents and men [*made*] no secret of their having applied for work.

As the men had not accepted the Company's offer by 6 p.m. on the 9th the Company sent notices to quit to the occupants of their cottages, and this had the effect of impressing upon them the fact that the company meant business and helped to bring them to time.

The Company have now selected their own men and the trouble now is to dispose of the men for whom there is no work. The Company have not yet engaged all the men for whom they can find work and it is impossible at present to gauge correctly the number of the unemployed, but I think it safe to say that it will range from 100 to 150. I hear the C P R can find work for 75 of them on the road between Dunmore and Gleichen, and, if so, that will relieve the tension somewhat.

Assuming that matters may be somewhat amicably arranged just now, it does not follow that there will be no recurrence of a disagreement between masters and men. It is sure that a branch of the Union will be established here and it is also sure that if the men can only catch the Company "once upon the hip" they will "feed fat the Ancient Grudge" they bear them ....

On the 28th. the mayor called a meeting of the Town Council and Board of Trade, and asked me to attend. A number of Sclavs had gone to him to ask for assistance, saying they were out of work and wanted to get transportation to Texas. They were a little cheeky, and said if they could not get relief they would steal. The Mayor thus brought the matter before the towns-people, a number of the Sclavs being present. A deputation which I was asked to join, was chosen to interview Mr. Galt on the matter and he agreed to give the men a free train to Great Falls, provided they would all go, and would see what terms he could make for them with the U S Ry. to Texas. It appears the U S Railways will not allow passengers to travel in box cars, at so much per car, which was what the Sclavs wanted but will reduce the fare from $52.60 to $41.60. A number of them came to see me yesterday and today and I told them this. It appears the C.P.R. can find work for about 70 men in a few days on the road between Dunmore and Gleichen and although the wages, $1.25, are not as high as they have been in the habit of earning, I am endeavouring to instil into the thick Sclavish skull, the principle that "half a loaf is better than no bread". The Sclavs say with good reason that in Great Falls, there is no more work to be had than here, and I think they have also visions of a chain gang institution for paupers, which they have in that land of Liberty.

Deane, Monthly Report, April 1894 (NAC, RG18, 91, 148-94)

Having interviewed several deputations of Sclavs & Hungarians, both gentlemen and ladies, at the beginning of the month and persuaded them there was nothing to be gained by their staying here: they finally made up their minds that they would go south. They had been told at the station that no more free passes would be issued and were in considerable perplexity. I got the names of some 80 souls altogether and as a personal matter, Mr. Galt consented to give them free passes to Great Falls. Some of these changed their minds at the last moment, but on the 2nd Inst 32 men, 7 women and 23 children went to Great Falls and one man, a Hungarian paid his way East. It is probable that these people have left $1000. worth of irrecoverable debts in town, the H.B.Co. being by far the biggest loser.

E.T. Galt to L.W. Herchmer, 15 March 1894 (NAC, RG18, 94, 285-94)

With reference to the recent lock-out in this place among the miners employed by this Company, I wish to record my appreciation of the valuable services rendered to this Company by the North West Mounted Police in the preservation of order and the protection afforded to property during the trouble which lasted twenty-nine days.

I wish further to say that this testimony would be wholly incomplete without referring to Captain Deane who by his personal influence, tact and good judgment did much to promote a settlement of differences between masters and men.

II-3 "Palmy Days"
Deane, Annual Report, 1897 (*SP 1898*, No.15, pp.57-58, 62-63)

The Police year opened most auspiciously on the 1st December, 1896, with a genial chinook which came just in time to save numbers of range cattle from certain death.

The loss in the district from the effect of the November storm was estimated not to exceed one per cent. It is true that the calf crop this year has been small and much below the average, but we had a very cold and unseasonable spring, and to that is attributable the loss of calves.

So far as winter pasturage is concerned, the opinion is gradually gaining ground that this district has much to recommend it. For lack of moisture the grass does not grow so luxuriantly as it does further west, but on the other hand it cures before the frost has time to affect it. The snow fall, again, is always comparatively light here, and thus, though the grass is short, the cattle can get at it without much difficulty.

A system of irrigation to the south of us is a mere question of time, and the ensuing year will probably see a beginning made of extensive works, wherein irrigation and colonization will go hand in hand. It will follow as a matter of course that this will become a great producing centre. We know that, given sufficient moisture, the soil will grow almost anything, and apart from cereals there will be in the mining country a great demand for garden produce of all kinds, in supplying which Lethbridge will have the advantage of being close to the market by means of the Crow's Nest railway.

An irrigation ditch some 70 miles long, with its ramifications, may be expected to cause some climatic changes, and ten years hence we may expect to see no longer a treeless landscape. It will take settlers of the right sort to do justice to the country, but an industrious man may earn something to keep the pot boiling from a very early date. Radishes and lettuces, besides eggs, poultry, and butter, will find a ready sale in the Kootenai.

It is, too, a practical certainty that broad gauge trains will be running into Lethbridge from Great Falls next summer over the A. R. & C. Co.'s and the Canada and Great Falls lines.

Business was very dull during the first half of the year, but it has increased with the progress of the Crow's Nest Railway until it is as good now as it was in the palmy days of the town.

The miners took advantage of the flowing tide last August to strike for increase of wages and other concessions. This was the outcome of a predetermined plan. Negotiations had from one cause or another come to a standstill, when a opportunity offered for my intervention, and I was able to be the means of bringing the two parties together again. I need not enlarge on this further than to say that the company conceded every demand made by the men except that of an additional ten cents per ton. Rather than do that they declared they would shut the mines down, and the men eventually resumed work, having good reason to be satisfied with the fruits of their agitation, which may be capitalized at about $8,000 per annum ....

We have devoted unceasing attention to the maintenance of order along the Crow's Nest branch of the C. P. railway while under construction. The heaviest part of the work on the whole line has been at Whoop-up, from about 5 to 8 miles distant from here. The line crosses the St. Mary's River at Whoop-up, and the bridge there will be 2,800 feet long. About six million feet of timber will have been used for bridging between here and Macleod by the time the road is completed.

The contractors have had a hard time of it. The soil in some of the cuts at Whoop-up is a very stiff clay, which a plough will not touch, and which is more difficult to blast than rock. The contractors are working this at the price of dirt, and some of them will have lost considerable money. I understand that on one section alone seven car loads of blasting powder have been expended, and that the contractor stands to lose very heavily unless he gets more than the price of dirt for his excavating.

The contractors have had a lot of trouble, too, with their men. They brought up men from the East, many of whom no sooner arrived here than they wanted to break their contract and leave their railway fare unpaid. A batch of men were charged before me under the Masters and Servants Act with deserting their employment, and I suspended judgment on the defendants undertaking to go to work. In some cases this answered well enough, while in others the men laid themselves out to demoralize the gang to which they were attached, and generally gave such trouble that the employers were glad to get rid of them at any price.

B. The Underside of Lethbridge

In spite of the concerts, dances, sports clubs, church activities, and the theatrical evenings in which Deane was instrumental, Lethbridge was not a genteel town. What frontier community is? As a centre which attracted speculators, miners, cowboys, rail-

waymen, and other laborers, it had its drifters, sharpies, and rough characters.

Moreover, all of its residents had migrated to the town from far afield. It was an ethnically heterogeneous community, with many of the miners tracing their origins to southern and central Europe. The disturbances which disrupted Lethbridge were by no means restricted to the miners or to non-Anglos. Yet, as already seen in Document I-22, Deane's views on "foreigners," as Anglos were prone to call them, were tinged with disdain.

Becoming immersed in the underside of Lethbridge was not especially edifying, but it was required of Deane whether he liked it or not. And today his reports about family, neighborhood, and ethnic squabbles and fights reveal much about the reality of Lethbridge society a century ago.

II-4 "Various Nationalities"
Deane, Annual Report, 1894 (*SP 1895*, No.15, pp.91-92)

To give an idea of the various nationalities composing the population of Lethbridge I may cite a placard which can occasionally be seen hanging up in the post office to the effect that there is "no mail to-day." This is expressed in no less than eight different languages, viz.: French, German, Slavish, Hungarian, a dialect of Hungarian, Danish, Italian and Chinese. There are some Swedes and Russians in town too, and the Hungarian dialect above mentioned seems to be a sort of Volapuk by which they can manage to communicate with one another. The Hungarians and Slavs were not a very desirable element, a great number were compelled to seek "fresh fields and pastures new," and they are not much loss. Some of them have great aptitude for collecting and hoarding shekels. A Slav, who left town in the spring bewailing his ability to pay his butcher and grocer was found after his departure to have carried off $700 in hard cash. His grocer managed to make him disgorge before he got entirely out of reach.

II-5 A Stabbing
Deane, Monthly Report, December 1893 (NAC, RG18, 74, 73-93)

On the 11 inst a Hungarian named Bolock was brought up charged with having stabbed a compatriot and fellow boarder named Mike Cako on the previous night. The wounded man was unable to appear so I took the evidence of the two witnesses and adjourned the hearing .... I was irresistibly reminded by the interpreter of the old saying at cricket when an eleven starts to play against an opposing eleven and their umpire. It seemed to me that the interpreter was very anxious to find the prisoner "not out" every time, and whether my conjecture is true or not, I will if possible secure another interpreter for the trial before the Judge. The wounded man was subsequently able to appear and give evidence on the 20th inst, when the case was sent for trial, the accused being unable to obtain bail. He had some compatriots with savings bank accounts who at first were willing enough to go bail for him, but when they assimilated the fact that if he should happen to walk off, they would lose their money, they did not appear to have much faith in human nature as represented by Joe Bolock [*who received three months hard labor*].

Out of this wounding which occurred on the night of Sunday the 10th inst. a report arose which gave us not a little work to unravel. A Hungarian girl named Alsatki who works for a Mrs. McNabb was sick for a few days and went home to her parents. While at home she heard her mother talking to some one and saying that the Hungarians had had a row, that a man had been killed and that the Hungarian had buried him in one of the coulees. When she returned to her place she told Mrs. McNabb, who told her husband, who told Const. Condon, who told Sgt. Hare, who told me. Sgt. Hare then began his enquiries and found that Mrs. Alsatki had heard it from her husband who is now in hospital with a broken leg — he heard it from John Swedy — he from George Gresik, and he from a man named McLean who had been told that a Hungarian had been stabbed on Sunday the 10th inst. and was likely to die. That is all there is "to" it as they say but no one knows what sensational story may not appear in a newspaper one of these days.

II-6 Wedding Violence
Deane, Weekly Report, 2 February, 1894 (NAC, RG18, 91, 148-94)

On Sunday evening the 28th ulto the Sclavs had a wedding and a Hungarian invited himself to the festivities. There seems to have been about 35 people there. Presently the Hungarian was assaulted and stabbed and made complaint at the Town

Station. Sgt. Hare, Consts. Condon and Wright, went to the house with the Hungarian, who pointed out two of the men who had assaulted him, one being the stabber. The house was very crowded and Const. Condon was taking out the two men whom he had arrested, Const Wright helping to make way through the door, when the crowd rescued the two men by jamming Wright into a doorway and Condon into the wall and pulled the prisoners away from them. The Constables identified two of the crowd who were most prominent and they will have an opportunity of hearing what the Judge thinks.

The stabber, John Vogtila, was tried under the Summary Trials Act and in consideration of all the circumstances, provocation &c. was fined $25 and costs or 2 months Impt. H.L. In the other cases I have entered a conviction and adjudged the defendants to come up for judgment when called upon. I have also ordered Andrew Popp and John Vogtila to find sureties to keep the peace for a year. They shook hands in my office and I dare say will live harmoniously after this.

II-7 "In Flagrante Delicto"
Deane, Monthly Report, October 1895 (NAC, RG18, 104, 131-95)

The miners['] "ladies" have been quarreling a good deal during the past month. Summonses and cross summonses resulted in a Mrs. Wells being fined $2 and costs on the 8th inst for assault, and on the 10th the Hungarian wives asserted themselves. It appears that a Mrs. Luzi Elek (anglice - Susan Alick) "improved the shining hour" of 7 - 8 a.m., after her husband had gone to work, by visiting a certain shack, occupied by a young blood, named Dan Tobias, who works at night in the mine. Chance, doubtless, led two Hungarian ladies to take a morning stroll whither Mrs. Alick had gone, and it happened, that when they entered Dan Tobias' shack, they found him and Mrs. Alick on the bed in flagrante delicto. About an hour later, when the several ladies had returned to their respective domiciles they began to call one another names and finally to throw chunks of coal at one another. Mrs. Alick charged one of the others with throwing cayenne pepper into her face, and it is true that there was a plentiful supply of that condiment on hand (about 1/4 lb was brought to Barracks in a dirty piece of cloth) but I know

from former experience, that Mrs. Alick's uncorroborated statement requires some admixture of salt, and she could not get any
one to support her theory, except that, after she had retreated
into her house, the other ladies threw stones through her windows, and broke sundry panes of glass. To cut a long story short,
what with having a worse interpreter than usual, and his diffi-
dence in translating Hungarian terms of endearment into matter of fact English, I was glad to escape from the strife of tongues
by ordering the ladies who had broken the windows to pay for
the damages and to dismiss the other charges.

David Akers, late 1870s
GA, C.C. McCaul sketch,
NA-670-3

Thomas Lee Purcel, 1908
GA, R.N.W.M.P. photograph, NA-258-2

*Akers and Purcel had been associated in various enterprises over the
years, including whisky running and coal mining. But their relationship
was not always cordial, and in 1893 a quarrel between the two over
some cattle led to the death of Akers at the hand of Purcel.*

C. The Killing of Dave Akers

Society on the Canadian Prairies may have had rough edges a century ago, but it certainly was not the Wild West of the movies with gunslingers and desperadoes in every hotel bar and behind every knoll. In fact, until he took over the Calgary Division in 1906, Deane seldom had a case of homicide to investigate. The Akers-Purcel case of 1893 was an exception.

Both men were old-timers in the region. Dave Akers seems to have been an amiable fellow who got along well with people. Deane was positively inclined towards Akers, in part because Deane admired good gardening, and for many years at Fort Whoop-Up Akers had grown the best cabbages in the region. In contrast, Lee or Tom Purcel was an irascible rascal who was involved in a wide variety of legal scrapes both before and after the killing of Akers.

II-8 A Dubious Tale
Deane, Special Report, 7 December 1893 (NAC, RG18, 1284, 368-93)

In connection with my telegram of the 4th Inst., and that of today, I have the honour to report that at about 2 45 p.m. on the 4th Inst, Lee Purcel came into my office, and gave himself up for shooting and killing David Akers, about 5 o'clock on the previous evening in his (Purcel's) corral on the Pot Hole about 30 miles from here [*near present-day Magrath*]. I gave him the usual and proper caution.

Having seen the Coroner and warned a jury, I started at 3.30 p.m. with Sgt. Major Macdonell and Purcel for the scene of the tragedy. I had no teams to convey the jury, my hay teams not having yet returned from Milk River. We arrived at Purcel's ranche at 8 p.m.; the roads were very heavy during the last 10 miles.

Constables Pierce and Thorn were there. Corporal Carter from St. Mary's detachment had been there and taken a sketch, notes &c. of the place during the day, and had left these two men, having started himself for Lethbridge to report to me.

The Coroner and jury with Corpl. Carter arrived about 10 a.m. next morning and the evidence of a couple of witnesses was taken on the spot. We all returned to Lethbridge the same day, interviewing sundry people on the road, and the inquest was continued and lasted all day yesterday.

The jury at about 11 p.m. returned a verdict of manslaughter. I believe the moot point was whether it should be that or something worse.

The story is briefly as follows: There has been a long standing quarrel between Purcel and Akers, about some cattle.

They have known each other for about 35 or 40 years, were vigilantes together in the olden times; were concerned in running whiskey into the country and to my knowledge Akers has provided Purcel with a home at Whoop-up, when otherwise he would have been out in the cold.

Akers claimed that he found a coal mine in the Pot Hole and went shares in it with Purcel. Subsequently he wanted to buy out Purcel, and the latter said he would take so many head of Akers' cattle in payment of his share. Akers told me that he never agreed to this, but Purcel took the cattle all the same, branded them, and killed and sold at least one steer. I believe they have been heard to threaten one another. Akers, some time ago, managed to recover the cattle and, about 3 months since, sold them to a man named Hyssop, on whose father's ranche, about 8 miles from here, they were running until a severe storm not long ago, drove them off, and then they came once more into Purcel's possession.

On Sunday, the 4th instant, Akers was on the Pot Hole looking about for his cattle, including 3 or 4 others that had not been included in the Purcel deal, and which had strayed with the rest. About 1 p.m. he arrived at a ranche occupied by a Mrs. Perry where he had dinner. The following is culled from my notes taken at the inquest. He said he had come from his old place at Whoop-up and was going to Tom Purcel's to fetch his cattle back — that Tom had taken them. He said he was fetching them for Mr. Hyssop. He was not in an angry but in a joking mood. Mrs. Perry said she hoped there wouldn't be any trouble between them, and he said she needn't trouble about that — there wouldn't. He said if he saw the cattle at Purcel's he wouldn't go near Purcel, but if not he would have to go and ask him where they were. "As I was laying the dinner things, Akers and my son Eber were talking about a revolver that Eber had. I heard something said about somebody being 'stood off' and I said to Akers 'What's that?, I hope there won't be any trouble between you and Tom' and he replied 'That's only what Eber said — I am not afraid of Tom Purcel and he won't harm me.' "

He left Mrs. Perry's house, probably about quarter to 4 p.m. and arrived at Purcel's at about 5. He was riding and had nothing but an ordinary jack knife in his pocket and a quirt, or Indian whip, in his hand.

Purcel was at this time working at his corral; his rifle was there too, as he had put a shot through the paunch of a bull that had injured his corral — the corral is 36 yards due east of the house. It is 12 sided and has a diameter of 15 yards, being near 6 feet high.

Purcel says he was getting some hay from a stack adjoining the corral to feed his horse and some calves, when he saw a horse standing outside the door of his house. He wondered who it was and presently Akers came out of the house, mounted his horse, rode over to the corral and began taking down the bars at the entrance. Akers said "By George, you old s-o-b- you've beat me out of my cattle and I've come here to kill you".

Purcel forbade him to take the bars down but Akers took them down and rode into the corral. This is Purcel's story — "Then he made at me with his horse, with his whip in his left hand. I tried to get out of his way by trying to get over the fence. My foot caught in the fence and he hit me on the head with the stock of his whip. I had a cloth cap on. I fell off the fence under the horse's neck and chin, and took along the side of the rail fence where the building stands, and he still kept coming after me. Hit me on the shoulder with the back of the whip — couldn't reach me with the stock of it. Then I happened to see my gun there — hadn't thought about it at all until I saw it and I picked it up and held it up cocked. I said 'Akers, if you don't keep away I'll shoot you'. I snapped the gun then; there was a blank cartridge in it. I dropped the gun down partly and kind of started along the fence and pumped a cartridge in as I was going and trying to keep away from him. He closed up on me in the corner by the calf pen, his right side was to me; he had his horse close up and was striking with the whip with his left hand over the horse's head. Once I punched the horse in the side with the cocked gun, I repeated, I suppose 6 times, 'Akers if you pound me over the head this way I'll shoot you'. He would say 'Shoot and be d—d you s-o-b- you daren't shoot'. He was within 2 or 3 feet or closer and I let the gun go. The horse turned round about half way and walked 20 feet across the corner towards the centre. He fell over the horse's neck forward on the near side on the ground."

He also said that if Akers moved at all he just turned over, but he couldn't say whether he did that. He never spoke nor moaned. Purcel left the body where it was, and the corral as it was, and after a little rode away. He spent the night at J. Pearce's ranche, when he told the people what had happened and they notified our St. Mary's patrol. I brought in the body in my waggon on the 5th inst., and on the following day, a post mortem examination was made by Doctors Mewburn and DeVeber, which showed that the bullet entered the belly, on the right side about 5 inches from the navel — passed through the lower lobe of the liver, opened the aorta and struck the third lumbar vertebra — grooved it to the left of the median line, then wounded the spleen and kidney and passed out between the 11th and 12th ribs on the left side, smashing the lower border of the 11th rib. The wound of exit is 5 1/2 inches higher than the wound of entrance. The bullet passed between the intestines without injuring them. There was a mass of intestinal covering about 3 inches in length, protruding from the wound of entrance. The bullet was found between the shirt and the vest at the wound of exit. Death was practically instantaneous.

... Purcel's story is, I think, to be received in some of its details with very great caution. A great number of witnesses were examined at the inquest whose evidence will not be receivable against the accused.

Dr. Mewburn examined Purcel's head and shoulder for bruises caused by the stock of the whip, but found none.[3]

---

[3] Deane's Special Report provided little basis for doubting Purcel's story except that Purcel had no bruises on his head or shoulders. It does not say, for example, whether the corral actually showed any evidence of damage caused by the bull, which was the reason Purcel gave for having his rifle out at the corral. Nor does it cast doubt on the plausibility of an unarmed man first threatening to kill and then attacking a man who was armed. In any case, the jury did not fully buy Purcel's story of self-defence. It found Purcel guilty of manslaughter "with a very strong recommendation to mercy on account of the prisoner's age [*i.e. 64*]. " The judge imposed a sentence of three years in the penitentiary (see Deane, Monthly Report, February 1894 in NAC, RG18, 91, 148-94). Purcel served his time, which he is supposed to have said was less than he had received for killing a calf, and returned to the region. He died about 1910.

II-9 "Hard Luck"
Deane, Monthly Report, December 1893 (NAC, RG18, 74, 73-93)

The case of homicide was specially reported on the 7th inst. on which day the late D. Akers was buried. He had had hard luck during his career. Born of Pennsylvania Dutch parents he ran away from home in his early days and went to California by water. In course of time he turned up at Helena in the gold digging days and left there with a bag of gold dust said to have contained $50,000 or $60,000. He was intending to go East to marry the girl he had left behind him. He and two other men were going down the Missouri in a skiff and at Great Falls the skiff and its contents had to be portaged. Aker's gold dust bag was enclosed in his roll of bedding, which when he came to open he found the money gone. He and his companions went to Benton where he had them searched &c but he never recovered his property and being dead broke and disgusted went westward again. It is said that he never communicated with his friends after this. He was one of the original whiskey traders in this country and lived in the historic Fort at Whoop up until his Indian woman and her numerous relations ate him out of house and home and he moved to the Pot Hole. He was a mild mannered well dispositioned old man who was generally liked.

D. Gender Relations

Police records in any jurisdiction contain much information about relationships between the sexes. The pioneer community of Lethbridge, with its male/female ratio of at least two to one, was no exception. Deane's reports tell stories both horrifying and inspiring, some sad and some even amusing. For example, in his December 1893 report, he recorded the complaint of a man that someone had reached through an open window and pulled the covers off his wife: "It did not seem to be clear how he was going to identify the intruder, and even if he expected to find a lustful eye the light was not well calculated to assist him in his search." But most cases could not be taken in such a light-hearted vein, for they often revealed great unhappiness on both sides of the gender line. They also show the existence of a strict moral code along with the reality of deviation from that code. Finally, the records reveal the hard lot of many women, their lack of autonomy, and their frustrating subservience to and dependence on men.

Deane was himself part of that male supremacy, bound to uphold a social structure in which women were dominated and controlled. But there are indications in the documents that he was not unsympathetic to the plight of women. It is also a curious fact that in many of the plays Deane produced for the stage it was the males who tended to be the fools while the females were more frequently portrayed as being controlled, intelligent, rational, and fully deserving of the right to determine for themselves how they would lead their lives and to whom they would give their hearts.

II-10 "Improper Overtures"
Deane, Monthly Report, December 1893 (NAC, RG18, 74, 73-93)

On the 1st Inst about 5:30 pm a man named Burns went into the central telephone office with a bag of fruit and a dollar bill. He found a little girl there not yet 14 years of age who is one of the operators. He gave her some of the fruit and put the dollar down for her acceptance, then began to kiss her and subsequently put his hand, as she said "in an uncommon place" indicating the sacred neighbourhood of the Mons Veneris. Upon that she managed to get away and her assailant was arrested in due course. In his defence he admitted kissing the girl but denied the other soft impeachment. He omitted however to give any explanation of the dollar bill circumstance ....[4]

A Hungarian woman has complained that a man named McNulty, respectable, and the father of a family, went into her house on the 26th inst, in the afternoon and kissing her made improper overtures which she rejected. He then went away and bought a pair of baby's shoes and a pair for herself and renewed his importunities, trying to put his hand under her petticoats &c but with no better success. This man is probably cached in the mine and we have not yet been able to get him.[5]

---

[4] Burns was sentenced to three months of hard labor (see Deane, Monthly Report, January 1894 in NAC, RG18, 148-94). Deane stated that the sentence imposed by the judge was more lenient than most people expected. One dollar was a typical rate paid to prostitutes at the time.

[5] The woman later asked that the charges be reduced from indecent assault to common assault. McNulty then emerged from his hideaway in the mine, pleaded guilty and was fined $5 (see ibid.).

II-11 Girls' Latrine
Deane, Monthly Report, September 1897 (NAC, RG18, 126, 5-97)

On the evening of the 20th inst. soon after 9.30, the occupants of the Barracks were startled by a loud explosion, which seemed to come from near the back of the Officers['] Quarters. Several of us went out and looked about, but nothing was seen or heard, and I concluded that some one had been experimenting with dynamite or other explosive.

Comparatively few people heard the explosion and the next thing I heard was on Monday morning the 27th inst. when Mr. Simmons, the Head School teacher, told me that the explosion had taken place, and damage had been done in the latrine used by the school girls. There was nothing to be seen from the outside, although the nails securing the Western end of the building were partly drawn. Inside there was an abrupt hole in the floor, measuring about 6 x 10 inches. The glass of the window was shattered and the ceiling of the West end was torn up. It is funny that the little girls should have used the place for nearly a week and have said nothing about its condition, which was not discovered until the caretaker went to scrub it out on Saturday the 25th inst.

Some of the boys during their holidays were working on the Crow's Nest Road, and one of them must have stolen a stick of dynamite and a fuse. This does not appear to be a difficult matter to do, and it is hardly likely that we shall discover the culprit now.[6]

II-12 "Promiscuous Fornication"
Deane, Monthly Report, July 1894 (NAC, RG18, 91, 148-94)

Within the last few days two complaints have been made to me of girls in town getting into trouble. In one case, that of a French miner named Bruchet who was in great distress about his second daughter who was enamoured of an Italian (married

---

[6] Fred White, the Comptroller of the Mounties, received copies of all periodical reports to the Commissioner. On this report he appended the following comment, dated 11 November: "I think the Dynamite explosion should not be lost sight of, possibly it was an effort to alarm people who made use of the latrine at night for immoral purposes."

man) miner. I believe and hope the difficulty is settled — the man went east by train last night, and the girl assures me that there is nothing wrong with her.[7] The other case is hopeless and a baby will appear on the scene ere long. I told her mother the other day that, had she appealed to me when the circumstances first came to her knowledge some months ago, I might have been able to do something but now I cannot do anything. The Presbyterian and Methodist ministers have been of late making a great deal of talk about prostitutes being allowed in town. If they would turn their attention to the juvenile depravity and promiscuous fornication that is going on under their own eyes and in their own congregations, they would be kept so busy that they would have no time to think of the professional ladies, who at all events are orderly, clean, and on the whole not bad looking. The Methodist congregation is exercised because its pastor is wicked enough to play cricket, which he does well. Not long ago the two ministers above mentioned formed themselves into a delegation and interviewed the Town Council in public session convened and talked about the "soiled doves" &c. The whole town was there to see and hear. The "doves" had a lawyer present to watch the case for them and I was told that the whole business was great fun. The Reverend gentlemen got no satisfaction from the Council and retired covered with ridicule. The Church of England parson had declined to join in the agitation at all. He said he would go with the other ministers to try and reform the ladies of easy virtue, but he did not believe in the step the ministers were about to take; they did not accept his invitation.

II-13 *Le Triangle*
Deane, Monthly Report, August 1893 (NAC, RG18, 74, 73-93)

On the 12th Inst a Frenchman named Prospere Vanhulle, was brought up charged with threatening to kill a compatriot named Desagher. Marriage has been distinctly a failure as far

---

[7] A sequel to the story appeared in Deane, Monthly Report, September 1894 in NAC, RG18, 91, 148-94. Deane recorded that Bruchet brought in a letter written by the seventeen year old girl in which she said she was going to drown herself. But it was discovered that the missing young woman had taken her best clothes and, putting two and two together, Deane arranged to have her picked up in Medicine Hat and sent back.

as M & Madame Desagher are concerned. Madame told her husband that she would like to live with the other man, and that he had said that he would kill Desagher. Presently M Vanhulle arrives at Desagher's house but scouted any idea of living with Madame Desagher. As he frankly said he could do his business very quickly and there was no necessity for his living with the lady altogether. He remarked, however, to Desagher, that he would kill him if he did not get out of the house (his own) and leave the woman (his own wife) alone. Desagher was badly scared without doubt for he left the house precipitately and spent the night with a neighbour. Thinking that the police did not do business on Sunday he did not complain to them till next day. The Judge ordered Vanhulle to be bound over to keep the peace for a year.

II-14 Tar and Feathers
Deane, Annual Report, 1895 (*SP 1896*, No. 15, pp. 91-92)

An unprecedented occurrence of lynch law in Lethbridge deserves something more than a passing notice, and it will be necessary to touch upon the circumstances that led up to it in order to explain the extraordinary expression of public approval that was evoked by the act. On the evening of the 13th of February, Charles Gillies blew his brains out. The coroner's jury returned a verdict of "suicide while under mental depression caused by domestic troubles." He had had good situations, but had lost them through drink. At this time he was out of work, and the wolf was at the door. The household, in fact, was kept going by a lodger named James Donaldson. "But for him," the woman said on one occasion, "we should have had nothing to eat." Gillies had, however, frequently complained to various people of undue intimacy between his lodger and his wife — an intimacy extending over a period of years — and not a little indignation had been aroused by the treatment which the husband complained of having received.

It is no disregard of the obligation *de mortuis* to say that, when the deceased Gillies re-admitted Donaldson to his household, he knew what his past experiences had been.[8]

---

[8] In a close parallel to the circumstances related in Document II-13, Gillies had, on one occasion, been turned out of his own house by the other man (see Deane,

Donaldson attended the funeral as chief mourner, and it has been said that this helped to precipitate matters.

Be that as it may, soon after midnight on the 15th of February a band of masked and armed men broke into the house on the outskirts of the town occupied by the two brothers Donaldson, who were in bed. Maxwell was covered by a rifle and ordered not to move; his brother James was pulled out of bed, tarred, feathered, dressed and led with a rope round his neck to the front door of the Lethbridge House. Maxwell was left in bed under guard of two men and was forbidden to stir for twenty minutes. James was pushed into the hall of the Lethbridge House, the door was temporarily fastened from without, and the masked gang dispersed. After that he was allowed to walk home without molestation. It was a rather stormy night, with drifting snow; a night on which few people would be about the streets, and no noise was made.

It was 1.15 a.m. when I was aroused by Maxwell Donaldson and on my telephoning to Sergeant Hare, who was in charge of the town police station, he replied that James Donaldson had gone home. Under all the circumstances it may be assumed that this outrage could not have taken place if Sergeant Hare had done his duty. So far from that being the case I am ashamed for the credit of the division to say that he permitted himself to disregard the obligations of his oath of office and that he was himself a member of the burglarious gang. The Donaldson brothers were unable to identify any of their assailants and decided to let the matter drop. James left town at once for the east, declining either to make or support a complaint. The incident, however, had gone to the papers and the family in the east insisted on the offenders being brought to justice if possible. The only stipulation that I made was that James should return to give evidence when necessary and, on my receiving an assurance to that effect from his father, the leader of the gang, Charles Warren, was arrested on a warrant which I had issued some

Special Report on the Suicide of Charles Gillies, 16 February 1895 in NAC, RG18, 106, 191-95). Deane was no supporter of Donaldson. Two years earlier, he had reported a case of the theft of hay in which Donaldson was implicated. Deane's comment on Donaldson was: "I know him of old and know that he will bear watching" (see Deane, Monthly Report, December 1893 in NAC, RG18, 74, 73-93).

time previously. Warren, I may say, is a native of the United
States. He had been here for a few months, doing no work and
having no visible means of support, but quiet and inoffensive
withal. He habitually carried a 6 shooter in his breast pocket,
and was asked to "captain" the gang because he was supposed to
have had previous experience in like exploits, and there was less
chance of his voice being recognized. As it happened, it was his
manner of speech that led to his identification. He was arrested
on the 7th of June. By that time two members of the party had
left the country, but four others were put in the witness box, and
invited to give an account of their proceedings on the night in
question. They all stoutly denied any knowledge of the affair,
and this practically disposed of an alibi on Warren's behalf. The
prisoner was committed for trial upon the evidence of Maxwell
Donaldson, who identified him by his voice, build, dress and
manner as the man who had stood at the foot of his bed, with a
revolver in his hand, and acted as the captain of the gang. The
feeling of sympathy with Warren was so strong here that change
of venue was applied for and granted, and he was to be tried at
Macleod on the 6th of July on two counts of burglary and two of
riot. I may say here that I had at the time sufficient evidence to
convict Sergeant Hare under the Police Act. It was in my power
to prove that he was seen immediately after the dispersion of
the gang, masked and disguised, with a carbine in his hand,
with feathers sticking to it; and he was offered the choice between telling what he knew and taking his medicine. He chose
the former alternative, and was put in the witness box at Macleod,
where he confirmed Maxwell Donaldson's evidence as to Warren
being the man who had stood at the foot of his bed, with a
revolver in his hand, etc. The result of the trial seemed to be a
foregone conclusion. The defence called no witnesses. Counsel
for the Crown waived their address to the jury. Counsel for the
prisoner dilated on the severity of the punishment for burglary,
which, he contended, this was not, in the ordinary acceptation of
the word; and the jury disagreed [*i.e. were unable to come to a
decision*]. James Donaldson was in such a state of nervous pros-
tration that he was unable to go into the witness box at all. A
new trial was ordered for the 10th of July, and on the evening of
the 9th Sergeant Hare deserted. He was at this time undergoing
hospital treatment for a broken arm, which was encased in

plaster. A subscription of $100 was raised for him by the persons most interested in his absence, and he was persuaded to leave the country. Of this $100, however, only $40 reached him, and he made various threats of coming back on account of the breach of faith; but his conspirators treated his threats with contempt, and nothing came of them. Warren was released on bail until the winter assizes, and took advantage of his freedom to cross the boundary: one of his sureties followed him. The case was called at Macleod on the 16th of November, but the prisoner did not appear, and his bail was ordered to be estreated. The prosecution has had its effect, and it is quite likely that there will be no further experiments here with lynch law.

II-15 Ending a Liaison
Deane, Monthly Report, December 1896 (NAC, RG18, 114, 25-96)

Early on the morning of the 24th instant, a brakesman on the C.P.R. applied to me to know how he could prevent his wife from leaving town by the Macleod stage, with the supposed object of ultimately joining Ex-Constable Archibald McKay, whose name has been frequently coupled with hers, and who was said to be about to leave town too.

I had heard of this liaison, and some feeling in town was arising in consequence. Some 5 or 6 men, sympathizers with the husband, looked to A. McKay on the evening of the 23rd, and would probably have handled him roughly, if they had been able to find him. I suggested to the aggrieved husband, that he should forbid the stage driver to carry his wife, and this he did, for later in the morning she came to me. I referred her to her husband, and instructed Const Lewis to tell A. McKay, that if he remained in town, evil might befall him which I might be unable to prevent. This McKay is a tailor, working for Mr. E.J. Hill, and this message brought up that gentleman [*Hill*] and the Methodist Minister [*to see Deane at the barracks.*] [A]pparently [*they hoped*] to convert me to the doctrine that the mob law, which [*they*] thought meritorious in the case of James Donaldson, and his tar, and feathers, was quite the reverse when brought in conflict with E.J. Hill's business interests. Mr. Hill asked if A. McKay could not have Police protection, and I replied "certainly", but that I had not enough men to guarantee his not being tied up, for instance, to a telephone pole, and given a sound flogging. I should probably not hear of the circumstances until after the occurrence, and one had to look for similar public sympathy in such a case as was accorded to the tar and feather gang. Mr. Goard, the Parson, I think, agreed with me. A. McKay left town for British Columbia on the 28th instant, and Dan McKay, and his wife, who is still here, have concluded a sort of armed truce.

II-16 "He Will Probably Kill Her"
Deane, Monthly Report, November 1894 (NAC, RG18, 91, 148-94)

On the 6th instant Thomas Elliott was committed for trial on a charge of unlawful wounding. On the Sunday previous he had gone home drunk, and beaten his wife to such an extent that she was not out of bed for some time. A wound on the head caused by a pitchfork, is the cause of the charge of wounding being laid. This man habitually supplies liquor to Indians. Sergt Hare found and destroyed a decoction of tea, and whiskey, which he had brewed for the Indian trade, and I thought it as well to keep him locked up instead of allowing him out on bail.

Deane, Monthly Report, March 1895 (NAC, RG18, 104, 131-95)

In Regina vs. Elliott, the man who wounded his wife with a pitch fork pleaded guilty, dropped a penitential tear, or two, and received a sentence of three months imprisonment with hard labor.

Deane, Monthly Report, October 1895 (NAC, RG18, 104, 131-95)

On the 16th Inst a Mrs. Elliott complained that her husband had nearly choked and threatened to kill her. He has already suffered imprisonment this year for assaulting his wife with a pitch fork, and a few days before the 16th the woman made a long complaint with a view to obtaining sureties of the peace, but at the last moment she weakened and asked me to let it lie over. Elliott now stands committed for trial for assault. He will probably kill her one of these days. It would be a good thing if the law could empower a Judge to order a judicial separation in such a case as the present. The man has treated his wife with great brutality. The woman can support herself and family, if the man will only leave her alone, but this he won't do. A whipping would do him more good than anything.

Deane's Monthly Report for November, 1895 (NAC, RG18, 104, 131-95)

The next Criminal case was that of Thomas Elliott, on a charge of wife-beating, and in this case the Judge [*Mr. Justice Rouleau*], acquitted the prisoner, saying that he looked upon the matter as a family quarrel, and that Elliott had already been punished, by being six weeks in the guard room.

E. The Flotsam and Jetsam of Society

As a former Royal Marine who had served at sea, Deane would have been well acquainted with the term "flotsam and jetsam," the rubbish discarded from ships and left adrift on the wide ocean. Society also had its discards, the people who were misfits — the beggars, the wanderers, the physically and mentally challenged, the mentally disturbed, the destitute. Such people came from all ethnic, social, age, and occupational groups. Some were fortunate in having someone to support and assist them. But most of those who ended up in the police records were isolates in society.

In dealing with these people, the Mounties played a dual role. On the one hand, they enforced the law, including restrictions against tramps and vagrants. On the other hand, in an era and place where social welfare agencies to care for unfortunates were scarce, the police were called upon to fill the vacuum. Mounted Police duties thus included elements of both social control and social welfare. Deane's reports provide ample evidence of the torment, both physical and mental, suffered by the discards of society. But they also demonstrate the ability of some to shift for themselves on the margins of society, even though the dominant elements in the community might not approve of the methods used.

II-17 Body in Badger Hole
Deane, Weekly Report, 3 August 1894 (NAC, RG18, 91, 148-94)

On the 31st ult I received a note from D.J. Whitney, a rancher, that he had come across the dead body of an Indian in a badger hole about 2 miles from his hay camp in the Ridge .... I at once telephoned to Corporal Carter to notify the Indian Agent and ask if he knew of any Indian being missing .... Corp. Carter saw Mr. Sanders the clerk, on the reserve, who told him that an Indian named "Packs-meat-on-him" had been missing since the 7th June last. It was also said that this Indian would probably have on his person a paper signed by Dr. Girard as to treatment in Hospital. On the 1st at 4 a.m. I started with the Coroner and Dr. DeVeber. D.J. Whitney's camp is a long 35 miles from here .... There was very little of the body to be seen. There was a hole about 2 feet square by two feet deep, in which were some bones, a butcher knife, a cartridge belt, a necklace, a few trinkets and a pouch containing a paper which was dated 1st June and signed by Dr. Girard as to medical treatment which would best suit the bearer's case. The head was some 30 or 35 feet away, there were tresses of long hair round about; the skull was quite bare save for a little dried up skin and so were the bones some of which were lying about, having evidently been dragged out of the hole by coyotes which had stripped the flesh off them. I had wired to Milk River Ridge for Interpreter Taylor to meet me at Whitney's camp and had taken one of our Indian scouts with me. Corp. Carter had also arrived there with an Indian from the Reserve to identify the remains if possible. The Coroner held his inquest under the shade of a friendly hay-rack, the jurors being gathered up from neighbouring hay camps. The jury returned an open verdict, as there was no object in prolonging the business at great expense, and at 6 p.m. just as we were about to pull out on our return journey Interpreter Taylor arrived, looking fagged out and almost too tired to talk, He explained that he with the Milk River Ridge men had been fighting fire all night and had been riding all day. Through him we learnt that the Indian "The Neck" from the Reserve recognized the necklace in the grave as that worn by "Packs-meat-on-him". That the deceased had killed a squaw and had been missing since the 7th June. He also knew of the paper which Dr. Girard had given to the deceased, who was said to be crazy. I don't know anything about the killing of the squaw but there is no doubt that the remains are those of "Packs-meat-on-him", who probably sat himself down on his haunches in the hole aforesaid and there died. Whether he accelerated death by any means is not possible to tell. The remains were put back in the hole and covered by the Coroner's authority. No marks of violence were on the skull. The Coroner will give me the letter and other exhibits and I am communicating with the Indian Agent thereanent. I reached home with my party at 1 a.m. on the 2nd Inst.

II-18 Escape by Conjury
Deane, Monthly Report, October 1896 (NAC, RG18, 114, 25-96)

The refugee Cree prisoner "Ca-qua-ta-ca-mick" who had been here for some time awaiting trial on a charge of horse stealing escaped from the Guard Room on the night of the 9th Instant. Corporal Hilliam was in charge of the Guard, and I investigated a charge against him of negligently conniving at his escape. The conclusion I came to was that the Corp'l had been outwitted and that he was not culpably negligent. I therefore ordered him to come up for judgment when called upon. The Indian had apparently been leading up to this for some time. He complained first of the Ball and Chain which he had to wear, but was not allowed outside the Guard room without it. He then at night took to covering himself up with the blankets, and close examination on the part of the Orderly Officer on his rounds was necessary to find out whether the prisoner was there or not, if he would not answer. On the night of the 8th Instant there were only two prisoners, "Ca-qua-ta-ca-mick" and Abraham Shattock, a prisoner at large, who was confined under the Lunatic's Ordinance.

At about 7.20 p.m. the Indian asked Constable Gray, one of the Guard, for a drink of water and thus put himself in evidence, knowing that the cells would be locked in a few minutes. He knew also that the cell at the back of his, being untenanted, would be left open. Having arranged a dummy in his own bed I believe that the Indian went into this empty cell, wherein, when an electric light is turned on, there is a small dark corner into which a small man could crouch without being noticed by a person walking along the corridor who did not actually walk into the cell. Corporal Hilliam admittedly went into the cell (the Indian's proper cell) and said "Are you there?" or words to that effect. He says he touched him and stooped down over him and heard his reply. The Indian answered with a grunt, and I believe that his mouth was at that time close to the other side of the partition and down at the level of where his head should have been on his bed. This is a well known illusion to conjurers and to me in my conjuring days. The voice would appear muffled as if it came through the blankets and a person who was not on the look out for deception would be at once satisfied. By similar means I have deceived hundreds of people in a large room when they were on the look out to discover how the trick was done.

The booted and spurred Guard gave ample evidence of their movements and while they were locking the dummy's cell and walking around the corridor the Indian in his moccasined feet would have no difficulty in getting back to his dark corner and Corporal Hilliam, having seen that Shattock was satisfactorily taken care of, would have no further misgivings.

The dummy's cell was never unlocked until next morning, and the Indian was free to make use of his opportunities. He escaped through the south west window of the prison corridor. There are perpendicular bars across the aperture, and these were not, as it happens, set into iron plates at the top or bottom. Shattock says the only thing he ever saw the Indian with was a piece of wire, and it is presumable that he effected his escape by means of this.

II-19 Clipsham the "Crank"
Deane, Weekly Report, 2 February [*actually 2 March*], 1894 (NAC, RG18, 91, 148-94)

On Sunday evening last, the 25th inst, I went with Dr. Mewburn to see a squaw who was living in a house in town with a man named Clipsham and with regard to whom some complaints of ill-treatment had been made. I may premise that Clipsham is a "crank" of the most aggressive kind on the subject of Indians, and their sobriety, morality &c. He has unquestionably done a great deal of good amongst them. I have known him to take a squaw with malignant tumours in her bosom into his house and feed, nurse and look after her at his own expense until she was well enough to go back to her Reserve.

As to the present occasion, some months ago a squaw named "Kate" who had left the hospital on the Reserve of her own accord, came here with a tumour in her womb. She was almost a skeleton and Dr. Mewburn said, when Clipsham took her to him, that she was not in a condition to be operated upon. Clipsham then took charge of her and the result of his nursing and feeding is shewn in the fact that she is now in good condition, almost fat: contrary to the expectation of the Doctor, who thought she would die. It appears that on Sunday, Clipsham wanted to inject some carbolic acid and water with a syringe that had been given to the woman on the Reserve, and she did not want it to be done. He attempted to coerce her, she screamed and the neighbours went in. The Indian Agent of the Blood Reserve was communicated with and came here on the 27th ult. Dr. Mewburn said the woman could be moved, so her friends took her back to the Reserve, and I intimated to Mr. Clipsham that his philanthropy in future will not be allowed to go to the length of having sick Indian women in his house, no matter how pure his motives may be.

II-20 Tramp Accused of Rape
Deane, Weekly Report, 16 July 1897 (NAC, RG18, 126, 5-97)

A harrowing story of rape or worse met me yesterday as I drove in from Macleod, as to which I may say there is not a word of truth. A tramp went to a house in the river bottom and asked a little girl for a drink of water. She gave him one and he kissed her. That is the whole truth. He pleaded guilty before me this morning to a charge of vagrancy, and I have remanded him for sentence until I can make some enquiries. He says he is an Engine driver and worked under Mr. Haney on the Onderdonk Section. I will ask Mr. Haney about him when I next go to Macleod.[9]

---

[9] Evidently the man's reputation did not turn out to be very positive — Deane later classified him as a "professional tramp" — and he was sentenced to six months imprisonment with hard labor in the Regina jail (see Deane, Monthly Report, July 1897 in NAC, RG18, 126, 5-97).

II-21 Offensive Vagrant
Deane, Monthly Report, December 1893 (NAC, RG18, 74, 73-93)

A man named Eckerd was locked up on the 8th inst. charged
with vagrancy and then developed the most offensive form of
dts[10] being extremely violent, shouting & screaming, smearing
his excreta all over his cell and making himself as generally as
great nuisance as possible particularly to the other unhappy
companions of his captivity averaging 8 in number. He got over
his bout in course of time and as no second justice of the peace
was available to try him for vagrancy, I allowed him to go on
promise of going to work or leaving the country.

II-22 Aristocratic Vagrant
Deane, Monthly Report, December 1897 (NAC, RG18, 126, 5-97)

A man, who gave his name as William McElroy, was brought
before me on the 27th instant, charged with vagrancy. He came
into town from the south on Xmas Eve, and was arrested next
morning. He is certainly an Englishman and an old soldier,
probably a begging-letter writer to boot, for he has a long list of
nobility and gentry in England. He knows just as much about
the vagrancy law as I do, and I could not but admit in my own
mind that his arrest had been a little premature. Having heard
the case I did not proceed to a conviction but adjourned the
hearing for 3 days to enable him to obtain work or leave town.

On the morning of the 28th instant, however, he was found
coming out of a dry goods shop into which he had broken in the
night and stolen several articles, besides about $20. in money.
He was duly committed for trial on the charge of burglary.

In the course of the day it transpired that he had stolen an
overcoat and a pair of fur-topped gloves from the Lethbridge
House, and had pawned the coat for $2.00. He was committed
for trial on this charge also. I think he has done this in order to
get locked up. If he had not some reason for getting out of the
way, he could hardly be such a fool as to burglarize a store in the
open way he did ....

---

[10] An abbreviation for *delirium tremens* caused by alcohol abuse and character-
ized by sweating, trembling, anxiety and hallucinations.

At the expiration of the 3 days for which McElroy's charge of vagrancy was adjourned, viz: on the 31st instant, he was brought up, and I convicted him, and awarded him 6 months imprisonment with hard labour. This, as I expected, touched the raw, for he immediately swore that he would not work while awaiting trial on his other charges; however he may change his mind.[11]

II-23 An "Imbecile"
Deane, Monthly Report, December 1895 (NAC, RG18, 104, 131-95)

Report was made on the 4th Instant by a section foreman at Grassy Lake that there was an insane man near there, living in a ditch, dependent for food solely on what the men at the section house gave him. Corporal Bullough went out with a warrant and brought him in. He is not insane as the word is commonly understood, but is incapable of taking care of himself and seems to be half witted. He cannot work and says he has come from Indiana State. I have written to the Chief of Police of Indianapolis, near where Shattock's relations are said to live, but have not heard from him so far. I am in correspondence with the Lieutenant Governor's office now about his disposal.

Deane to Lieutenant Governor, 23 October 1896 (NAC, RG18, 134, 164-97)

I have the honor to forward the enclosed report by Doctor Mewburn on Abraham Shattock who has been for some months in custody here under the Lunatic Ordinance.[12]

This man has been very slowly but very steadily improving for a long time past. He does little odds and ends of work around barracks as a prisoner at large, and is happy and contented, but

---

[11] Deane was known to refuse food to prisoners who would not work, citing the principle: no work, no grub. Evidently, McElroy did work, but while cleaning the hospital, got hold of a chloroform bottle, drank quite a bit of it, and nearly died as a result. He then received a three year sentence for burglary and was sent off to the Manitoba penitentiary (see W.S.M. Morris, Annual Report, 1898 in *SP 1899*, No.15, p.93).

[12] Mewburn's conclusion was that while Shattock "is quite harmless and cleanly in his habits, he would be classified as an imbecile."

he could not earn his own living if thrown out in the world. He would certainly become a charge upon some Municipality or possibly upon the Government again.

He belongs, as I have previously reported, to the State of Indiana, and in order to curtail the expense to which the Canadian Government is put, I would respectfully suggest that he should be discharged from custody, be given a free passage to Great Falls viz $10. (ten dollars), and $5 (five dollars) to help him along.

I propose to notify the Chief of Police at Great Falls of his arrival there, and judging from a message which I have already received from that official, he would look after Abraham Shattock.[13]

II-24 A "Lunatic"
Deane, Monthly Report, July 1896 (NAC, RG18, 114, 25-96)

A Lunatic arrived here by train from Great Falls on the 2nd instant. His fare to Lethbridge had been paid, and he had been given in charge to the conductor. I made an exhaustive enquiry into his case. He has been heard to boast, when in his cups, that he is the son of an Earl, and he has a mother (known as Belle Bilton) living in Calgary, and a brother there who keeps a candy store. His relations will not have anything to do with him. He lived for some time on Buffalo Lake, near Edmonton, with the wife of a Half-breed named Paul Faillant, and came southward last November to try and get work for the winter. Paul Faillant was drowned in Calgary, and on the same day his wife and daughter were drowned in Buffalo Lake. Willie St Aubyn Burdett seems reasonable to some extent, but there is a screw loose somewhere, and he is not fit to be at large. He seems to have degenerated into a Squaw man [*white man with an Indian woman*], and I should judge that sexual excesses, or masturbation, or both, are responsible for his present condition. Pursuant to Lt. Governor's orders he was despatched to Brandon Asylum on the 23rd inst.

---

[13] While the Territorial Government covered the $15 cost of transporting Shattock, it seems that the Police were unable to recoup the $213.15 incurred in maintaining him for ten months, a fact which was to make the Mounties loath to look after unfortunate individuals like Shattock in the future (see correspondence in NAC, RG18, 134, 164-97).

II-25 An "Insane Person"
Deane, Monthly Report, April 1897 (NAC, RG18, 126, 5-97)

A shoemaker, named Craney, is now in custody as an insane person. He has a recurrence of an attack which he had some 9 or 10 years ago, and is afraid that his mind is gone. He is also afraid that he will be unable to keep his hands off his family, whom he is tempted to put to death in order to save them from starvation. We have brought his tools up and induced him to do a little work at his trade to try and take his attention off his troubles, but he is not fit to be at large yet. Asylum treatment would of course be best for him.

II-26 "Cut His Throat With a Razor"
Deane, Monthly Report, September 1897 (NAC, RG18, 126, 5-97)

At this [*construction*] camp [*for the Crow's Nest line*], No. 1., of Stewart's, on the 16th inst., a man named Tom Ward cut his throat with a razor. He only joined the camp that day from the steel gang, and he must have lain for some time during the night before the cut was discovered. He was sewn up and brought into Hospital and was thence discharged into our Guard Room on the 28th inst. No cause is assigned and he has $75.00 of American money in his possession. An asylum is the proper place for him, I should judge, but I will leave it to the judge to dispose of him.[14]

II-27 "Stealing a Ride"
Deane, Weekly Report, 24 April 1896 (NAC, RG18, 114, 25-96)

While Cst Wright was searching the east bound C.P.R. train at the Montana Junction on the night of the 20th inst he came across four young Germans, who were stealing a ride in a box car half full of coal, and took them into custody. They were brought up on the 22nd, and I awarded them 3 days imprisonment. This is the first complaint of the kind that has been made here, and these men are not tramps. They all hail from Edmonton where they were frozen out, in fact the story they tell does

---

[14] Ward received a one month's sentence for attempted suicide.

not constitute a very good advertisement for the South Edmonton District. One man who had $14.00, said he had a homestead, shack, and stable, his wheat was frozen, and unsaleable. Two of the others are brothers, they had $1.75 between them, and had left home to try and get work, and send money home to Father and Mother with five children. The other fellow had nothing. They had walked to Calgary, and hearing that they could get work here, had walked on here where they arrived on the 20th very tired. They are trying to work their way along to the Mennonite Settlement in Manitoba, where they think they are sure of work. For my part I hope they will be able to steal a ride now and then. The C.P.R. authorities wished the case prosecuted, or I should have let them go.[15]

II-28 Death of a Boy
Deane, Monthly Report, October 1896 (NAC, RG18, 114, 25-96)

A boy about 10 years old had both thighs broken on the evening of the 27th Inst. A train consisting of an engine, one car of coal and 5 tanks each containing 2000 gallons of water left the A.R.& C. Co's yard here en route to No 3 shaft. The boy was taking a ride on the rear tank. When the train had reached the yard it backed at the rate of about 7 or 8 miles an hour and the Yardmaster, who was in charge of it, expected that a certain switch which he had left in a certain way, would shunt the train on to No 3 Shaft track. Instead of that somebody had altered the switch and the train was diverted on to a track which led towards a long coal shed where the narrow and broad gauge ran on the same sleepers, and where a C P R car was standing loaded with rails at a distance of 207 yards from the switch. As soon as he saw that the train was on the wrong track the Yardmaster signaled the Engineer who reversed his engine etc., but it was a down grade, and the momentum was such that the

---

[15] This would have been directly contrary to a circular sent out by the Commissioner in May 1895, which ordered a crack-down on "tramps" stealing rides on railways (see NAC, RG18, 1346, 199-95).

engine could not hold the train, which ran into the car of rails before mentioned and shunted it 27 yards from its standing point. These distances were given in evidence by the Master Mechanic. The Yardmaster saw there was going to be a collision, told the boy to jump and jumped himself. The boy did not jump, and when the tank struck the car the effect was to jerk the rails towards the tank and pin the boy there. He had both thighs broken and died the same night. He never rallied from the shock and was in no pain.

An inquest was held next day and the Yardmaster, a Mr. Burnett, explained his reasons for having allowed the boy to ride on the tank with him etc., and said that the accident was attributable to somebody having tampered with the switch. He was of opinion that boys must have done it. The Railway hands had had considerable trouble with children trespassing on the Railway, riding on cars etc. He laid down the Railway law to be that a man should leave a switch as he found it.

It subsequently appeared from evidence that two of the Company's officials, had, in furtherance of what they conceived to be the Yardmaster's intentions, altered the switch. The Yardmaster did intend to haul out the car of rails but not just at the time, and by transgressing the switch law the two persons concerned brought about the accident.

The foreman of the jury was one of the Company employees, and the verdict of the jury was as follows:

"That the said George William McLean came to his death accidentally while riding on the A.R.& C railroad.

"And we consider that more efficient steps should be taken to prevent the re-occurrence of such accidents, by prohibiting any boys from riding on the cars or engines of the Company."

... I think it was a case in which the public interests demanded such an enquiry as a Coroner only could hold. The Company appear to think that because the boy died in his bed, and because every one knew that two broken thighs were the cause of death, that it was not only [un]necessary but offensive to them to enquire into the cause of the broken thighs. The enquiries showed that a person who had no sort of business to touch the switch sent the deceased to his death. It was a piece of interference which, while not criminal, goes with other incidents to show the laxity of railway discipline.

II-29 "Juvenile Depravity"
Deane, Weekly Report, 14 June 1895 (NAC, RG18, 104, 131-95)

There is a most extraordinary case of juvenile depravity here. A miner, named Mark Johnson, a widower, has a little boy, 8, who is as nice looking and nice mannered a little fellow as one would wish to see, he has a kissable face and takes the hearts of women by storm. He knows his catechism off pat, says his little prayers before he goes to bed, folds up his little rags neatly as he takes them off, and is generally a remarkable instance of pious precocity. His father drinks at times, but keeps a clean house, and I believe the boy is as well looked after as he can be by a father who is away from home all the time whenever the mines are working, and who comes home tired at night. This youngster, however, has got into the habit of staying from school and home for days at a time. He goes to various houses and says he has got nothing to eat etc, and people generally take him in and feed him and pet him etc, and the boy has found out that it pays, besides making a change in the monotony of life. The other night he broke into a house near the Barracks. The occupants were not at home, and he took a pane out of the kitchen window and went in, got some food &c out of the cellar and left. He admits this, but denies having taken a silver spoon which is said to be missing. The puzzle is what to do with a boy like that. His father says he can do nothing with him, and the boy is rapidly turning into a hardened criminal. He is such a shrimp that it is difficult to look at him without laughing, but all the same the criminal taint is there, and it is a pity there is no Reformatory to which he could be sent. He would be worth a fortune to a London cracksman [*burglar*].

III
"SUBMISSION TO CONSTITUTED AUTHORITY"
MACLEOD AND LETHBRIDGE DIVISIONS 1898-1902

Between 1898 and 1902, Deane's position was really that of a senior superintendent with supervisory responsibility for both the Lethbridge and the Macleod Divisions, even though there were often titular commanding officers for one or both divisions.[1] The territory was huge, covering the southern section of the old territorial district of Alberta and encompassing perhaps forty thousand square miles. As the Macleod Division had more men and was closer to the major problems of the era, Deane concentrated on it. He would spend the middle part of the week at Macleod and take an elongated weekend in Lethbridge where his home remained on the grounds of the barracks. But while his responsibilities increased, Deane's reports indicate that the nature of the job retained many familiar features.

A. The Crow's Nest Pass Railway

By 1897, the CPR had purchased the railway from Medicine Hat to Lethbridge and had concluded an agreement with the federal government to extend the line west through the Crow's Nest Pass into the interior of British Columbia. The CPR was interested in the potential of both metal mining in the B.C. interior and coal mining in the Pass. For southwestern Alberta, the enterprise had important short and long-term economic benefits. During construction of the line, the Mounted Police had special responsibilities, their jurisdiction even extending several hundred miles into B.C along the route of the steel.

Chief amongst the issues drawn to their attention were problems related to railroad construction workers, or "navvies" as they were called. These men were part of the unorganized, tran-

---

[1] The amalgamation of the two divisions was actively considered at this time (see NAC, RG18, 198, 799-00).

*sient, largely unskilled segment of the North American work force
at the turn of the century. Lacking security of job, location, and
material assets, they paid a heavy price for the progress brought
by their labor. Their problems ranged from inadequate medical
service, to dangerous working conditions, to delays in wage payment even after employment ceased. There were a staggering
number of illnesses, injuries and deaths suffered by workers
while the railroad was being built. Although there were several
cases of murder/manslaughter, most of the deaths were caused
by diseases such as typhoid and pneumonia, and by various
construction accidents, such as the case of the worker who was
blown up while attempting to thaw sticks of dynamite.*

*One fatal accident was quite bizarre. At a siding near Pincher
Creek, some twenty miles west of Macleod, a batch of cars became
detached from the engine. Being closer to the mountains, this
location was of higher elevation than the territory to the east and
the cars rolled backwards, evidently attaining a terrific speed
before slamming into the engine of another train a few miles from
Macleod, killing the engineer and fireman. The letter presented
as Document III-2 was a response to a letter sent to Prime Minister Laurier by the Presbyterian Minister, J.A. Jaffary, in which
he objected to the fact that no inquest had been held, supposedly
because the Mounted Police refused to make the request.*

*Although the Mounties concluded their special duties with the
construction of the Crow's Nest Pass line in November 1898, the
completion of the railroad did not end the legacy of violence
connected to it. The men involved in the fight related in Document
III-4 were CPR employees who lived in a railway boxcar at
Haneyville, the train yard and station just outside Macleod. The
danger of work along the line was compounded by the isolation of
most workers. Thus, such an apparently inconsequential matter
as mail delivery took on great significance.*

III-1 "Four Men Died"
Deane, Monthly Report for Macleod, April 1898 (NAC, RG18, 143, 17-98)

On the 31st [*March*] ... Mr. [*Michael J.*] Haney [*supervisor of
construction for the Crow's Nest Pass Railway*] wired to me from
Whoop-up, that whiskey was being sold, in the railway camp

Bridge Construction Gang on the Crow's Nest Pass Railway, 25 April 1898
GA, Steele and Company photograph, NA-659-81
Building railroad bridges required muscle, skill and courage. Some of the nameless men who provided the labor were captured here. The faces of the men reflect their sombre mood. Perhaps they were remembering that four of their colleagues had been killed in an accident eighteen days earlier, as Document III-1 relates.

there on the Indian Reserve. I wired to Inspector Morris to telephone to Sergeant Higinbotham, to go from St. Mary's to Whoop-up, at once, and report to Mr. Haney — next morning Mr. Haney wired that a man named Falkner, had been stabbed in the throat, in one of the boarding cars. I sent Constable McLean from here at once, by train, and wired Inspector Morris ....

Later, on the 1st. instant Mr. Haney wired "we are having trouble in getting the men here to work, and are dismissing a number in consequence, there may be trouble, can you send some police from Lethbridge, to stay a day or two until we get matters adjusted?"

I wired again to Lethbridge to send Serg. Higinbotham, and two constables to Whoop-up, and sent Inspector Casey from here, by train of that night. The appearance of the police quieted matters and on the 2nd. Mr. Haney wired me that one man would be sufficient: I therefore withdrew all but Constable McLean ....

The trader who was supplying the liquor was W.D. Hill, a brother of E.J. Hill, a merchant of Lethbridge, but I think the trouble partly arose from the nature of the work at Whoop-up. The piles which have been driven there are 70 feet high, and there have been a great number of accidents ....

One of the bridges in the Whoop-up bottom, while in the course of construction, was blown down, by a very high wind on the 7th. instant, and four men died as a result of the accident.

III-2 No Inquest
Deane to Commisioner, 17 August 1898 (NAC, RG18, 154, 441-98)

The Rev. Mr. Jaffary represents the views of a very small portion of the community in the complaint which he makes to the Prime Minister.

The engine was disconnected from the train at Pincher Creek siding to do some shunting.

Whether or not the brakes were securely set is an open question, but the fact remains that the train of cars thus left by themselves started off as stated, and crashed into another train with the result that the engineer and fireman lost their lives.

The brakesman of the runaway train disappeared as soon as the cars started and has not been seen since.

The Canadian Pacific Railway Company were rather desirous of having an inquest held, and the Coroner was aware of this. The Company would have liked to place the responsibility for the accident, but to have pressed the point would have served to evince distrust of their employees, and they did not desire to go to the length of making the affidavit required by Mr. Anderton.

The Coroner considered that the deaths were the result of a pure accident, and did not consider an inquest necessary.

The Police had no information to lead them to form an opposite opinion.

Sergeant Camies distinctly denies that he refused to make an affidavit. He was never asked to do so.

He consulted the Coroner, ascertained his views, reported them to me, and there the matter ended.

I do not know what particular regulations govern Mr. Anderton's conduct as Coroner.

He seems to me to be a law unto himself, and to be desirous of accepting as little responsibility as possible.

His practice is not to form his own judgment independently, but to wait until someone, no matter who, makes the affidavit which he considers essential.

III-3 "Criminal Negligence"
Deane, Monthly Report for Macleod, June 1899 (NAC, RG18, 161, 86-99)

On the 3rd inst., W.J. Essery, a brakeman, was killed at "Haneyville." A scantling, forming part of a scaffold projected over the track, and while deceased was braking on top of a box car, this scantling threw him between the cars which ran over him. The Coroner's Jury found that, "William Jaffray Essery came to his death in the execution of his duty as a brakeman for the Canadian Pacific Railway Company at Macleod on 3rd day of June, 1899, by being struck by a scantling projecting from coal chute, the property of the said Canadian Pacific Railway, being thrown between cars and run over by said cars and we the said Jury find that the Canadian Pacific Railway Company is guilty of criminal negligence for causing the death of the said William Jaffray Essery."

III-4 A Bloody Fight
Deane, Monthly Report for Macleod, January 1901 (NAC, RG18, 204, 89-01)

In the afternoon of Sunday the 27th. instant, on notification by the C.P.R. agent here, two Italians were arrested for fighting. Their names seem to be A. Venere and A. Maruglio. They had injured one another considerably but it is not clear which was the aggressor. Venere was taken into the hospital here with 7 knife wounds in his body. Some six inches of bowel protruded from his abdomen, and he had an ugly cut on the left side of his breast which had penetrated to the lung and caused an escape of air. These two are obviously dangerous wounds but the patient is doing uncommonly well. Venere's story is that he was lying on his bed in the car where they were living and the other man came to him and began stabbing him. He picked up an axe and began defending himself.

Maruglio, who was confined in the guardroom, is suffering from a broken finger on his right hand and two of his ribs on his right side have been broken and forced into the lung from which air escaped. His story is that he was lying in his own bed in the car when Venere came and struck him with the axe, first in the side and then in the hand, when he took to using the knife in self-defence.

Maruglio had $950 on his person and Venere $845.

Both men were sober.

The car was in great disorder with blood marks in places. The axe and knife are in our possession. [*Neither man was convicted.*]

III-5 The Mail Did Not Go Through
Deane, Monthly Report for Macleod, August 1898 (NAC, RG18, 143, 17-98)

Const. Robinson ... reported that complaints had been made to him by the men along the line of construction to the effect that their mail never comes to hand, and that, since Mr. Tuttle's contract expired they do not know where to go for their letters. Const. Robinson's enquiries elicited the fact that the mail sack is left at the station and every one who desires to examine it, turns the mail out on the floor and picks out his own.

There is no one to sort or deliver the mail or is responsible for it, although the workmen are charged 25 cts per month per head as "Mail Fees."

Mr. J.D. Higinbotham of Lethbridge has been sent to Macleod, by the Post Office Inspector, to overhaul the Post Office here. I understand that he has found large quantities of mail matter, which have never been sorted or delivered, but had been thrown aside to take care of itself.

B. Cultures in Conflict

From its establishment in 1874, Macleod had been the most important Mounted Police centre other than the headquarters which, from 1882, were located in Regina. Situated in the heart of territory dominated by the Blackfoot nation, the Macleod Division was expected to pacify the natives and establish the Dominion of Canada's concept of law and order so that whites could settle and carry on agricultural and commercial activities. With the signing of Treaty No. 7 in 1877, the decimation of the buffalo, the incursion of whites into the area, and epidemic and chronic diseases running rampant through the population, the Blackfoot people became increasingly dominated. Most whites took for granted the gradual elimination of Indian tribes as separate peoples, but time has proved these expectations wrong.

The native people, though gravely weakened, were not merely passive victims in the cultural transformation of the Canadian Prairies. They used a variety of techniques, from negotiation to confrontation to evasion, in their attempt to thwart external direction and domination, and to avoid ultimate extinction. They also demonstrated their adaptability, for along with their endeavors not to lose their old ways they accepted many of the new. Whites, on the other hand, seem to have become so enamored with the concept of "progress" that they had little room for tradition, especially that belonging to a different people. But the bias of white leaders towards native customs is understandable not merely because Social Darwinian views were entrenched in white society at the time, but also because these people were attempting to create cultural unity in a heterogeneous country. Not only Indians but also other non-whites and even white ethnic minorities, including French Canadians, came under pressure to acquiesce in the creation of a nation shaped in the Anglo-Canadian image.

The documents in this section demonstrate numerous facets of the cultural conflict undergone by the native people at the turn of the century. One sees the chiefs of the Blood tribe, notably Red Crow, attempting to maintain control over their affairs in the face of encroachment by missionaries and the government's Indian Agents. In this endeavor they consulted the Mounted Police, partly to register their complaints and partly to determine precisely how far the police would allow them to go before interfering.

Deane was perfectly happy to have these discussions. Officially, he did not discourage the visits of Indian delegations "because it is a matter of expediency to obtain and retain the confidence of the Indians and to learn what they have in their minds."[2] But there was more to it, for in subtle ways he informed Blood leaders how to go about modifying traditional ceremonies so that they would not run afoul of the law. His actions can be explained partly by the fact that he had few problems with the native people. As he stated in Annual Report for Macleod 1899: "The Indians deserve all possible praise for their behaviour. Taken as a body they give less trouble than white men." In addition, Deane was offended by sanctimonious and interfering agents and ministers, including the young Anglican parson at St. Paul's Mission on the Blood Reserve, Arthur B. Owen, who raised the astonishing charge against the Sun Dance related at the end of Document III-8 and who had already impressed Deane "as having more zeal, than breadth of mind, or tact."[3]

The issues raised by the Blood chiefs in their discussions with Deane included economic and political matters, but the most prominent were cultural, especially those related to the dances which were integral to native religion. Although but one of many, the Sun Dance was the most famous because it was the most complex and the most unusual to whites who thought it demonstrated the primitive and barbaric nature of Indians. In condemning the Sun Dance, however, whites conveniently overlooked various brutal and humiliating rites of passage of young males in white society at the time, such as the practice of "fagging" at elite schools or of initiation practices in the military. The double standard of whites was also shown in prohibiting natives from giving away their property, while at the same time extolling the virtues of capitalism, one tenet of which was the right to dispose of property as the individual saw fit.

As shown in Chapter I, Deane was no supporter of the Sun Dance per se. Yet he could see that such practices were expressions of traditional Indian religion. And while he accepted the dominant view in white society that these were "superstitions" that should not be perpetuated, he believed that they would dis-

---

[2] Deane to Commissioner, 12 February 1901 in NAC, RG18, 205, 136-01.
[3] Deane, Monthly Report for Macleod, July 1898 in NAC, RG18, 143, 17-98.

appear with the passage of time and therefore did not need to be forcibly suppressed. In the 1890s, the Indian Agent on the Blood Reserve made a concerted effort to prohibit Sun Dances, but they were not easily eradicated. In 1896, an arrangement was made between the Blood people and the Indian Agent to hold races in place of a Sun Dance. But this substitution did not prove satisfactory, and ceremonies of some sort were held in 1900. Whether they merited the title of Sun Dance is an open question. Indian Agent J. Wilson had not asked the police to suppress the activities, but months later officials in the Department of Indian Affairs complained of Deane having allowed a Sun Dance. It was convenient to blame Deane, but the fact was that not even Indian Affairs' officials had either the will or the power to prevent the ceremony.

Blood Indian Delegation at Fort Macleod Barracks, 28 June 1898
GA, Steele and Company photograph, NA-118-13
The occasion for this picture, as detailed in Document III-6, was the desire of the Bloods to convince Deane of the legitimacy of a rite of the Medicine Pipe Society. Their visit was a success. Deane intervened with the Indian Agent on their behalf, and they proceeded with the eleven day ceremony unmolested by the police.

The partial triumph of the native people in the matter of dances was threatened by the increasing emphasis of whites on weaning Indian children away from their roots by having them placed in boarding schools, thus removing them from family and tribal influences. As Document III-9 reveals, Deane was happy to assist and, in his Annual Report for Macleod for 1900, he even raised the question of whether it was not time to make school compulsory for Indian children.

III-6 "Learning the Lesson of Submission"
Deane, Annual Report for Macleod, 1898 (*SP 1899*, No.15, pp.26-28)

The Indians have been remarkably docile and well behaved. Those whom we employ as scouts do the duty that is required of them uncomplainingly and well, and the Indians as a whole are steadily learning the lesson of submission to constituted authority.

A deputation of Bloods, headed by "Calf Shirt," came to see me on the 8th June and protested their children being taken way from them and sent to school. I told them it was done for their children's good, that the agent had his instructions from Ottawa, and that they must be obeyed. They then complained that they were not allowed to hold Sioux dances, but it appeared the agent had not forbidden them at all, provided that the Indians did not give away their property, and did not hold them on Sundays.

A picturesque bevy of both sexes paid me a visit again on the 29th June. It seemed that some one had inadvisedly coupled the word "arrest" with "Red Crow's" name, and the old chief keenly resented the connection. He and his following came to ask me what he was to be arrested for. As a matter of fact I did not know, and it took me the whole of a long hot afternoon, with the aid of the best interpreter in the country, to get at the facts, and to pour oil on the troubled waters.

There is, it appears, an eminent secret society among the Indians, known as the Medicine Pipe Society, entrance to which entails due formalities of election and contribution. Women are as eligible as men. This society holds certain superstitions of a religious character; the wife of an Indian, named "Heavy Shield," at one time on her death bed, as she thought, vowed that she would purchase a certain Medicine Pipe in the event of her recovery and so become a member of this society. In course of time she regained her health, as it happened, and desired to fulfil her vow. There is but a limited number of Medicine Pipes (15) among the Bloods, and that which she was eager to acquire was in possession of a squaw of "Red Crow's," who was equally anxious to part with it upon receiving its value in kind (viz., 15 horses) according to the custom of the tribe.

"Red Crow", as president, felt bound to call the members of the society together to consider the election of the new applicant, and the prescribed formalities extend over some 11 days, there being 4 distinct dances. He convened the meeting at a time, unfortunately, when the Indians should have been setting about their haymaking operations and this naturally displeased the agent who pointed to the clause in the Indian Act forbidding "giving away" dances. Any one who knows anything about the Indian agent's difficulties must know that he is at times exasperated almost beyond endurance at the intractability of his wards, but it is an aphorism to say that in the last resort the application of a statute must perforce be referable to the courts of law, and it is a measure of common prudence to anticipate the verdict of a jury if possible. Whether this particular transaction on the part of the woman be looked upon in the light of a thank offering, from an Indian's religious point of view, or whether it be considered analogous to the initiatory fee payable on joining a secret society, the fact remains that there are the Indians' superstitions which cannot be eradicated in one generation — how are they to be dealt with?

"Red Crow" said, inter alia, that he was too old to give up his own prayers, and would not do so. He desired the prayers of the sisterhood for his wife. He liked the Christians' prayers, but he liked the Indians' prayers too.

It seemed clear to me that if the Indians were honest in their promises that there should be no dedication or exchange of property beyond that directly required for the acquisition of the Medicine Pipe, no court would hold that the Indian Act had been infringed. They promised unreservedly all I asked, and agreed to give up agitating about a Sun Dance this year (which was in the minds of some of them), and I agreed to ask the Indian agent to allow the Medicine Pipe to pass on this one occasion out of consideration for "Red Crow" and his advanced age.

I made inquiries afterwards and was informed that they had strictly kept their promises and, after the 11 days formalities were completed, had returned to their homes.

It is some years since a Medicine Pipe dance has been held, and it may be many more before they desire to hold another ....

At the time of the treaty payments, when a number of the Indians were in town, some thoughtless young men amused themselves at the Indians' expense by what is known as "hokey-pokey." This consists in dropping a few drops of bisulphite of carbon on to a pony, the result of which is to drive a short haired animal to distraction, and to run the risk of incurring considerable danger and damage. The Indians of course resented this, and some arrests were made. Charges of Cruelty to Animals were heard in the courts, and although a nominal penalty was inflicted, the defendants were cautioned to discontinue this particular amusement in future.

III-7 Red Crow's Complaints
Deane, Monthly Report for Macleod, July 1899 (NAC, RG18, 161, 86-99)

On the 27th inst. a party of twenty-five Indians came here to see me, their spokesmen being "Red Crow," "Many Dust" (a minor chief) "Many White Horses" and "Calf Chief".

"Red Crow" said he comes to the Police for advice. That the conditions of the Treaty have not been fulfilled. He would like me to obtain a copy of the Treaty and to read it up. When the Treaty was made, he was duly elected chief and was told that the Indians of his tribe should make any representations through him.

He says a meeting was lately held on the Reserve and was called without his knowledge. He was not notified of it until the day of meeting. He was not there himself, because when the Agent sent for him at the last moment he thought he was not being treated properly. He says it was not a representative meeting, as he had been told that only a few of the Upper Agency Indians were present. The Agent is reported to have said to "Eagle Bearer" that it did not matter whether "Red Crow" was there or not, provided a majority of the Indians were present and that "Red Crow" was getting too old to act anyhow. "Red Crow" says that from what he had been told of the proceedings he does not approve of what was done.

He wishes to have a new meeting called after due notice given, to discuss matters of which he will give notice. These matters are as follows:

1stly The question of the C.P. Railroad running through the Reservation. "Red Crow" says that before Christmas he and his councilors decided to charge the C.P. Ry. $15.00 per head of Indians. Mr. Wilson was informed hereof but "Red Crow" has heard no more about it and he wishes to have the question settled.

2ndly re. the expenditure of $3000.00 paid by stockmen, now standing to the credit of the Indians (as Mr. Wilson is said to have told them), for permitting cattle to graze on the reserve.

3rdly The Indians wish to know why a fence has been run across the Reserve which they claim has restricted the Reserve to which they are entitled. "Red Crow" objected to the fence from the first, as he could see no necessity for it. Four strands of wire have been put on this fence and he has tried to get wire over and over again. The Indians are wondering where the money is coming from to build the fence. "Red Crow" says the mounds are sufficient to mark the boundary. He says Mr. Wilson explained to him, when he ran the line, that the older Indians who were present should explain to the rising generation where the true boundary ran. He says the fence does not follow the true line but leaves room here and there between itself and the boundary for a nice little ranche. The Indians are wondering for whom these places are being reserved.[4]

4thly Lord Aberdeen and the then Indian Commissioner [*Hayter Reed*] promised "Red Crow," in consideration of his hav-

---

[4] The fence, which ran along the southern boundary of the Blood Reserve from Cardston to Big Bend, was controversial, and not just from Red Crow's perspective. From the very beginning, Deane feared it would be a constant source of trouble. As he expressed in his monthly report for Macleod for July 1899, "There is not a single gate in it from one end to the other (20 miles), and it is quite certain that people will not go several miles out of their way when the remedy is so easy and the chance of detection so slight." By the end of the year, Deane's fears were confirmed, for the fence was in shambles, and it was practically impossible to detect the culprits (see NAC, RG18, 176, 11-00).

ing to entertain Indians etc., that he should receive an extra
ration and have the privilege of drawing it between the regular
days of issue. This extra issue amounted to 3 rations, one each
for himself and his two wives. About three months ago this extra
grant was stopped. "Red Crow" wants to know why and by
whose order.

I told the Indians that I would send Mr. Wilson a copy of the
representations that they had made to me besides forwarding a
copy to you and they then left.

III-8 Red Crow's Last Sun Dance
Deane, Monthly Report for Macleod, May 1900 (NAC, RG18, 181, 163-00)

A deputation of Indians came to see me on the 16th inst. to
ask if they might have a Sun Dance. They said Mr Wilson had
referred them to me. I told them that I had nothing to do with
giving them permission and that if they persisted and Mr Wilson
called upon me to stop the dance I should have to do so. They
said they wanted to pray to their own divinities, and one of them
remarked that he could not see why, if the priests could practise
their religion on the Indian Reserve, the Indians could not practise their own.

Deane to Commissioner, 12 February 1901 (NAC, RG18, 205, 136-01)

[*By the time of a meeting in June, 1900*] they had clearly
determined to have a Sun Dance, and I told them that it was
against the law. They talked about wanting to say their prayers
and I said, "No white man would be allowed to go into church
and stick skewers into himself the way you do." They said they
had dropped all that. One of them said that they did not want
Policemen about them when they were saying their prayers, and
this was said in a manner that might or might not cover a
threat. I thought it was intended to convey a threat as they all
waited intently for my reply, which I did not make for some little
time. A little later I told them that if any Policeman went to
their prayer meeting it would be myself. They all burst out
laughing and said that they would be glad to see me. I told them

at intervals throughout the interview that I had no power whatever to give them permission to have a Sun Dance which was
contrary to the law, and that if Mr. Wilson should call upon the
Police to stop it, we should have to do so.

Corporal Bryan distinctly remembers hearing me tell them so.

Joe Healy, an Indian, was interpreter, but I have no reason
to suppose that he did not interpret correctly ....

I attach a copy of the notes which I took of their representations.

Macleod, June 7th. 00.

Chief — "Red Crow"

Minor Chiefs. "Morning Chief," "Day Chief," "Bullshield,"
"Running Wolf," "Eagle Rib," "Wolf Skull," "Heavy Shield," "Calf
Shirt," "One Spot" and Indians.

"Red Crow" says his following are well dressed, they have
bought their own clothing. He wants the Government to do
something for his people. They all work hard to get their own
implements and things, and they want the Government to help
them out. Mr. Laird made the first treaty with the Bloods. Red
Crow would like him to come up here, he would like to see him.
Mr. Laird promised to give the Indians implements. "Red Crow"
thinks he is ashamed to come here, as he never has been here
since he was appointed Commissioner [*in 1898*]. Mr. Laird promised to treat him very kindly. "Red Crow" says that he does not
get enough rations.

"Red Crow" went to see Mr. Wilson, but he skipped out and
would not see him, this was last Monday, the 4th. June. Mr.
Wilson sent Dave Mills to say that he wanted to see "Red Crow".
"Red Crow" said he was busy but would go on Monday. He went
there and "Jack" told him that Mr. Wilson had told the Agency
people they should go away as the "Old Chief" was coming down
to see them. "Red Crow" could not find anyone at the Agency.
There was no one there. Mr. Wilson said he was going out to the
Bull Herd in St. Mary's Coulee. "Red Crow" is not satisfied in
that he has been slighted by Mr. Wilson. He thought he was
appointed for the purpose of attending to the Indians and hearing what they have to say.

"Day Chief" says it is four years since they tried to stop
Indians having the Sun Dance, a lot of them were not satisfied to
give it up. The Government have given prizes for races since

then. Mr. Wilson told them he would not give them another steer to kill for the races after last year. If Mr. Wilson takes back his promise as to giving the Indians beef, the Indians are entitled to take back any promise as to not having a Sun Dance. He, the speaker never gave any such promise. All minor Chiefs present also say they made no such promise. It is not working time yet. They want to be allowed to form their Summer Camp and get together and pray. The Indians have had a great deal of sickness during the winter. They consider themselves entitled to have a Sun Dance, since the steer for the 1st. July races has been denied to them. The Queen's men have beaten the others [*undoubtedly a reference to the South African War*] and they want to celebrate it with a Sun Dance.

"Calf Shirt" went with "Red Crow" on Monday and saw Mr. Wilson going off. "Red Crow" had sent "Heavy Shield" to say that he was coming. Mr. Wilson also told "Black-foot-old-woman" to go away from the Agency when he told other people to go away. "Jack" heard him tell him. He felt hurt at the slight to "Red Crow".

"Eagle Rib" said that there were Churches all over the country — it is lawful for everybody to pray except for the Indians.

"White Buffalo Chief" says, he does not want Police horses and Scouts sent out to where the Indians are having their prayers ....

"Bull Shield." The days are coming for the Horns Society to have their prayers. They think the Horns Society is as good as the Bible. He wants me not to break up their camp. The Indians would like to see Mr. Laird, they have waited a long time for him to come. When working time comes they are willing to drop what they are doing now and do their work. He asks me to ask Mr. Wilson to give them time between sowing time and haying time.

... "Many White Horses" says "We have dropped the cutting and the mutilating at the Sun Dance, but we will have a prayer and have a little fun."

"Sleeps-on-top" says he was very sick and got better, now he wants to have his prayers.

June 8th. 1900. 12 noon

... "Red Crow" wants a scout to be present to hear what he says. Delay of 1/2 hour while "Green Grass" is being found. "Green Grass" is to be spokesman. There are prayers all over the world. You go to Church. (Meaning me). "Red Crow" believes in his own praying. He wants to be allowed to have his prayers. They only want it once a year, the next month is the time. They have been asking so long, they want to get it this time. They are going to buy their own [*cattle*] tongues and they don't want them cut.

"Red Crow's" wife says it is the true praying when the tongues are not cut. They are afraid of them when they are. If Mr. Wilson should give them tongues, the Indians don't want them cut.[5]

Deane, Monthly Report for Macleod, August 1900 (NAC, RG18, 181, 163-00)

"Red Crow" accompanied by some minor chiefs, viz. "Heavy Shield," "Calf Shirt," and "Black Horse's Horse" came in on the 16th inst to make certain complaints. The old chief said that for ten days during their late religious ceremonies, in camp assembled, he did not receive his rations. Also said that some 12 head of cattle which the Indians had acquired by exchange of 15 horses had been taken away from them. This matter seemed to be somewhat involved, and I have even now no clear idea as to the extent of the complaint ....

S/Serg't Hilliard reports on the 29th inst. that Head Chief "Red Crow" died on the previous day.

Deane, Monthly Report for Macleod, December 1900 (NAC, RG18, 181, 163-00)

While travelling here in the train on the night of the 4th inst, with the Rev. Mr. Owen, of the C[*hurch*] of E[*ngland*] Mission on the Blood Reserve, he told me that he had been to Ottawa and among other things spoken of the Indians' Sun Dance. "Joe Healy" had asked him "For God's sake don't let my girls out of your school while the dance is going on." After a good deal of

---

[5] A whole buffalo tongue had been the main sacrament of the Sun Dance, and part of the ceremony had been to cut the tongue into strips. See H.A. Dempsey, "The Blackfoot Indians," in R.B. Morrison and C.R. Wilson, eds., *Native Peoples: The Canadian Experience* (Toronto: McClelland and Stewart, 1986), p. 416. With the buffalo gone, beef tongues were an acceptable substitute for the occasion, but only if they were uncut.

The Joe Healy Family, c. 1895
GA, detail of NA-190-2

Joe Healy was often utilized as a translator and Mounted Police scout. In his youth, he was orphaned and had taken the name of a benefactor, John J. Healy, a noted whisky trader at Fort Whoop-Up. In all probability, he was the first Blood to receive a formal education and was an important intermediary between natives and whites. Evidently, the Healys were the only Blood family that celebrated Christmas in the 1890s. Thus the concern Healy raised against the Sun Dance, as reported near the end of Document III-8, may have been based on Christian antagonism to traditional native religion. But he may simply have wished to keep his daughters — Suzette on the left and Aimee on the right — away from the exciting ceremony just in case things got out of hand. In any event, the family's apparel, from Joe Jr's smock to Mrs. Healy's umbrella, indicates that the Healys were not averse to adapting to changing circumstances.

pressing as to the significance of the request, Joe Healy said that a Sun Dance was known to the Indians as "the breaking-in-season," and that all young girls, even those of tender age, who attend the Dance and are caught in the neighbourhood are held down and raped by any number of men. I have long understood that the Indian customs permit of the raping of young girls, but I never heard that it was the special feature of the Sun Dance, or indeed that it had anything to do with it. Mr Owen was skeptical, and Healy said that Mr Wilson knew it, and he met someone in the Indian Department at Ottawa who also knew it. Ex-Sergt Major Spicer was the best informed policemen on Indian customs that I have ever met, and if he had known he would surely have said so. I told Mr. Owen I would like to have the information at first hand if possible, and he promised to see what he could do. In all the arguments against Sun Dances that have been advanced from time to time, it is funny that this all-powerful reason has never been made known to the Police by those who were cognizant of it.[6]

III-9 "Hand Over Their Children"
Deane, Monthly Report for Macleod, August 1900 (NAC, RG18, 181, 163-00)

On the 1st, 2nd and 3rd inst, I exhausted the subject of recent obstructions on the Railway within the limits of the Blood Reserve.

On the 1st inst. I went with "Piegan Frank"[7] and his grandson, aged 11 years, to the Strong Ranche. The boy pointed out a spot where, about 3 weeks previously, he had been present with 3 other boys, "The Lizard," "Slap-mouth" and "Shines this way," when "The Lizard" placed across the south rail of the track a [*train car*] brake-shoe which was lying near by, and one of the other boys put 3 stones on the same rail. They all went then a little distance up the hill and lay down to watch results ....

The brake-shoe in question, we found a few yards from the exact spot indicated by the boy and I brought it in. The boy said that the east bound train came along, knocked off the obstruction and made sparks.

On the same afternoon I went to where a tire of a dump cart had been found across the north rail of the track, a mile or so

---

[6] No doubt, therefore, Deane was not surprised when specific first hand evidence failed to be submitted.

[7] Piegan Frank was a Mounted Police Scout who impressed Deane enormously with his dedication and effectiveness.

further eastward, by the train No 22 of the 31st July last. A haying camp of Indians was close by. We had ascertained from the section man that he suspected Indian children, as he had previously found them placing things on the rails and had removed them. "The Lizard," the suspected boy was in this haycamp, and I examined him and his people. He is the son of an old Indian named "White b[u]ll" who is practically blind, and his mother consoles herself with a lusty young man called "Nice old Woman," who obtruded himself somewhat. "Tom Daly" an English speaking Indian (whom I had to engage for the afternoon's work as I had no other interpreter) told me that "The Lizard" was crazy, and that some people say that he is suffering from a complaint of "too much father." At any rate the whole family protested that they had seen no such thing as a tire anywhere about there. Except a very little child, who said he had seen one, but whom his mother promptly suppressed.

I issued a warrant for the arrest of the 3 boys before mentioned and they were brought before me on the 3rd instant.

"Shines in the Night" [*the grandson of Piegan Frank*] did not now give the same testimony. He varied it by saying that only "The Lizard" and himself were present and that only the brakeshoe was placed on the line by "The Lizard". He also said that this took place last year. He knew nothing about God or truth or falsehood, so could not be sworn, and his Grandfather subsequently remarked that "they had got him scared" to account for his varying his story.

While reading to "The Lizard" what the witness had said, he blurted out that it was "Shines in the Night" the little fellow himself who put the shoe on the rail and that they were there together last year. This confirmed the witness's story to some extent, and "Piegan Frank" was in a position to prove that the two boys with the lodges of their respective families were camped near the spot in question about 3 weeks previous to the enquiry and not last year at all. I found by experiment that "Shines in the Night" could with difficulty lift the brake-shoe, whereas "The Lizard" being bigger and older (14 or 15 years old) was the much more likely offender of the two.

There was thus of course no case to send before a higher court, but a happy solution of the difficulty presented itself. The parents of all the boys concerned were much frightened and afraid that their progeny would go to the pen[i]tentiary <u>etc.</u> They had gone to the Rev. Mr. Owen of St. Paul's Mission[8] on the Blood Reserve, entreating him to save the children from the pen[i]tentiary, and to take them into his school. He came to see me. When I found how matters stood, I told the anxious relatives that if they would formally hand over their children to Mr. Owen, with the understanding that they would be kept in his school until they became 18 years of age, I would let them go. They jumped at the chance and I think the case was satisfactorily settled. The boys will be out of mischief and the Indians are impressed with the gravity of the offence.

C. The Town of Macleod

The town of Macleod had developed adjacent to the Mounted Police post. Situated close to the Blood and Peigan reserves it became a judicial centre and a distribution point for the ranching country for miles around. Unlike Lethbridge, its ultimately victorious rival for regional dominance, it lacked mining and industrial enterprises. But there was always an esprit de corps, *a western frontier outlook, that characterized the residents of Macleod. It was an approach to life which probably derived from the atmosphere created by the cowboys and natives frequenting the town. Deane learned about this feature of Macleod back in 1884 when the residents of the area closed ranks to wreak vengeance on an undercover Mounted Policeman whom Deane, then the Acting Adjutant in Regina, had sent in order to nab illicit liquor dealers.*[9]

The West has often been viewed as a land of opportunity, and so it was. But it also contained a number of losers in the gamble of life, some of whom sought aid from the police. The popularity of the Mounties was enhanced by their helpfulness as a welfare

---

[8] This is especially noteworthy because, in their 1898 interview with Deane, the Indian delegation expressed a special objection to the school at St. Paul's Mission "on the ground that some of the pupils there practice immorality" (see Extract from Deane Report, 30 June 1898 in NAC, RG18, 154, 443-98). Perhaps the fact that Owen was an inveterate opponent of the Sun Dance helped to fuel the animosity of the Blood representatives.

[9] See R.B. Deane, "The Story of Joe Bush" introduced and annotated by W.M. Baker, *Alberta History,* 40: 4 (Autumn 1992): 2-15.

agency. But desperation led a surprisingly large number of people to attempt suicide. Indeed, in the police records for the decade of the 1890s, there are far more suicide cases than murder cases.

Document III-15 provides an insight into the arena of prostitution. The excess of males over females in western Canada in pioneer days is simply one of the reasons that its urban centres had thriving houses of prostitution. Indeed, perhaps the most recurrent theme of Deane's reports from 1888 to 1914 was prostitution. Macleod was quite typical both in the existence of prostitution and in having its town council inveigh against the trade from time to time. An incident in the red light district, such as a suicide, was sure to draw the attention of town officials to the "evil" of prostitution, but campaigns to end the trade were seldom wholehearted. As a result, prostitution was only temporarily repressed.

Houses of prostitution offered varied entertainment, not merely sexual services, and it was said that cowboys in particular liked to take their time and enjoy music and conversation during their visits. These houses may have afforded an employment opportunity to women in an era when few paid occupations were open to females, but it was one full of peril. While the story of these "businesswomen" was not always a tale ending in disaster, a tragic ending was not uncommon.

III-10 The Wild West ?
Macleod Gazette, 14 September 1900, enclosed with extract from Deane, Monthly Report for Macleod, September 1900 (NAC, RG18, 197, 766-00)

A WILD TIME

Gallagher Resists Arrest - A Fusilade of Shots - The Lariat as a Weapon - Criminal Bravado.

The even tenor of life, which is such a characteristic of Macleod, was rudely disturbed last Wednesday afternoon, and for a couple of hours there was quite an exciting time in and around the town. A young lad named Gallagher had spent most of the afternoon in town, and for want of something better to do had occupied the time at his disposal in taking in a variety of liquid refreshment, and as he began to feel his oats (in this case his rye) proceeded to make a general nuisance of himself. As he

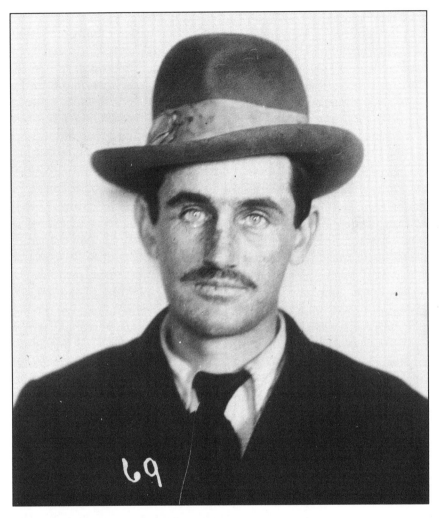

Joseph Gallagher, 12 July 1904
GA, N.W.M.P. photograph, NA-258-1

As Document III-10 illustrates, Joe Gallagher had immense difficulty in combining drinking and controlled behavior. This photograph was taken by the Mounties on the day he was again taken in, this time for a mad tear around Claresholm that lasted two days. During an escape attempt the same day, he would have shot the corporal in charge except that the hammer of the handgun hit an empty chamber. Instead, Gallagher was himself shot in the arm. Infection set in, and he lost the arm. This loss probably had something to do with the decision of the court to give him a suspended sentence on the charge of attempted murder.

was exceeding the latitude usually allowed on such occasions Constable Dooley took him in charge. He was to all appearances perfectly amenable and professed the greatest willingness to accompany the constable to the Barracks. It seemed, however, that he was only acting a part, and seizing the first opportunity he made a break for liberty and succeeded in reaching and mounting a horse that was standing close at hand. Once mounted he treated the constable to a choice volley of bad language, and on Mr. Dooley attempting to again take him in charge he wheeled his horse around and galloped down the street. In a minute or so he came charging back again at full gallop, whirling a lariat in his hand. As he passed the policeman he made a furious throw at him, which if successful would in all probability have ended that gentleman's career once and for all. With considerable presence of mind Mr. Dooley ducked his head and the loop of the rope only jerked away the little forage cap that perches so becomingly upon the head of our local guardian of the peace. Gallagher then seemed to make up his mind to have a good time of it while he was about it, and galloped up and down the street swinging his rope and inviting Dooley to come out and be roped. It was of course useless to argue with a man in his condition, and instead of responding to his invitation, Mr. Dooley telephoned to the Barracks for assistance, and in a very short time two mounted men were in town. The onlookers who had been taking in the show foresaw a speedy conclusion to Mr. Gallagher's vagaries. But not so with the man himself.

The policemen at once gave chase and on seeing that one of them was pressing him close, Gallagher wheeled round and swinging his rope jerked his pursuer to the ground. The lad in the red coat was as near his death as ever he will be, but the other policeman galloped up and with their pistols they managed to intimidate Gallagher for a minute until the rope was slipped off, and he is not likely to forget in a hurry the sensation of the rope around his neck. As it was, he received a nasty twist, and has been reported unfit for duty. Gallagher then made for the open prairie, with the policemen who had been joined by an Indian scout, in hot pursuit, but the fugitive was mounted upon an excellent pony that could run right away from the heavier police horses, and at one time it seemed as if he were going to ride clean away from his pursuers. There was, however, not much excitement for him in a simple race, and before he had gone far he turned and came back at the policeman, whirling his rope as before. They, however, had seen his skill with the rope and (small blame to them) did not wish to come to an ignominious end by means of a rope in the hands of whiskey-crazed boy and on his approach they dismounted and tried to induce him to submit quietly or else take him unawares. This, however, was not his game, and he kept warily out of reach. They mounted again, and aided by the scout and some other policemen on foot, tried to surround him just on the outskirts of the town. An attempt was made to frighten him by firing some blank shots, but there was no scare in him, and charging down on one of the policeman he flourished what the man asserted was a gun. It is supposed that he was armed but had no ammunition for his gun but the policeman seeing a revolver flourished at him at unpleasantly close quarters, did what nearly everyone else would have done under similar circumstances, drew his gun and fired. Gallagher now appeared to be determined to hurt some one and as they could not run him down on account of the superiority of his horse, the policemen opened fire at his horse in the hopes of disabling it. But it is not very easy to hit a horse going at full speed, with a heavy revolver especially when the marksman is on a horse himself, and despite the miniature fusilade that was kept up for a few minutes, Gallagher seemingly oblivious of the bullets dashed past the police and made for the river. As he galloped close past a policeman who was taking a snap shot, he shouted, "Wait till I get a gun and I'll show you fellows how to shoot." Owing to the superior speed of his horse he reached the river considerably in advance of his pursuers and dashing into the water was soon out of sight among the bushes.

The police followed him up and crossed the river after him but abandoning his horse he plunged into the bushes and as evening was closing in, it was impossible to see him and the pursuit had to be abandoned. A guard was, however, set at the various fords as it was thought likely that he would try to recross under cover of darkness and attempt to secure another horse and try to make his escape to the boundary. About ten o'clock Gallagher appeared at Mr. Robins' ranche where a policeman was watching for him and quietly went with him to the Barracks.

Altogether Gallagher managed to make more excitement in Macleod than has been seen for many a day. A large number of people ran around from place to place to witness the efforts of the police to capture Gallagher and doubtless several visitors from the east who saw the affair will have a wonderful yarn of the "wild west" to relate when they get home again. In spite of all the shooting that took place very little harm appears to have been done. Gallagher's horse is said to have been grazed by a bullet and one of the policemen shot a comrade's horse in the foot.

Constable Dooley, against whom Gallagher's animosity seemed to be directed, is to be congratulated on the tact and forebearance which he showed all through the affair although he must have been severely tried. The two mounted men did their duty as well as might have been expected but they were recruits, new to the country and the work. It was, however, the general opinion that any one of the old hands in the force well mounted would have run Gallagher down in short order. The whole affair is to be deplored. It was an example of lawlessness bad for the community and although the young man appeared to be half crazy with liquor a few months in the guardroom will give him plenty of time to reflect upon the error of his ways besides acting as a deterrent upon any one inclined to follow his example.

III-11 Destitute Mother
Deane, Monthly Report for Macleod, February 1899 (NAC, RG18, 161, 86-99)

On the 24th. inst. a half breed woman named Mary Johnson, being destitute applied for relief. She has two children and one sick baby by Philip Whitford who has a wife in the north. She has tried to get work but has not been able to support herself and family, so I gave her a week's rations and requested Asst. Surgeon Haultain to see the sick child. He did so and reported as follows:

"The baby has bronchitis and such an affection cannot improve in a tent with the temperature from zero to 15 or 20 below [*farenheit*], where they allow the sheet iron stove to go out at night, I brought the babe and mother in with me to our hospital, where they will be well looked after until recovered."

III-12 Constable and Wife in Distress
Deane, Monthly Report for Macleod, December 1898 (NAC, RG18, 143, 17-98)

On the 12th. inst. a Mrs. Cox was brought in as a vagrant and taken into hospital for treatment. She is the wife of Reg. No. 3313 Constable G. Cox and followed him to Pincher Creek in the summer. I know not how true it is, but I hear that a subscription was got up in Halifax to get her out of that place. At all events on her arrival, Const. Cox, who had been a very satisfactory servant to Inspt. Davidson, became drunken and worthless. He was returned to duty and sent into the post, and on the night of the 19th inst. he left his post as sentry and went to the shack, situate 800 yards to the south of the Barracks' enclosure, which he and his wife called home. The woman had been on a prolonged drunk, had no clothes and was very ill. Some of the men did what they could for her, and to save her life, Inspt. Cuthbert ordered her to be arrested as a vagrant. She was set on her feet and the vagrancy was of necessity dismissed when brought up. Const. Cox was sentenced to six months imprisonment with hard labour and is ordered to be dismissed the Force.

III-13 "Attempted Suicide"
Deane, Monthly Report for Macleod, February 1900 (NAC, RG18, 181, 163-00)

A Miss Lefevre, who seems to have had an unfortunate life in battling against a hard world, but against whose reputation there is not a whisper, recently took poison in a fit of despondency and was with difficulty brought round. In her delirium she seems to have made statements to the prejudice not only of herself but of other people, and the inevitable gossip monger duly circulated some scandalous reports based thereupon. A person who poses as a friend of Miss Lefevre's laid an information against her for attempted suicide, and Insp. Irwin is listening to the details.

I imagine that the case will be sent for trial, but the Crown Prosecutor will probably think it expedient to carry it no further. Meanwhile the poor girl's reputation is still unimpeachable.[10]

III-14 "Blown His Brains Out"
Deane, Monthly Report for Macleod, November 1899 (NAC, RG18, 161, 86-99)

On the 11<u>th</u>. inst. Const. Harrison shot himself in the room adjoining the veterinary surgery at the time of morning stables. An inquest was held by Coroner D. J. Campbell in the forenoon. Spec. Const. Porch, sick stable orderly, testified that he was in the stable, heard a pistol shot in Const. Harrison's room, went in and found him on the floor. He had put the muzzle of a pistol inside his mouth and blown his brains out. Dr. Haultain was sent for but life was extinct.

The bullet had struck the ceiling and had fallen to the floor. I was called upon for evidence and stated that criminal charge [*never specified*] was pending against the deceased as to the nature of which I desired to say as little as possible and that information would have been laid that day. So far as I knew Const. Harrison had no more reason to anticipate such action on that day than on any other day during the previous week. The Coroner's Jury found that the deceased came to his death by a shot fired by his own hand while temporarily insane.

III-15 "Close Up All Houses of Ill Fame"
Deane, Monthly Report for Macleod, August 1898 (NAC, RG18, 143, 17-98)

On the 18th inst., I received communication from the Town Clerk's Office to the following effect:

---

[10] Attempting to commit suicide was a criminal offence, but charges were seldom laid. For example, the case of an apparent attempted suicide of a Macleod waitress in April 1899 did not go to trial because the attending physician refused to give evidence (see A.R. Cuthbert, Monthly Report for Macleod, April 1899 in NAC, RG18, 161, 86-99). In the instance of Miss Lefevre, Deane's prediction was substantially correct, as the case was thrown out at the preliminary hearing (see Deane, Monthly Report for Macleod, March 1900 in NAC, RG18, 181, 163-00).

"At a meeting of the Municipal Council of the town of Macleod on 15th inst., the following motion was passed:

"That this Council request the Officer Commanding N. W. M. Police to close up all houses of ill fame inside the Municipality as soon as possible."

I replied that the matter would have my early attention. I sent word to the women that they had better move outside the limits in order to save themselves trouble and expense, and if they should want time to complete their arrangements, I would see that they had it.

Inspector A.R. Cuthbert,[11] Monthly Report for Macleod, September 1898 (NAC, RG18, 143, 17-98)

In my weekly report of 14th September I stated as follows:

"Some time ago the Town Council of Macleod requested the Officer Commanding at this post to remove from the municipality the houses of ill fame. On taking over Command of the Division, no decisive action having yet been taken, I informed the Town Council, for obvious reasons, that should houses of ill fame be removed from the municipality, they would not be allowed to exist in the district and outside the municipality; thereupon a council meeting was held, their previous action reconsidered, and the matter left to the discretion of the Police. It is needless to add that the best course is to leave them within the municipality where they can be under a certain amount of control without more than the usual Police supervision."

Deane, Monthly Report for Macleod, June 1899 (NAC, RG18, 161, 86-99)

On the 1st inst., Ida Jahr, known as Daisy Walker, a keeper of a house of ill fame, was found dead in her bed; circumstances pointed to poison. An inquest was held and the verdict was practically suicide ....

The Town Council of MacLeod wrote to me as follows on the 6th inst.:

---

[11] Cuthbert filled in as C.O. during Deane's absence on leave.

"Dear Sir,

At a meeting of the Town Council held last night, I was instructed to request you to take such steps as you may consider necessary to rid the town of all women of ill fame.

Yours truly,
(Sgd) Chas. H. Baker,
Secretary Treasurer."

We took the necessary action, with the result that one woman consented to leave town, another said that she will leave as soon as a certain case in which she is interested has been heard in the Supreme Court, and the third (who is suffering from venereal disease and thus unable to do business just now) says that she is living by herself, is a property owner and tax payer and defies prosecution. The Town Council are content to let the matter remain at that for the present. [*Within a month the houses were running again.*]

D. The Mormon Community

Adherents of the Church of the Latter Day Saints, or Mormons, formed one of the largest distinct groups in southwestern Alberta. Under the leadership of Charles Ora Card, they settled just north of the American border in 1887, named a town after their leader, and gradually spread out from that point and thus came within the territorial boundaries of both the Macleod and Lethbridge Divisions of the Mounted Police.

Mormons were instrumental in the development of agriculture in southern Alberta and were renowned for their expertise in irrigation. As Deane put it in his 1892 Annual Report: "It is generally conceded that what Mormons do not know about irrigation is not worth knowing ...." They provided technical expertise and labor for the building of a large irrigation system that commenced in 1898 after many years of frustration. Mormon settlements followed the path of the "ditch" as it was affectionately called.

Deane was quite positive towards Mormons because they were generally a peaceful, orderly, productive and cooperative people who accepted and celebrated the Canadian polity. But he also found them cliquish, inclined to look after their own affairs, and not prepared to assist the police, especially when a member of the Church was under investigation. The most contentious issue, of course, was that Mormons were rumored to practise polygamy, in spite of its official abandonment by the Church in 1890. There were some instances of plural wives in Canada, but evidence was scanty and cases were difficult to prove.

III-16 "Most Capable Men"
Deane, Annual Report for Macleod, 1899 (*SP 1900*, No.15, pp.18-19)

It is ... the Cardston district which has made the most rapid advancement, and the immigration of Mormons next year is expected to run into the thousands.

I am informed by a Mormon gentleman, who is in a position to know not only the numbers of Mormon settlers, but the names of each and where they are settled, that the population of Cardston and its district is about 1,300 at the present time.

At Magrath, where there was not a single house last January, and which is now a thriving little village, there are 270 souls. Magrath is in the Pot Hole country, and on the irrigation canal, which extends from the intake, above our St. Mary's detachment, to Stirling, a point 18 miles south of Lethbridge, on the Canada and Great Falls Railway.

Stirling itself was no more than a name at the beginning of this year, but it is now a village of some 230 souls. Cardston, the Canadian headquarters of the brotherhood, will, in all probability, always be an important distributing point, and urgently requires barrack accommodation for a detachment and quarters for an officer and magistrate. Business men do not care to exercise judicial functions where their customers are concerned.[12] The village authorities are willing to contribute a site, and are desirous of having a police detachment there.

It may not be uninteresting to briefly describe the Mormon system of immigration into this country. Certain brethren in the

---

[12] This was Deane's veiled way of expressing his view that Mormons did not wish to sit in judgement of other Mormons in public but preferred to "keep matters within the fold of the Church" (see Deane, Monthly Report for Macleod, September 1900 in NAC, RG18, 181, 163-00).

United States were selected to become pioneers of the movement and were informed that the interests of the Church required them to migrate to Canada.

Some of them were very comfortably settled where they
were, and had no personal desire to begin life afresh in a new
country, but allegiance to the Church demanded the sacrifice,
and they "pulled up stakes" and came.

They seem to have as little to say as to their destination.
Some were ordered to build up and occupy Stirling, others
Magrath, others this place or that, and the business in hand
proceeded with the regularity of discipline. During the summer
there was some dissatisfaction in connection with the excava-
tion of the ditch, and a general stoppage of work was threatened.
The president of the Mormon brotherhood [*C.O.Card*] came over
and set the machinery going again. "The Church," he said in
effect, "has undertaken this contract. The honour of the Church
is at stake. The brethren will resume their labours," and they
did.

It goes without saying that selection has been made of most
capable men. A speaker at the Hon. Mr. Clifford Sifton's meeting
at Magrath said, "We will make your country blossom like the
rose," and no one who knows the people and the experience they
have gone through doubts their ability to fulfil the prediction.

III-17 Practising Medicine
Deane, Monthly Report for Macleod, July 1899 (NAC, RG18, 161, 86-99)

Under date of the 18th. July Inspr. Moodie reports as follows:
" ... On the 17th. inst. I went from St. Mary's to Cardston and
saw Dr. Brant re. death of a child of one Howard Hinman. Dr.
Brant had left word at the detachment asking me to call. He
informed me that the child was ten or eleven months old — had
been ill for about a fortnight and been attended by Mrs. J.A.
Hammer, wife of the Bishop, and that he (the Doctor) had not
been called in and could not state cause of death. He also stated
that women are in the habit of attending cases of all descriptions, some of which have turned out fatal — also that in such
cases it is too late to do good when at last he is called — and in
other cases the delay has made it much more difficult to pull the

patient through. I told Dr. Brant that I would report the matter ...."

This has long been a very sore point with Dr. Brant and he has previously written to me about it. I have simply drawn his attention to the law of the land. Births and deaths are required to be registered, and there is no difficulty in setting the legal machinery in motion if the Ordinances are transgressed.

Deane, Monthly Report for Macleod, August 1899 (NAC, RG18, 161, 86-99)

Adverting to my report of July and the representations of Dr. Brant of Cardston to Inspr Moodie re. medical treatment or rather non-medical treatment of Mormons' children by midwives and others, Dr. Brant early in the month made a statement in writing which Inspr Moodie forwarded to me and I sent the Coroner. Mr. Anderton told me that complaints of a similar nature had previously reached him and he proceeded to investigate the case of a child who had been attended by Mrs. J.A. Hammer and had died without medical assistance being sought. I furnished to the Coroner transport to Cardston on the 4th. inst and he returned on the 7th. inst. and said that Dr. Brant would not give evidence to support the written complaints that he had made and that the holding of an inquest was unnecessary. He gave Mr. Card, however, and the Mormon midwives to understand that in future they must give up the practice of medicine, not being duly qualified practitioners.

III-18 Polygamy
Deane to Commissioner, 17 March 1899 (NAC, RG18, 169, 305-99)

I have the honour to forward the enclosed copies of reports from Reg. No. 2797, Corpl. Bolderson, who is on duty at Cardston, re. polygamous practices of Mormons.

It is an open secret that sundry Mormons have one wife in Canada and one in the United States, and it is quite possible that some of the latter may be imported in the future.

Charles McCarty is a prominent man amongst the Mormons and may be expected to move backwards and forwards a good deal between Canada and the United States.

According to Corpl. Bolderson, this man lived in one room last winter with two women, sisters apparently, one of whom was known as Mrs. McCarty and the other as Mrs. Maude Mercer.

In the summer of 1898 Corpl. Bolderson, at Mr. Card's residence, met the woman who had been known in Cardston as Mrs. Maude Mercer, and was introduced to her as Mrs. McCarty, which mistake he says "appeared to cause some consternation," and was explained away.

This Mrs. Maude Mercer later went to Utah with the said Charles McCarty and an extract from the Salt Lake Herald, notifying their arrival at American Fork, was republished in the "Cardston Record" of 8th. February.

The publication of this paragraph has attracted notice, and the Mormons watch us so closely that, as Corpl. Bolderson shows, it was difficult for him to obtain a copy of the Record of 8th. February.

It would be easier to begin working up the case on the other side of the line, as this could be done without attracting attention here. We are not likely on this side to be able to obtain evidence of the marriage ceremony, if any, to which McCarty and Mrs. Maude Mercer were parties, and thus the less interest we appear to take in the Mormons' customs the better.

[Attached to Deane's letter were copies of two reports to Deane from E.H. Bolderson, the first dated 12 February 1899, as follows:]

"I have the honour to submit the following report for your information:

"Last winter I noticed two women were living for a time in Cardston in one room with a man named Charles McCarty. During the past summer McCarty introduced me to one as his wife. The second one passed as Mrs. Maude Mercer.

"Later in the summer I called at C.O. Card's residence on business. Card was out, and a young woman newly arrived from Utah was busy entertaining the woman known as Mrs. Maude Mercer. The late arrival immediately introduced me to Mrs. Mercer as Mrs. McCarty, which appeared to cause some consternation. The supposed mistake was rectified and I was told Mercer and not McCarty.

"The young woman mentioned has since returned to Utah.

"Since then whilst discussing polygamy with Mark Spencer of Cardston, who is not by any means a good Mormon from their standpoint, he was telling me, in confidence, what men resident in Cardston had two wives (1 here and 1 in the U.S.). I asked Spencer 'What about McCarty?' He said 'Well McCarty seems to think sisters are all right, but only one has children.' The sisters referred to by Spencer are the women I mentioned as having been introduced to, and both as Mrs. McCarty.

"Charles McCarty lately went to Utah, taking with him the woman known here as Mrs. Maude Mercer, and in reference to this I enclose a copy of the Cardston Record containing an extract from the Salt Lake Herald ....

"Extract from the 'Cardston Record' of February 8th. 1899.

"'American Fork, Jan. 26th. — Charles and Maude McCarty from Cardston, Alberta, Canada, are visiting here at present. Mr. McCarty is working in favour of the big irrigation scheme of which Mr. Card is at the head. Two hundred settlers with teams are wanted. — Salt Lake Herald.'

"One of the lady clerks in H.S. Allen and Co's store asked me if I had noticed the item.

"McCarty lives somewhere near the Pothole and has not been through any marriage ceremony in Canada as far as I can ascertain.

"Taking the facts of the introductions, Mark Spencer's remarks and the newspaper item, would convince me, with my experience of these people, that Charles McCarty is guilty of polygamy under Sec.278, Crim. Code 1892.

"These two women being sisters and passing under different names, have in the ordinary course a reasonable excuse for living in the one house, and further, no Mormon would give evidence in a case of this kind unless cornered very tightly.

"McCarty is expected to return in the early spring and will probably bring back the woman he took away, who will resume her place as Maude Mercer.

"Dr. Brant, who is not a Mormon, but who has lived in Utah for years, tells me he is pretty sure another man living near Mountain View has two wives resident in Canada. He will report to me or Sergt. Cotter, the name and particulars as soon as he finds out. Dr. Brant's suspicions come from a Mormon source. A Mormon having in course of conversation remarked to him

'Two or three of these fellows with two wives will come in here and the Police will get on to it and everybody will get down on us all because of a couple of those fellows'.

"These people are up to all kinds of dodges to shield polygamy, which necessity taught them in the U.S.A. and if it once gets a footing in Canada will be very hard to stamp out, perhaps next to impossible."

[Bolderson's second report, dated 11 March, 1899, began with the tale of how difficult it had been to obtain a copy of the newspaper in which the implicating notice had appeared:]

"... After an unsuccessful attempt to obtain the paper from private source I was forced to apply at the Record office, where I was informed that copies of the paper of any date except Feb. 8th. were to be had. This story I thought improbable and finally (by purchasing all the back numbers from the end of January to date) the editor, rather unwillingly to all appearances, produced a copy of the 8th. ultimo.

"I have no doubt that the editor found, after the paper was published, that he had made a slip in putting the paragraph in. (C.E. Snow, editor, is the son of the President of the whole Mormon Church.) Since I made my report to you, I learned from Mr. Hammer, the Bishop here, that he had written to McCarty in the U.S.A. to say that if the woman he had with him was his wife to leave her behind. He professed not to know whether McCarty was a polygamist or no, but did not deny that he was. Hammer told me that the Rev. Gavin Hamilton had written to Ottawa about McCarty. From Mr. Hamilton's conversation with me on the subject of polygamy and without asking him the direct question, I am led to believe that he did not make any report. This only leaves the conclusion that the Bishop's action was caused by the Record item.

"In conversation with Robt. Ramsbottom (C.O. Card's partner) who has lately joined the Mormons and who came from Brandon, [*he*] told me a few days ago that Card had received several letters from Utah asking whether settlers would be allowed to build two houses, one to shelter a polygamous wife, so that the man could support his family, and that they [*were*] told 'No'.

"I have reason to believe, however, that this is exactly what a man near Willow Creek is doing, one woman supposed to be his deceased brother's wife. His name I have not yet found out, but will see Sergt. Cotter in whose district Willow Creek settlement lies.

"It may seem strange that I am able to obtain such information from the prominent men in the Mormon Church who generally advocate the holding of outsiders at a distance.

"This I can scarcely explain, as when I first came here they complained of my being too strict, but [by] my establishing for myself a good reputation and rendering small services socially I have obtained from them a certain amount of confidence. This I found was the only way to do anything with them at all. I mention these latter facts, as outsiders have at different times made statements that I was un-necessarily friendly, and I wish no action of mine to be misconstrued, with regard to Mormons or Mormonism."

III-19 A Fiesty Woman
Deane, Annual Report for Macleod, 1900 (*SP 1901*, No.28, p.12)

On June 7, in response to a pressing telegram from Sergt. Cotter, Inspector Irwin was sent to Cardston to try a case. A man had made some filthy remarks in connection with the name of some young lady who was visiting there from the United States — how such a remark could have reached her ears I am at a loss to understand, but at any rate she made her slanderer kneel down at the muzzle of her revolver and make her an ample and public apology, which "on dit" he did without any loss of time. The young lady then contributed $10 to the State coffers for assault.

E. A Cattle Smuggling Operation

By the turn of the century, Deane was one of the most experienced officers in the Mounted Police. As a result, from time to time he was given the responsibility of investigating and preparing special cases. Deane enjoyed these breaks from ordinary routine and liked the challenge presented by complex and difficult cases. The investigation described in Document III-20 was wonderfully successful and resulted in commendations from the West-

*ern Stock Growers' Association and from both Commissioner
A.B. Perry and Comptroller F. White. Unfortunately for Deane,
the individuals who were convicted and fined in the case and who
had long shown their hostility to the Mounted Police, had powerful friends. Before the year was out, Clifford Sifton, the Minister
of the Interior, demanded that Deane be transferred. This was
bad enough, but Deane also felt that the government had cheated
him out of a portion of the monetary reward due to him.*

Spencer Brothers' Ranch Hands, 1899
PAA, A-412
*The territory near the 49th parallel south of Medicine Hat is awe-
inspiring in its magnificent barrenness. Not surprisingly, accusations
were rife about cattle and horse theft, smuggling, and other nefarious
activities in the region. As Document III-20 shows, Deane was successful
in bringing charges for evasion of import duties against the owners of
the outfit who employed the cowboys in the picture.*

  *Document III-20 is an excerpt of the draft of the 1902 Annual
Report that Deane submitted to the Commissioner. The operation
had taken place as part of the Lethbridge Division, but by the end
of the year Deane was no longer in command of that Division.
Commissioner Perry knew the perils of publishing Deane's ac-*

count and deleted this portion from the printed version. In a note to the Comptroller, Perry provided his reasoning: "Considering the contentious nature of this portion of this report dealing with the round up of the Spencer Bros' cattle it would be advisable to cut it out altogether. In any case it has nothing [to do] *with Maple Creek District." Nevertheless, his superior officers knew that he had been unjustly treated, and they attempted to make it up to him in the years that followed. As for Deane, he had, as he put it, "the grim satisfaction of knowing that I had worked up a case in which there was not a single flaw, and which could not fail to be upheld by every tribunal in the Dominion.*[13]

III-20 A Crime That Simply Added Up
Deane, Draft of Annual Report for the Maple Creek Division, 1902 (GA, M3799, folios 59 and 60)

In March last [*1902*] I proceeded with Mr. J.C. Bourinot, Special Preventive Officer, to a ranche near Pendant d'Oreille Coulee on the Milk River the proprietors of which had been charged with smuggling some hundreds of American cattle into Canada. The lease held by the said firm comprises four townships on the banks of the Milk River, two of them being townships numbered one, adjoining the international boundary line, and the two others adjoining being townships numbered two. The range is thus conveniently situated for access to the American or the Canadian market.

This firm had had some trouble with the American Customs officers in 1901 respecting a shipment of about 170 head of cattle shipped by train from Galata in Montana, and a deposit of some $2300. or so was made by the consignors before the shipment was allowed to proceed. Most, if not all of these cattle were fattened on the Canadian range, were conducted to the line by a Canadian round-up and driven off to the railway under the personal direction of the senior partner of the firm. There is evidence to prove all this ad nauseam.

---

[13] Deane, *Mounted Police Life*, p.178. Deane provided a detailed account of the entire operation and its aftermath on pp. 154-181 of his book. Additional material on this and related cases are located in many Mounted Police files, but especially useful collections are located in NAC, RG18, 346, 21-08 and in GA, M3799, folios 59-60.

Mr. Bourinot was charged by his Department with a message to the firm in question and delivered it to the managing partner thereof. That gentleman denied that there were any smuggled cattle on their range, and we returned to our respective headquarters.

Persuant to instructions from the Department of Customs Mr. Bourinot returned to Lethbridge in May, and on the 14th. of that month he and I, with a small party of Police, accompanied a round-up party of 13 men, which travelled across country in a due easterly direction until we arrived at the range to which we were bent. On arrival Mr. Bourinot informed the management that we were taking charge of the cattle on the range and that we were provided with means of rounding them up. Our operations were considerably delayed by weather as it was on the night after our departure from Lethbridge that the series of rain storms began which culminated in the floods of that period.

We reached, on the 18th. May, a point on the said range where we found a rider stationed to prevent the Co's cattle from going *North*: he had been stationed there for some time for this purpose. Just prior to the time of our arrival, also, two men had been stationed at the S.E. corner of the range where, in conjunction with some miles of fencing running along the international boundary westward, it had been their duty to prevent cattle from going *South*. The number of men employed altogether on the range at the time of our visit was nine, and it was accounted to be "a big outfit".

It will thus be apparent that the range was well guarded, and that cattle thereon had every inducement to remain, even in the event of their evincing an inclination to leave their magnificent pasturage for a southern climate.

A feature that presented itself, as we proceeded in our work, and which was remarkable was that the range was so "clean", that is free from cattle bearing brands other than those of the owners.

There is no truth in representations which have been made that there were thousands of stray American cattle on the range in question. During the five weeks that I was on the range I did not see 500 head of American cattle other than those that we were in search of. It was notorious that the leaseholders had systematically driven American cattle off the range. On one notable occasion, in February 1901, as is duly chronicled in the Police reports of the day, they drove from 1500 to 2000 head of strayed American cattle (which were not trespassing on their lease) across the Milk River when the ice was known to be rotten, notwithstanding remonstrances that were indignantly made at the time.

The managing partner had told Mr. Bourinot and myself previously that the firm claimed to own between 6000 and 7000 head of cattle — he could not give closer figures than that, and no books were kept shewing purchases or importations, except as to 1230 head (854 of which were calves under 12 months) which had been imported from Montana and entered at Customs, between 24th. April 1900 and 21st. April 1901.

Between the 18th. May and the 10th. June we gathered a herd of rather more than 1400 cattle branded with the American brands of the firm, besides sucking calves. Some of these "suckers" were big fat yearlings, bearing the Canadian brand which had been affixed in the course of the *previous year*, while their mothers bore the American brand only. In the course of our peregrinations we dropped from day to day 15 cows to allow them to calve, and at the last we found ourselves with a herd consisting of close on 2000 head, including calves, many of which had travelled about 70 miles; I may add that we never lost a single calf from first to last.

The number of cattle, three years old and upwards, to which the firm were in the ordinary process of nature entitled, due allowance being made for such calves as might have qualified as three year old animals since their entry on 25th. April, 1900, amounted to 398 cows with calves and 26 steers. The 26 steers were the product of a duty paid entry on the 25th. April, 1900, and did not become three years old until after the 25th. April, 1902. These were all handed over to the firm, and of the remaining herd we cut out

      30 steers over 5 years old
      172 steers over 3 years old and under 5
      170 cows with calves
      <u>234</u> dry cows
[*total*] 606 all over three years of age

The manager objected to one steer and 18 cows as not being three years old, and to save time and unnecessary talk we conceded the animals, leaving a total of 587 which were duly seized.

It may be supposed that we were not simple minded enough to start out on an errand of that nature without having reliable expert opinion ready to hand, and the men upon whose opinions we acted are well known men of proved capacity and unimpeached integrity. We had gone a step further, and provided a competent veterinary surgeon, so that if necessary an animal in dispute might be thrown and its mouth examined. We did not, however, desire to "strain at a gnat", and wherever our experts said that there might be a doubt we conceded the point and the animal.

The managing partner, both verbally and in writing, acknowledged the age of the 587 head of cattle received by him to be aged three years and upwards, after having been invited to subject to mouth examination any animal to which he took exception. This invitation was in no case accepted.

It will be observed that no steers, other than calves, had been entered at Customs, and the fine large beef steers which we found on the range could not fail to attract the attention of any person who was in any way connected with cattle.

All sorts of irrelevant statements have been made by interested parties in connection with this matter — and as the pens of Mounted Policemen are restrained by discipline I will merely say that the Departmental case for the Exchequer Court, if the defendents should think fit to betake themselves thither, is complete and unassailable — their statement of defence would, if it were made public, cover its authors with ridicule in the stockmen's world, and the imputations which, in a desperate effort to drag a herring across the trail, have been cast upon men who performed a simple act of duty in the service of the State are as silly as they are cowardly and mendacious. [*The conviction was confirmed after an appeal to the Supreme Court of Canada.*]

IV
RUGGED INDIVIDUALISM
MEDICINE HAT AND SOUTHEASTERN ALBERTA
1902-1906

Deane did not fight his removal from Lethbridge to Maple Creek in 1902, although the citizens of Lethbridge repeated the protest against his transfer that had been successful a decade earlier. A year after his departure, they presented him with a glowing testimonial and a fine gold watch and chain. At first, the top brass of the Mounted Police contemplated establishing a criminal intelligence department to be headed by Deane, but the concept was premature. Instead, he became the Commanding Officer of Division A. This was not quite the demotion that it might seem. To be sure, it was a small division without a lot of activity, but it put him in close proximity to Regina and enabled him to act for the Commissioner on occasion, to take on special cases, and to revise the Rules and Regulations of the force two decades after he had originally prepared them.

However, the years from 1902 to 1906 were not happy ones for Deane. As well as resenting the treatment he had received from his political bosses, he also had a series of personal troubles. He was well into his fifties and suffered from various ailments including sciatica, rheumatism, respiratory problems and Dupuytren's Contracture. The latter not only resulted in a stiffening and clenching of his right hand which eventually required a three hour operation but also was likely related to Deane's having a toe amputated. He no longer played cricket or participated in theatrical productions. There were family problems as well. When Deane was removed from Lethbridge, his son Percy was dying in Los Angeles of consumption, and Deane did not even have the financial resources either to go or to send his wife.

On a happier note, the eldest boy, Reginald Burton, had become a physician and had moved to Maple Creek where he provided medical services for Division A of the Mounted Police. In Maple Creek, therefore, the senior Deanes were close to grandchildren. His daughters had also married. The younger one, Lily, had become the wife of Superintendent P.C.H. Primrose of the Macleod Division. But Deane's wife of over thirty years was in failing health. She did not wish even to make the short trip from Maple Creek to Lethbridge without her husband, when Lily's first child was born in 1902. By the end of their sojourn in Maple Creek, Mrs. Deane had declined badly. She went to the coast for treatment but died there, without her husband, just before Christmas, 1906.

No doubt, these personal problems affected Deane's perceptions of his time with Division A. He found Maple Creek itself "a funny little Methodist-ridden place ...."[1]* He was bored, did a lot of riding just to pass some time, devoted his attention to such mundane matters as putting the barracks and guardhouse in shape, and read the service and took the collection at the Anglican Church when the vicar was absent. On the other hand, he no longer had to shuttle back and forth between two centres. Nor was he saddled with a Mounted Police commissioner whom he detested, for in 1900 L.W. Herchmer was forced into retirement by Prime Minister Laurier and was replaced by A.B. Perry who, by 1904, succeeded in having the designation "Royal" added to the name North-West Mounted Police.*

The Maple Creek Division covered the western portion of the District of Assiniboia in the old North-West Territories. As such, it encompassed the southeastern corner of what became the Province of Alberta in 1905. The documents in this chapter focus on that Alberta portion of the division. In 1906 that sector was removed from the jurisdiction of the Maple Creek Division and turned over to the Lethbridge Division.

During this period, Deane's monthly reports became more abbreviated and routine. Only in part was this a consequence of little going on. The very function of monthly reports was being transformed, for in order to keep track of specific cases it was becoming the practice to organize files on the basis of individual case reports. Reports on particular criminal cases, for instance, were submitted to Deane but were no longer addressed to him. This did bring greater order to the organization of police work, but unfortunately, many of the old case files are today either missing or incomplete. Deane himself was instrumental in the re-

---

1 Deane, *Mounted Police Life,* p.97.

organization, but the change meant that his monthly reports were less complete and lacked rhetorical flourish. Fortunately, other Deane materials reveal the rugged individualism that character-ized the time and region, albeit police files present mainly its negative aspects.

A Garden Tea Party In Maple Creek, c. 1906
GA, NA-3668-10
Maple Creek was not London, not even Regina or Lethbridge, but that did not stop people from dressing up for social gatherings. This sunny party, with tea and berries, may have been the last for the first Mrs. Deane (second from left), for she died not long after this picture was taken. Her failing health was one of the reasons for Deane's discontent about being assigned to the Maple Creek Division.

A. Non-treaty Indians

As in the Lethbridge Division, the Maple Creek Division had no substantial Indian reserves within its boundaries. The small number of Indians within the territory were non-treaty Indians who attempted to sustain an independent livelihood. Unfortunately, some suffered from the same problems that plagued not only Indians on reserves but also white pioneers on the plains: i.e. disease, destitution, and alcohol abuse.

The law forbidding alcohol to Indians under any circumstances was likely counterproductive, since it seemed to promote an "if damned for an ounce, then be damned for a quart" attitude. In any case, the episode recounted in Document IV-3 was typical of the messy altercations which formed the basis of the all-too-prevalent stereotype of the "drunken Indian." On the other hand, the tenacious struggle of the non-treaty Indians to avoid becoming wards of the state won a degree of admiration from Deane, and his reports reveal evidence that undermines the image of native people as impoverished and intemperate.

IV-1 Smallpox
Deane, Annual Report, 1903 (*SP 1904*, No.28, p.20)

At the beginning of January it was reported to me that a camp of non-treaty Indians, numbering 101 souls, was affected with smallpox. The health officer of the district, who happened also to be the Acting Assistant Surgeon to the police [*Reginald B. Deane*], had already taken charge of the camp, and quarantined its inmates. Persuant to instructions, I then arranged to make the quarantine effective by stationing a N.C. officer and interpreter within the precincts of the camp, and issued rations of beef, flour and tea to each family, as the Indians were by their seclusion precluded from earning their livelihood for themselves. The health officer vaccinated all the Indians that required it, and the usual precautions as to disinfection, &c., were strictly carried out. As a result the disease did not overstep its limits, and was effectually stayed without casualty.

IV-2 "Morbidly Afraid of Accepting Assistance"
Deane, Annual Report, 1904 (*SP 1905*, No.28, p.25)

During February and March, with the concurrence of the Indian Department, we issued rations of beef, bacon, flour and tea to some Salteaux Indians who have never taken treaty and who live mainly on Maple Creek.

Deep snow prevented them from following their usual calling, namely that of hauling firewood into Maple Creek from the Cypress Hills, and they were contemplating the destruction of their own log houses and selling the material for fuel, when their extremity came to my ears. They are inclined to be quite independent, and look askance at any assistance from the Indian Department for fear the acceptance thereof should be a stepping stone to the curtailment of their liberty. In conjunction with Interpreters Hourie and McKay, I had a long talk with them with the idea of inducing them to have their children taught something whereby they may be able to make a decent living later in life, but advice seems to go in one ear and out at the other.[2]

Deane, Annual Report, 1905 (*SP 1906*, No.28, p.24)

The non-treaty Indians living in the neighbourhood of Maple Creek are well behaved and give no trouble at all, but they are in great poverty and if we should have a hard winter it will go very hard with them, and some of them are not unlikely to starve to death.

If we do not happen to find out their condition they will say nothing as they are morbidly afraid of accepting assistance from the government lest they should be compelled to go and live on a reserve. One is disposed to think that life on any kind of reserve must be better than they life they lead, but they cannot be persuaded to think so.

IV-3 Resisting Arrest
Inspector W. Parker, Crime Report (submitted to Deane): Assault on Peace Officers by Ka-cess, a Cree Woman, 26 April 1906 (NAC, RG18, 309, 120-06)

On the 25th. instant Sergt. Quinn laid an information against Ka-cess and charged her that she at Medicine Hat on the 24th.

---

[2] The relief provided was minimal. As Deane put it, when submitting his claim for reimbursement from the Indian Department: "we fed none that were not actually in extremis, and gave them no more than was necessary to sustain life." The recipients were not only wary but also unclear about who was giving them the rations: "one unusually ignorant Indian asked if the grub had been sent by the American Government." See NAC, RG18, 276, 454-04.

April, 1906, did assault two peace officers, Const. Ellwood, of the R.N.W.M.P. and Town Constable McCorkindale of the town of Medicine Hat, engaged in the lawful execution of their duty with intent to resist and prevent the lawful apprehension of herself and other Indians for committing an offence by being drunk and disorderly.

The accused was arrested and brought before Insp. Parker.

John McCorkindale stated as follows: "On the evening of the 24th. instant I accompanied Const. Ellwood to the Indian camps east of town. I saw the accused in the camp fighting with a man. Const. Ellwood took hold of her and I got hold of the man and separated them. I was holding the man down when the accused picked up an axe and made for me with it, but Const. Ellwood knocked her down. She got up and picked up the axe again. I caught the axe, took it away from her and threw it away, and took her in charge, and was taking her along the line of tents, when Iron Eagle, an Indian, caught hold of her, and pushed her into a teepee. Const. Ellwood then arrested Iron Eagle and put the nippers on him. I then went into the teepee after the accused and put her out in front of me. I then turned to look at two other drunken Indians in the teepee, and I then saw Const. Ellwood and Iron Eagle on the ground, struggling. The accused picked up another axe and made another swing at me with it. I then tried to separate Const. Ellwood and Iron Eagle, when the accused came again with the axe. Const. Ellwood was choking as Iron Eagle had him by the throat with his left hand, his right hand by the back of the neck. The accused was still coming with the axe, another Indian had a knife, and several drunken Indians were around. I drew my revolver and shot Iron Eagle in the right leg, and then made a rush for the accused, knocked her down and took the axe away from her. When Iron Eagle was shot he released his hold on Const. Ellwood, and Ellwood got up in dazed condition. We then brought Iron Eagle to the Barracks.[3] I had permission from Chief of Police Marwick to accompany Const. Ellwood to the Indian camp.[4] The accused and Iron Eagle were drunk."

---

[3] Iron Eagle's injury was a flesh wound, not even serious enough to prevent him from walking the one mile from the Indian camp to the barracks.

[4] Ellwood had been sent by Parker to investigate alleged drinking in the Indian and Métis camps. As Sergeant Quinn was not available, the town constable accompanied Ellwood.

Const. Ellwood was the next witness and his evidence was about the same as McCorkindale's. This closed the case for the prosecution, and the accused declined to give any evidence or to call any witnesses, stating that she knew nothing about it.

She was committed to the guardroom at Calgary to await trial upon the above charge at the next sitting of the Supreme Court to be held at Medicine Hat.[5]

IV-4 "No Complaints of Their Conduct"
Deane to Commissioner, 5 April 1906 (NAC, RG18, 1574, 69/4-06)

I have the honour to forward ... a report by Sergt. Redmond, from which it may fairly be inferred that there is no ground for the imputation against the Indians who are now living near Fort Walsh.

The Indians in question are non-treaty Crees, numbering about 30 souls. No complaints of their conduct have ever come to my knowledge. Until lately they have lived in the vicinity of Graburn,[6] but it now seems that they intend to live in the Four Mile Coulee.

I happened to see some of these Indians in town yesterday. One of them changed three $10.00 bills into smaller currency and still had money in his purse. They were well dressed and well behaved, and the fact that the partner of the man who made the complaint has not heard of their having done anything wrong is significant.

B. Robbery on the Range

Other than a couple of towns and a few villages, the entire territory covered by the Maple Creek Division was ranching country. An irony of Deane's forced transfer to Division A was that in Maple Creek he was as close to the Spencer Brothers' ranch as he

---

[5] Six persons were convicted of liquor violations stemming from this case, with the supplier of the booze getting four months (see NAC, RG18, 1583, 145-06).
[6] Due east of present-day Elkwater at the current Alberta/Saskatchewan border, the location was named after Constable Graburn, the first Mountie murdered in the line of duty.

had been in Lethbridge. That case had been well publicized, and cattle operators knew that Deane was no one to trifle with, for over the years he had gained considerable expertise on the ins and outs of the industry. He knew about nefarious techniques for accumulating stock; he was cognizant of the difficulties created by the 49th parallel; and he was not averse to mounting his horse to check out rumors of illegal activities. His Maple Creek reports indicate that such activities were practised there as elsewhere. It was not even necessary to name the perpetrators in public documents, for the cases and individuals were well-known in the region. Indeed, the present-day reputation of the cowboy/rancher as an upright, honest, straight-shooter was not so prevalent around the turn of the century. Perhaps it should not be too surprising that certain individual ranchers acquired stock in questionable ways when the stock growers' round-up itself followed rather dubious practices.

Blackfoot Indians at Medicine Hat
GA, NA-2003-55

This group was just passing through Medicine Hat, for there were no reserves of any consequence in the district. Nonetheless, off-reserve and non-treaty Indians were no strangers to the area. The women and children here, taken with the snow melting on a sunny day in the early 1900s, demonstrate that travelling was a family affair for native people, not just restricted to adult males.

IV-5 "Here a Calf, There a Calf, Here and There a Calf" Deane, Annual Report, 1904 (*SP 1905*, No.28, pp.16, 19-20)

A prominent stock owner was convicted at the spring assizes and sentenced to three years in the penitentiary on three separate charges of cattle stealing, and this has, I think, induced "rustlers" on the prairie to pause and consider before taking chances which might prove to be adverse ....

The case of calf stealing alluded to above well exemplified the old adage "when thieves fall out honest men come by their own." Had they not "fallen out" this matter would not have become known and they might have become well-to-do ranchers by perseverance in their art. The minute details would not interest the general public but a rough outline of the plan designed by the thieves may repay perusal.

A certain cattle dealer in May, 1903, imported from Manitoba a number of calves which he proposed to sell to persons requiring "stockers." He had rather bad luck with this importation, for some got away from him before they were branded, and a much larger number got away from his herders in a bad storm. There were then upwards of 100 unbranded calves on the range and the possibilities were too obvious to be neglected. A local stockman, owning two or three ranches with fenced pastures extending to whole sections of land, whom I will call A, conspired with two employees, whom I will call B and C, to acquire some of these motherless and masterless calves. The *modus operandi* was to brand a certain proportion of the calves with A's own recorded brand, and these would constitute his share, while the other proportion were to be branded 7 11 7 which would form the share of the other two conspirators. This 7 11 7 (seven-eleven-seven) brand was invented by C, and was not a recorded brand. He explained that he invented it because a lateral line would at any time connect the two perpendiculars of the figure 11 thus converting it into a letter U, and a slight extension of the top of the first figure 7 would convert it into a T — the converted brand would thus read T U 7; this was also unrecorded [*but formerly had been C's brand*].[7]

---

[7] See Deane et al., Crime Reports: The John Lawrence — Cattle stealing in NAC, RG18, 274, 387-04.

I was never able to satisfy myself as to the reason of these men breaking up their connection, but this is what happened. B and C had a scheme on foot to take up and brand certain calves on a particular Sunday, and A and B came together and gave information to me.

The result was that two constables watched the Sabbath morning operations and arrested C red-handed — he was handling the branding-irons and apparently directing the operations. He was subsequently convicted and sent to the penitentiary for three years upon very simple and indisputable evidence,[8] but while he was awaiting trial in the guard-room here he gave away the story of the conspiracy between himself and A and B. B got wind of it and left the country, while A was tried and convicted here last March and dispatched to join his confrère at Stony Mountain.

Particulars which came to light in the course of the trial indicated that the "rustling" of calves had not been confined to the principals in this performance, and a feeling of insecurity has since existed in more than one thitherto unsuspected quarter.

Deane, *Mounted Police Life in Canada*, pp. 102-103

The verdict [*in the latter case*] was hardly expected by the general community, and came as a kind of shock to its nerves. The first comment that came to my ears, after pronouncement of the sentence, was a conversation between two ranchers as follows:

"Well, Joe, what do you think of this?"

"It would have done more good, Pete, if it had happened fifteen years ago."

That epitomised the general opinion of the neighbouring stock-owners, who had lost "here a calf, there a calf, here and there a calf," and had never been able to obtain redress. The convict, in this instance, was a pillar of a Nonconformist church and a man of means, who was very assiduous in his religious attendance and duties. After a few months' confinement in the penitentiary, he was suddenly released by order of the Minister of Justice, and took up his former abode as if nothing had

---

[8] Material about this case is located in Deane et al., Crime Reports: A.J. McConnell — Cattle Stealing in NAC, RG18, 255, 394-03.

happened. The train that conveyed him westward towards his home carried also the Chief Justice who had tried and sentenced him, and of the latter queried a passenger:

"Do you know that ———— is in this train going home? He says he is not on ticket of leave and seems to have been given a pardon. Have you heard anything about it?"

"No," said the Chief Justice, "and, what's more, I don't believe it."

The passenger's statement was, however, true enough, the convict had simply been released, and the local authorities had no information on the subject. It had for some time been no secret that the minister of the nonconforming church in question had been very active in making supplication to the Government to quash the righteous sentence, and the result showed that he had not laboured in vain.

It was a different proposition, however, a few months later when the same reverend gentleman came to us to complain that his son, a young man, who had recently started a ranch of his own, had had some half-dozen bags of oats stolen from his stable while the owner was absent. The theft was traced to another young rancher, who was trying to earn a living for himself, and then nothing would content the minister of the gospel but his pound of flesh. He insisted on prosecuting the thief, who was convicted in a court of summary jurisdiction and sentenced to imprisonment. It makes all the difference whose ox is gored.

IV-6 "The Prairie Species That Preys Upon His Neighbours"
Deane, Annual Report, 1905 (*SP 1906*, No.28, pp.19-20)

In last year's report I mentioned the case of an individual whose character and antecedents had been known to me for years, and who was welcome to take all the rope he wanted. Nemesis has overtaken him quite recently .... A rancher near Medicine Lodge [*slightly south and west of present-day Elkwater*] first saw a foal that had just been born to a mare of his on the prairie on August 18, and kept the pair in view until the 28th of the same month, on which day the bunch of horses to which the mare belonged disappeared. The owner looked for them all day, but they could not be found.

On August 30, Corporal McLean, of Medicine Lodge detachment, visited a ranch, the owner of which was away from home. As he was some distance from home, he wanted supper and a night's lodging, so he determined to wait, and in the meantime looked about him. In the corral he noticed a mare and colt. The mare's hind legs were hobbled, and she would not allow the colt to suck, albeit it was obviously only a few days old. At about 5:30 p.m., the owner came home with a load of hay. The corporal made a casual remark about the colt, and the owner said it was a maverick — that is, an unbranded colt whose owner was unknown. The corporal proffered his services in the unloading of the hayrack in return for his prospective night's lodging, and in the hay was found the newly slaughtered carcass of a sheep. A casual question as to where he procured the sheep induced the reply that he had bought it from a herder. The following day Corporal McLean spent in making inquiries from the neighbours as to whether any of them had lost a colt — on the day following that, the owner of the mare reported that the foal was missing. In company with witnesses who knew the colt, the party visited the ranch. The bunch of horses, including the mare, was driven to the corral and the mare and colt claimed one another. The corporal arrested the ranch owner, who was duly committed for trial at Medicine Hat. We took the trouble to make inquiries of all the sheep herders in the district, and each and every one denied that he had given or sold a sheep as stated. The ranch owner in question rather boasted of the circumstances that he had, since he had been in Canada, been arrested on eight different occasions and was yet unscathed. He is a prominent example of the prairie species that preys upon his neighbours — here a sheep, there a colt — and hardly anything too insignificant to acquire. (Since the foregoing was written the accused has been tried at Medicine Hat, and sentenced to two years in the penitentiary.)

IV-7 "A Ready Way of Making Mavericks"
Deane, Annual Report, 1903 (*SP 1904*, No.28, pp.17-19)

A decision of considerable interest to stockmen was delivered by Chief Justice A.L. Sifton at Medicine Hat on November 20, the circumstances being as follows:

A German settler, near Josephburg [*slightly north and west of present-day Elkwater*], who cannot speak English, had a fourteen-month old steer, which had stayed about his place until it was driven off by the May snow storm and was lost. He heard in course of time that the Plume Creek round-up had gathered it up, and went to the captain thereof to claim it. He could not, however, make himself understood, and shortly afterwards his English-speaking son claimed it. The captain of the round-up pooh-poohed his claim, admittedly took no steps to ascertain whether the claim was well founded or not, and the steer was in due course sold by auction as a maverick (or unbranded animal) for $19.

Another German settler of the same locality lost a heifer under somewhat similar circumstances, and this was sold by auction at the close of the round-up for $16.50. This case differed from the first, in that the owner did not know that his animal (which was unbranded) had been taken up by the round-up, and did not make any claim for it.

I may remark, parenthetically, that there is no law which requires an owner to brand his cattle unless he pleases, and his property rights are obviously not impaired by any such omission.

Upon the foregoing facts being brought to the notice of the Police, a criminal charge of theft in each case was laid against the captain of the Plume Creek round-up, and he was duly committed for trial.

The Medicine Hat and Maple Creek Associations, which are separate organizations from the Western Stock Growers' Association, did not take this view of the matter, and engaged counsel at Calgary to defend their representative at his trial.

They held that an unbranded animal on the range is an incentive to theft by some person or other, and seem to think that if they brand and sell him for their own benefit they are removing the creature out of harm's way, are performing a useful service to the community at large, and are not infringing the law of meum and tuum. I happen to know that there is by no means unanimity of opinion as to their methods, even within their own ranks, and it may not be out of place briefly to describe the operations of a round-up so far as to emphasize the point I wish to make, which is this. If the claim of the associations in question be conceded, that unbranded animals, commonly called "mavericks," gathered by a round-up, are by right of custom the property of the Stock Association concerned, and may be applied to payment of the necessary expenses of the round-up which gathers them, it becomes material to consider the ease with which, and some of the methods in which, mavericks may be made.

I will assume that the rounding-up has been completed, and the cattle are gathered at the rendezvous in readiness for the cutting out. The first class of animals to be cut out are the cows with calves. That is an operation that requires great care, and in a properly conducted round-up only the most capable and knowledgeable and best mounted men are allowed to enter the herd. Two men apply themselves to each cow and calf, riding on each side and a little behind the animals, which are quietly conducted out of the day-herd (as it is called), and headed towards the "cut" which they are intended to join. There are mounted men in charge of each cut, and others all around the day-herd, whose duty it is to see that unauthorized animals do not break out or in. A very little harrying of a cow and calf in the day-herd will result in the calf being separated from its dam. This may be done unintentionally, and when it has happened the only recourse is to let the cow stay in the herd until she shall have reclaimed her calf. But suppose, for the sake of example, that the herd has been harried a good deal, and that some cows and calves have been separated: it is a mere matter of detail to cut out the cows and leave the calves until the close, when there will then appear so many unbranded calves (mavericks), which become the property of the association, and are sold accordingly. I should explain that at this stage the calf of which I speak has not yet been branded, and if it became separated from its branded mother, there is no way of telling who its owner is.

A prominent stock owner has this very season spoken of cows having been driven across a river while their calves remained on the other side. That is a ready way of making mavericks. A calfless cow with a distended bag is no unusual sight on the range, and we know that all the calves have not been killed by coyotes and wolves.

It is to be noted that a round-up does not necessarily confine its attentions to cattle which are the property of members of the association which it represents, as ought to be the case, unless it can show express authority to the contrary. There is no greater autocrat on the continent than the captain of the round-up, as has been abundantly shown in court during the last few weeks, but if owners suffer from unauthorized handling of their cattle it is not because there is any ambiguity in the law. The Stray Animals' Ordinance provides that any person who (1) takes, rides or drives off any horse or head of cattle belonging to another; (2) when taking his own animals from pasture, without the owner's consent, takes or drives off the animal of any other person grazing with his own, is liable to a penalty not exceeding $100.

To return, however, to the Supreme Court at Medicine Hat. The facts were all proved as charged.

The accused said he was appointed captain of the round-up by the Secretary of the Medicine Hat Stock Association, and took no steps to ascertain whom the cattle in question belonged to.

It was shown that the proceeds of the auction sale in each case were handed over to the secretary of the eastern branch of the association. A letter from the said secretary to the purchaser of the stolen heifer was read to the effect, inter alia, that if they should get a few more "pay" cattle they would clear their expenses.

The secretary of the Medicine Hat Stock Association said that he had been in the country nearly 30 years, and that it had always been customary to sell mavericks to pay round-up expenses. He said also that the association had for years been trying to get the custom legalized, but had failed so far.

Other witnesses, who had acted as captains of round-ups in former years, testified as to the custom, and said that they would have acted exactly as the accused had done. One witness went the length of saying that he would not have considered it his place to take any trouble to ascertain the ownership of the cattle in question. He considered it was the owner's business to make and prove his claim.

Counsel for the defence laid great stress on the fact that there was no felonious intent, and that the money went to general round-up expenses and not to the personal benefit of the accused. He said that although the acts complained of may have been illegal, and he did not intend to justify them on legal grounds, yet it was not criminal as applied to the accused, who happened to be captain this year, and merely followed the custom of his predecessors. He contended that the law is imperfect, in that cattle should not be allowed to go unbranded on the prairie, and so become a temptation to people of weak mind.

The judge agreed that punishment by way of imprisonment was not necessary, and considered that the requirements of the case would be met by the record of a formal conviction against the accused, and he would be released on suspended sentence. He said that there was no question that conviction was proper, and that the secretary and members of the association were equally guilty with the accused. They were well aware that the sale of mavericks was unlawful, because they had for years been making efforts to have the custom legalized. As to the intent, he commented on the fact that a direct benefit accrued to the Stock Association by application of the amount realized by sale of the mavericks to their expenses.

He said in effect that people have a perfect right to allow their cattle to range on the prairie unbranded if they please to do so, and that a round-up has no right to gather cattle which are not the property of members of the association, without the consent of their owners.

An order was made in each case for the return of the stolen animal to its original owner.[9]

C. Prostitution in Medicine Hat

Prostitution was just as fixed a feature in Medicine Hat as in any other prairie urban community, and just as problematic. Houses of prostitution offended the sensibilities of self-appointed moral guardians of society and not without justification, for they were frequently sites of drunk and disorderly behavior or worse. In any case, it was an issue that Deane had to deal with time and again no matter where he was posted. Ministers were frequently the ones who complained, but one police investigation was in response to a letter from C. White Mortimer, the British Vice Consul in Los Angeles, who complained of witnessing shocking

---

[9] Additional information on this case is to be found in Deane et al., Crime Reports: Theft of Herman's Steer in NAC, RG18, 255, 394-03.

behavior by some drunken, foul-mouthed, and disorderly rowdies in Medicine Hat. The Mounties found little substance to the main charge, but on a subsidiary matter they uncovered an unreported shooting in one of the brothels.

In April 1904, the Attorney General's office of the North-West Territories was alerted through private correspondence that two houses of ill-fame, several restaurants, and most hotels in the Hat were involved in the illicit sale of intoxicants. The informant also claimed that brothels were sources of an outbreak of venereal disease. According to the informant, one of the town's doctors stated that he had treated more than one hundred cases of syphilis in a two month period. Because the police had not eradicated the supposed source of the disgrace, the correspondent, whose name was not divulged to the Mounties, charged that "vice flaunts itself in high places." Deane and company were put on the defensive, but they responded vigorously and certainly had the last laugh on this matter.

IV-8 The Reverend's Complaint
Deane, Monthly Report, December 1902 (NAC, RG18, 232, 203-02)

The Rev. W. Nicoll had complained to me about the existence of a house of ill-fame at Medicine Hat. He did not wish to have the occupants imprisoned, but wanted them to be "run out of town." On enquiry I found that the house in question is from two to two and a half miles from the town of Medicine Hat on the left bank of Seven Persons Creek in quite an out of the way spot. Mr. Nicoll said he made his appeal on behalf of his congregation. Sergt. Macleod interviewed his church wardens, and they knew nothing of the matter.

IV-9 Disorderly House of a Madam Named "Archie"
Sergeant W.B. Macleod to Deane, 20 February, 1903 (NAC, RG18, 1526, 126-03)

There is some truth in the statement by the clerk that Keesee had frightened the inmates of Archie Wilson's house of ill-fame. This report is the first I ever heard of the occurrence. I went down to interview the women yesterday and they told me that no one had ever taken possession of the house, but I happened to be talking to a young fellow in the country today about Keesee and he told me that Keesee was at the house one night when he was here for a few days several weeks ago, and was drinking a good deal. He (Keesee) pulled a revolver out of his pocket and shot through a stove in the room. The concussion put the lamps out and there was a great deal of confusion, but the woman, Archie Wilson, never reported the matter. The first I heard of any shooting taking place in the house was when Boyd and Stillwell went there with revolvers and fired them, each of whom were fined $10.00 and costs.

This house of Archie Wilson's has been in operation since last spring and has never been raided, so that I think if it be raided in the near future it might encourage the keeper to report any disorderly conduct in her place.

IV-10 Venereal Disease
Deane to Commissioner, 28 April 1904 (NAC, RG18, 1533, 7-04)

I have the honour to inform you that this is the first time that the suggestion has been made to me that Syphilis is being disseminated through the medium of the houses of ill-fame at Medicine Hat and I have no reason to believe that the report has any foundation in fact.

As to the doctor who confides so unreservedly in Mr. Nicoll[10] as to his medical business [*if he*] would give the Police a "pointer" now and again, some useful results might be attained.

I wonder whether Dr. Elliott[11] would mind asking his private correspondent to furnish the name of one man who has acquired Syphilis at one of the "sporting-houses."

---

[10] Deane mistakenly assumed that the unidentified correspondent cited by the Attorney General's office was the Anglican minister. His mistake was understandable since Nicoll had recently complained to Inspector Starnes about the women coming to town and flaunting themselves so that even young children pointed them out and talked about them (see Starnes to Deane, 28 April 1904, in NAC, RG18, 1533, 7-04).

[11] Elliott was the one who had received the letter from the Medicine Hat informant and then turned it over to the Deputy Attorney General.

I understand that one of the clerks at the hotel has been at Banff for some time under treatment for Syphilis which came to him from an entirely non-professional quarter.

Inspector Starnes on his return from Medicine Hat told me that Mr. Nicoll had spoken to him about the women, and I have only waited for Corpl. Wilson to fully recover from his attack of appendicitis before giving him instructions in the matter.

However, Inspector Starnes will proceed to Medicine Hat and take the matter in hand. He says that the women have come more prominently into public notice since Corpl. Harvie's and Mr. Paddock's escapade.[12]

As to the complaint of Mr. Nicoll that the women advertise themselves in the town, it is to be observed that the Municipality has by-laws and a staff of constables to enforce them.

Inspector C. Starnes to Deane, 30 April 1904 (NAC, RG18, 1533, 7-04)

In connection with the attached file and in accordance with your instructions, I saw Mr. Nicoll. This gentleman informs me that he did not write to Dr. Elliott or anyone else on the subject in question. That after the conversation he had with me he did not intend to do anything further in the matter and was satisfied that something would be done. He also says that all the previous correspondence on the subject was written by himself officially, and that he would not write about it privately.

I then interviewed the three practicing doctors of the place as to the amount of syphilis in Medicine Hat, and got from them the following statements:

Dr. C.E. SMYTH states:

"During the past year I have treated about half a dozen cases of syphilis; gonorrhoea is somewhat more prevalent. By taking the patients['] statements I can trace many of these cases to the houses of ill-fame. I think these venereal diseases have increased in town since these houses have started, although the town was never free of it before. For several years when I came here at first there were none of these houses, this was from 1898 to

---

[12] Paddock had helped Corporal Harvie and two other Mounties to desert (see Document IV-16).

1899. I have never been called to any of these houses for cases of venereal disease. I could not give the name of any patient that I have treated, it would be a violation of medical ethics."

DR. CHAS. F. SMITH says:

"I have been practicing in Medicine Hat for the past nine years. In that time I have treated about ten cases of syphilis, and about five last year. Of this total number only two have been traced to the public houses at present in existence here. I have treated quite a number of cases of gonorrhoea and soft chancre, the source of infection in the majority of cases was non-professional. I am satisfied that as far as the present houses are concerned they are conducted as far as the spreading of disease as carefully as it is possible to do. I frequently am called to make examination and specially in Stella Hattley's house. She is exceedingly particular as to the health of her inmates. I could not give the name of any person I have treated. It is privileged information; it would be neither professional nor legal."

DR. J.G. CALDER says:

"During the last six months I have treated more cases of syphilis than I have treated in the last 16 years. Of the two kinds of chancre I have treated about 50 cases, the majority of which were syphilis. In addition there have been a great many cases of gonorrhoea, certainly more than a hundred. Last night alone I saw two cases of primary syphilis and two cases of gonorrhoea. Previous to the time that the two houses of ill-fame now in existence came here, syphilis and gonorrhoea were very rare. I have traced the majority of these cases to the girls in these two houses. I think the cause of this is greatly due to carelessness on the part of the inmates in these houses. There is no doubt that even although they are infected themselves, if they would use proper antiseptic precautions, and be properly looked after by the mistress, the danger of infecting others would be very much lessened. But where the landlady is careless, allows the women to get drunk and neglect themselves, the danger of infection is very great. I have been repeatedly asked to inspect them and have always refused to do so, because the girls are allowed to do too much drinking, and so many of the girls are addicted to the use of cocaine and morphia, that they were very often in a condition that I could not expect them to take any care of themselves at all. I have often mentioned this to people in town, but made no report to the Police. I could not give the name of any man who has been infected, without his leave. I do not know of any of the girls being infected at present, as I have not enquired the names of the girls in the last cases."

I cannot recall anyone in particular who spoke to me on that subject in such a way that I should have thought it necessary to report.

Inspector Starnes to Deane, 4 May 1904 (NAC, RG18, 1533, 7-04)

In answer to yours of yesterday I have the honour to report that since my last report and after the houses of ill-fame had been raided, I found out that Mr. Benson, J.P. was the one who must have written in connection with the matter. I met him the night before last and he complained to me that I had taken the cases.[13] He said that he considered it was a reflection on the local magistrates. He told me that he was in favour of the total suppression of these places, and that on a previous occasion he had spoken to me about this, a few days before I went down to Maple Creek. I then recollected that in a general conversation on meeting him on the street, he had touched on this subject and expressed his views, but it was after Mr. Nicoll had spoken to me, it was in a casual way, and as I was going to report on the matter anyway, I did not attach much importance to it. After recalling the fact of speaking to me, he told me that a medical man had told him that there were 100 cases of syphilis in two months. Of course this must be Dr. Calder, and his statement does not quite agree with this large number.

To-day I sent for the keepers of these two houses, and warned them in the spirit of your letter. They both were very much disposed to do what they were told. Both will have all their women examined medically and bring the certificates of examination to the office tomorrow. They also said that they would not allow their women to go to town on any pretense, that there was

---

[13] As a fee was attached to convictions in such cases, local J.P.s were thus deprived of an opportunity to make easy money, and they complained to Deputy Attorney General Horace Harvey. Copies of the correspondence are located in NAC, RG18, 1533, 7-04.

no necessity for it, that if they wanted to go out driving they would go out in the country. These keepers would themselves come about once a week and make the necessary purchases without attracting attention.

They both complained that sometimes men went to their places drunk, broke the doors in and virtually took possession of their places, to kick things around generally. I told them that whenever this happened they should report it, and steps would be taken to stop it.

Deane to Commissioner, 10 May 1904 (NAC, RG18, 1533, 7-04)

I have the honour to forward a report from Inspector Starnes giving the names of inmates and frequenters of the two houses of ill-fame at Medicine Hat who have been dealt with under the Vagrancy Act.

I also enclose copies of Medical Certificates which show that on medical examination the female inmates have been found free from contagious disease. These appear to dispose of the unfounded statement of Dr. Elliott's unknown correspondent, who would seem to be Mr. Benson, J.P.

Deane to Commissioner, 16 June 1904 (NAC, RG18, 1533, 7-04)

I understand from Corpl. Wilson that even the "Kickers" are satisfied with the state of affairs as regards the women in Medicine Hat. Corpl. Harvie encouraged them to get out of hand, but they are now seldom or never seen in the town and when they do go they dress and behave quietly.

It is the easiest thing in the world to get them into order and to keep them so if the N.C.O. will treat them firmly and consistently.

Dr. Calder is a "blow-hard."[14]

---

[14] Deane was in such good spirits with the outcome of this episode that in a postscript he even made light of his own physical ailment: "I have got a touch of sciatica which makes my downsitting and uprising a matter of some formality!"

D. Death by Water

Mounted Police files record a variety of violent deaths. Alexander Deutschman was attacked and trampled to death by range cattle while he was on foot. The four year old son of Sergeant Quinn died from drinking a quantity of carbolic acid. Fred Guggesburg hanged himself.[15] Yet it was supremely ironic that in this arid section of the Prairies, part of what has been called the Great American Desert, water was involved in a number of fatalities during Deane's term as C.O. of Division A.

Waiting for the Ferry, Medicine Hat
GA, NA-2003-23
This pre-1909 photograph shows teams and wagons waiting to be taken across the South Saskatchewan river. As Document IV-11 shows, however, even such a mundane activity as using the ferry could result in tragedy.

---

[15] Materials on these three deaths are to be found, in order, in NAC, RG18, 289, 136-05: NAC, RG18, 1571, 49/68-06; and in NAC, RG18, 1556, 49/74-05.

IV-11 Accidental Drowning
Sergeant D.G. Quinn to Deane, 11 June 1905 (NAC, RG18, 300, 516-05)

I have the honour to report that on the afternoon of the 10th. instant, about 3.30 p.m., Wm. Green, who runs the steam laundry here [*Medicine Hat*], was accidentally drowned while driving across the ferry.

Mr. Green was on the ferry in his buggy with his child a little boy. There were three other buggies on the ferry at the time. The ferry had just started when one of the horses in front of Green's horse got frightened and backed up and Mr. Green's horse had to back up also and backed the buggy off the ferry. The ferry could not be stopped quick enough, and the current of the river swung the buggy around and pulled the horse off the ferry also. Mr. Green threw the child to one of the men on the ferry who jumped into the water. The child was saved and the horse and buggy started down stream. The horse headed for shore and in some way got loose from the buggy. Green jumped out of the buggy and let the horse go. He went down and never came up again. Eye witnesses state that no danger was felt for him, as he was making for the shore and was about two horses length from shore when he went down. Several rushed to his rescue, but he never came up again, and the water is so muddy he could not be seen. The river is high at present and is running very swiftly. Search parties have been at work ever since, with boats, grappling hooks and nets, but have failed to find the body.

It is the general opinion that the body has been carried away in the under-current which is very swift.

He leaves a wife and three children, also a brother and other friends, and was a very much respected young man, being about 30 years of age.

IV-12 "She Said She Was Going to Drown Herself"
Inspector W. Parker, Crime Report (submitted to Deane): Suicide of Ellen Louden, 28 April 1906 (NAC, RG18, 1570, 49/32-06)

On the 22nd. instant the body of Ellen Louden was found in the river about four miles west of here [*Medicine Hat*]. The body was brought to town and Coroner Smyth notified. He issued a warrant for a jury and Sergt. Quinn warned the following: J. Benson, T.J. Fleager, R. Nelson, P. Robertson, J. Houson and G.B. Borridale. The coroner and jury met at 10 A.M. in the Court House. The jury was empannelled and the body, which was naked, viewed.

Samson Dutton said: "I live near Stair on my ranch. The deceased was my wife's sister. She had been stopping at my place for a week previous to the drowning. Her own home is about two miles from my place and about three miles west of Medicine Hat. On the evening of the 18th. instant [*she went out*] and did not return. I thought nothing of it as she often went to Mrs. Brier's place. Next morning I went to Brier's and made enquiries about her and found that she had not been there. I then went towards the river and saw Mrs. Hunt on the other side of the river. She called to me and said that a woman was in the river last night and must have been drowned, and that I would find the clothes further up. I went to where Mrs. Hunt directed and found the clothes which Ellen Louden was wearing when I last saw her the evening before. I hunted along the river and went to town with the clothes, and notified the Police. I also notified R. Louden, her brother, and James Louden, her son. She had two sons and lived with James. She has been in bad health for a long time and was not of very sound mind for the last two years. She was 56 years of age. The last time I saw her alive was at about 5 o'clock on the evening of the 18th. instant. She has been at my place often and sometimes appeared to be all right."

James Louden says: "I have seen the body which is that of my mother. She has not been in good health for some time, and was some times out of her head. I saw her three days before the drowning. She looked very well and I thought she was getting better. Only once did I hear her say she would do away with herself. That is a long time ago."

J. Brier says: "Yesterday afternoon I was out with a search party looking for the body of Ellen Louden. We found the body in about 6 inches of water on the north side of the river, face downwards, there were no clothes on the body."

Dr. Woodward, who made the post-mortem examination, said that to the best of his knowledge the woman came to her death by drowning.

The inquest was adjourned till the 24th. instant.

Mrs. Samuel Hunt says: "I live on the south bank of the river about six miles up from Medicine Hat. On the evening of the 18th. instant about 6.30 p.m. I saw a woman walking on the flats across the river from my house. She was walking and had a stick which she was swinging around. She called across the river to my children, asking them if the river was deeper on our side. The children told me and I watched her to see what she was doing. She was at the edge of the river. I went down to the river and called to her. She said she was going to drown herself. She undressed and got into the water. This was about 7.30. I told her to get out of the water and to put on her clothes and go home. I did not know who she was. She said she had no clothes and no home either. It was getting dark and I could hardly see her in the water. My husband came home and he went to the river with me, but we could not see her. I called but got no answer. I sent my daughter to town with word. We had no boat and no way of getting across the river, which is very wide at that point. She must have been in the water about 15 minutes, and that was the last I saw or heard of her."

This concluded the evidence and the jury retired and after 5 minutes returned the following verdict "That Ellen Louden committed suicide by drowning while temporarily insane."

IV-13 Another Body Found
Inspector W. Parker, Crime Report (submitted to Deane): Drowning of J.W. Russell, 29 April 1906 (NAC, RG18, 1570, 49/33-06)

On the afternoon of the 22nd. instant Thomas Louden, while on the river searching for the body of his mother, Ellen Louden, found the body of an old man floating down the river, just off Police Point. Louden was in a boat and brought the body to shore, then came to town and reported to the police .... The body was that of J.W. Russell, age 73, who has been missing since the morning of the 7th. inst. .... On the 24th. instant the jury met at 11 a.m. and the evidence of Mrs. Russell, daughter-in-law of the deceased, was taken. She stated as follows: "On the evening of the 6th. instant Mr. Russell went to bed after supper, but at about midnight I saw him walking in the yard and asked him what he was doing. He said he could not sleep. At about one o'clock I got him to go to bed and that was the last I saw of him. At about two o'clock I heard him breathing as if he were sleeping and I went to bed and to sleep. At seven o'clock next morning when I got up he was gone. He has been living with us for the last four years, and has not been very well all winter, and kind of stupid for the last few weeks. My husband is working for the C.P.R. and has been away for some time. On the morning of the 7th. instant, after I missed him and could not find him anywhere, I told Mr. Brown, a neighbour, and he made search and notified the Police."

Dr. Woodland gave evidence and stated that from his examination of the body, Russell came to his death by drowning.

Fred Russell identified the body as that of his father, J.W. Russell.

The jury returned the following verdict: "That J.W. Russell came to his death by drowning, whether accidental or otherwise it is impossible for us to say."

IV-14 Infanticide?
Sergeant D.G. Quinn, Crime Report (submitted to Deane): Re. Body of Child Found in Saskatchewan River, 14 May 1905 (NAC, RG18, 289, 136-05)

Late this afternoon some boys, who had been along the river bank [*at Medicine Hat*], came to the Barracks and reported that they had seen the body of a child washed ashore. The Coroner Dr. Smythe was at once notified and proceeded to where the body was about a quarter of a mile north of the railway bridge on the east side of the river and a little below the hospital about half way between the C.P.R. bridge and the Police Point. The body was that of a male child, and was decomposed quite a bit, and has been, the doctor says, in the water for some days. The skin was partly torn off by the beating of the water on the stones, and was washed ashore only by the strong west wind that had been blowing all day, as, if there had been no wind, the current in the river is so strong at present, the body would have been carried down stream. The body was naked. A plain linen pillow slip was found near the body, but there were no marks on it. The doctor states that the child was new born when cast in the river, and he says may have come with the current quite a distance. The body was handed over to the Coroner to the under-taker to be held for further examination tomorrow .... I searched along the river banks and shore for any other evidences that might throw light on the subject, but it got dark and I had to give up the search.

Deane to Quinn, 15 May 1905 (NAC, RG18, 289, 136-05)

Is the child of a white woman, halfbreed or Indian? Make enquiries as to whether any pregnant woman in your neighbour-hood has been delivered of a baby lately. Notices will be sent westward when you have gained all the information you can. It means murder.

Quinn, Crime Report (submitted to Deane), 15 May, 1905 (NAC, RG18, 289, 136-05)

The inquest was held in the Court House at 4 p.m., Dr. Smythe presiding. The evidence of one Christian Schneider was taken as to how the body was found and where it was found. He had gone fishing in the afternoon and found the body and then sent some boys to notify the Police. The evidence of Dr. Smythe, who held a post mortem examination on the body, was taken. He stated that the body was that of a male child, that it was 18 inches long and weighed about 5 lbs., that it was a new born child of white parents, that it had perished soon after birth from neglect, and was dead before being cast in the river. The cord, about 8 inches long, attached to the navel, had been broken off. He stated that he thought the child was born alive, but had died a short time after birth. There was no mark of violence, and he believed it died of hemorrhage. The child must have been in the water at least a week, from the state of decomposition and the coolness of the water for the last week .... The jury ... returned with the following verdict. "That the infant child came to its death through neglect at birth or soon thereafter ...."

This concluded the case except that the body was ordered to be buried.

IV-15 Alleged Murder at Seven Persons
Sergeant W.B. Macleod, Telegram to Deane, 8 November 1902 (NAC, RG18, 239, 671-02)

Reported murder at Seven Persons, no particulars, am leaving by train [*from Dunmore Junction*].

Extract from Medicine Hat Diary (submitted to Deane), 8 November 1902 (NAC, RG18, 239, 671-02)

Sergeant Macleod left this p.m. on Crow's Nest train for Seven Persons to investigate a report started by an Italian named Figlio that he had seen a man kill another near Seven Persons' bridge and put the body under the ice in a pool of water.

Macleod to Deane, 10 November 1902 (NAC, RG18, 239, 671-02)

I have the honour to report that I returned this morning from Seven Persons.

I went with Const. Holmden to the place where the Italian said he had seen the man thrown into the water. It is a stagnant pool under the railway bridge. The ice is very thin but we cut away a good deal of it and there is no sign of a body in the place.

I left Const. Holmden to cut the rest of the ice as it was so thin yesterday we could not stand on it any longer. I examined it all over when I went first but there was no sign of its having been broken anywhere before we started. I saw the conductor of the train that the Italian took at Seven Persons but said the man was evidently a tramp as he had not paid his fare, and he did not see him on the train.

I have not heard from Lethbridge yet as to whether the Italian is there or not.

Deane to Macleod, 11 November 1902 (NAC, RG18, 239, 671-02)

Your report re. alleged murder at Seven Persons is incomplete. But for your diary which says that an Italian had said that he had seen a man kill another and throw the body into a pool, I should not know what was the matter.

I assume that you got this information 2nd. or 3rd. hand? From whom did you receive it, and where and from whom did your informant receive it? Where did the Italian, Figlio, come from and whither has he gone? What did you do to catch him? You would have been justified in having him arrested on suspicion of being connected in the alleged murder. Are there any reasons for supposing him to be other than sane? About how big is the pond - how deep? It is a pity you could not take the Italian to the spot and find out all particulars. Where was he when he saw the murder? What was he doing and how came he there? How far from him were the others? Does he know who they were? Where did they come from? What became of the man after he had put the body into the pool? Is it quite certain that there is no body in the pool?

If you sent any messages or telegrams in connection with this matter copies of them should be sent here to complete the record.

Macleod to Deane, 8 November 1902 (NAC, RG18, 239, 671-02)

In respect to my telegram of this evening I have the honour to report that I received a note from here this morning asking for a Policeman to come out. There was a freight train coming so I sent Const Holmden. This evening at 6.25 p.m. I received a telegram from him stating that it was reported here [*Seven Persons*] a murder had been committed near here. The story as told by an Italian named Figlio is as follows:

Figlio was crossing the Seven Persons' bridge about two miles from here on the evening of the 7th. [*actually the evening of the 6th*] inst. when he heard a cry from a man. On looking down he saw a tall man strike another over the head with a gun, then shove him through a hole in the ice and throw a large stone on him. The tall man told him to come down but he would not, and then he said, "If you tell anyone what you have seen I will kill you also". Figlio went to Seven Persons' section house, and the tall man followed. Figlio took refuge in the water closet and the other came to the house, looked in the windows, and went off a few hundred yards till a freight train passed. He came to the train, looked in some cars and then went east.

When the section foreman came out yesterday morning he found the Italian, Figlio, on the door step, and in the evening he told this story.

The foreman tried to induce him to stay till he could send word to me but Figlio left about 12 p.m. last night on the passenger train for Lethbridge stating he intends to go on to Havre, Montana.

I have telegraphed the Officer Commanding "K" Division [*Lethbridge*] to locate and hold him if possible.

Const. Holmden went to the pool below the bridge, which is about twenty yards long by ten wide. He shovelled off a large patch of snow and examined the snow and ice carefully but there was no sign of blood or of the ice having been broken. He asked all the people living in the immediate vicinity about the matter but could get no information as to any one having been seen near the bridge ....

The Italian could give no other description of the assailant other than that he was tall and had a large moustache.

Deane to Macleod, 11 November 1902 (NAC, RG18, 239, 671-02)

Your report dated 8th. inst. at Seven Persons has been delivered here by a belated mail train.

You should make absolutely certain that there is no body in the pool, or neighbourhood, and, if not, the explanation probably is that the man Figlio is out of his mind — possibly he saw the crime committed elsewhere and cannot get it out of his mind.[16]

E. Desertions

The Mounted Police was a para-military body with a commensurate code of discipline. Not all members took kindly to the organization or its restrictions. Some men were insubordinate; others bought themselves out; others deserted. Of the last group, some wished to escape the daily grind, others were in trouble of one sort or another and did not want to "face the music," some sought better economic opportunities, others deserted in order to

---

[16] Lack of further information in the file suggests that no body was found and that no murder had taken place.

join their lovers, while still others left on a whim. In short, the Mounted Police consisted of men who were entirely human. Within its ranks were to be found men of all variety of character, from cowardly to heroic, along with the full range of skills, intelligence, incompetence, and stupidity. What is actually so admirable about the Mounties in the pre-1914 era is the job they were able to do with limited resources, including the quantity and quality of their manpower. Credit for this must go to the leadership within the force and to the many quite ordinary individual policemen who rose to the challenge. But even the mystique of the force, which was established very early and was built up year by year, could be a pressure on its members. The expectations of themselves, of senior officers, even of the public, grew apace. The image that developed certainly gave the Mounties high standards, but in reality it was not possible for each member of the force always to live up to the high demands that were placed upon them.

It is noteworthy that Deane took great pride in the Mounted Police. He was in a position to compare the Mounties to the Royal Marines and other Imperial units; he knew full well the foibles and ineptitudes that existed within the force; and, repeatedly, he had been refused personal advancement. Yet he still gave the Mounties high grades for performance. As a commanding officer, Deane allowed his men considerable autonomy to do their jobs. He went easy on them for minor misdemeanors, but came down hard on repeat offenders, those who proved incapable, and those who committed serious breaches which threatened the discipline of the force, brought it into disrepute, or undermined its law-enforcement capabilities. Desertion was near the top of his list of serious offenses.

Desertion was like an endemic disease that would break out periodically. In some instances, it infected groups of Mounties, while at other times one escape would trigger others a little later. An example of this infection is revealed in Document IV-16, for of the four desertions discussed, three were connected in a most complex manner. The first Mountie to desert was assisted by a man named Paddock who boarded horses at a ranch at Elkwater Lake. As Paddock's involvement was not known immediately, he went to Medicine Hat where he came into contact with a second policeman who wanted to leave the force. The two of them then decided to spring a third Mountie from the police cells in the Hat. The third man was up on charges of dereliction of duty while at Medicine Lodge detachment. As the detachment was just six miles from Elkwater Lake, Paddock undoubtedly was well acquainted with the third Mountie.

The four desertions in April 1904 reveal the following offenses committed by Mounted Policemen: theft of various sorts, drunkenness, consorting with a prostitute, dereliction of duty, escape from a guard cell, aiding a prisoner to escape, false arrest or false pretences (depending on interpretation), and bestiality — aside from desertion itself. In the one case which was unconnected to the other three, the Special Constable was virtually banished from the country by Deane and then reported as having deserted. The price paid by the other three was negligible. The first Mountie simply escaped scot free; the second received a one year sentence for allowing the third Mountie to escape and for desertion, and a three year sentence for horse stealing, but all this was reduced to three months after political intervention; and the third was found not guilty by a jury. Paddock was given six months for helping the first Mountie to escape but, after the jury decision in the case of the third Mountie, the charge against Paddock for aiding numbers two and three was dismissed. Paddock's hired hand, a man who had been directed by Paddock to assist, was given a sentence of one month. Not surprisingly, Deane was absolutely livid about this outcome.

IV-16 Four in a Month
Deane, Monthly Report, April 1904 (NAC, RG18, 269, 224-04)

Corpl. Harvie: Sergt. Redmond on the 30th. March last was sent to Medicine Hat to take over that detachment from Corpl. Harvie, and his orders were to send Corpl. Harvie to Maple Creek as soon as he had taken over the detachment. Corpl. Harvie boarded the east-bound train at Medicine Hat en route to Maple Creek on the 1st. instant, but got off at Irvine, and went south from there on the following morning, in company with a young Englishman named Paddock, to Ferguson's ranche, where he changed his uniform for civilian clothes furnished by Paddock, and left on the 3rd. instant mounted on one of Paddock's horses, and accompanied by Paddock's hired man (Roske) as guide, for Montana. He has not since been heard of.

Roske received one month's imprisonment for his share in the transaction.

Since Crpl. Harvie's desertion another charge has cropped up against him for which he can be extradited. It seems that when Oscar Yates was arrested and sent to Macleod, the Drowning Ford Ranche Company owed him money. The manager thereof, J.H. Spencer, handed $30.00 to Corpl. Harvie to be transmitted to Oscar Yates and took his receipt for the same; this receipt is now in my possession. The money in question did not reach Macleod, and this may possibly explain Corpl. Harvie's desertion.

Gray and Taschereau: Const. Gray had been locked up at Medicine Hat on a charge of absenting himself from his duties,[17] and on the night of the 10th. instant Const. Taschereau secured the key from the sleeping Sergeant's room and released Gray from the cell where he was confined.[18] They took the Medicine Hat team, buckboard, harness, 2 saddles and 2 bridles, and arrived with this outfit in company of Paddock at Ferguson's ranche[19] on the following morning, the three of them seated in the buckboard. They rested the horses here for about two hours, then saddled up the Police team with the saddles which they had brought with them, and started for the south, accompanied by Paddock and Roske, Paddock riding a horse of his own and Roske one belonging to McLean.

Roske returned the Police horses, saddles and bridles to the

---

[17] The charge against Gray was that he had gone AWOL and had holed up at a ranch with some booze and a prostitute (see Inspector C. Starnes to Deane, 9 April 1904 in NAC, RG18, 3225, 1904 - HQ-717-K-1 Gray). The file contains much information about the case from beginning to end.

[18] The escape, though bold, was not as ingenious, skillful and exciting as that perpetrated by three prisoners, including McConnell the calf thief discussed in Document IV-5, from the Maple Creek guardroom in 1903. In that instance the escapees bent walls, removed bolts from hinges, and removed a barred window, all without the night guard hearing any suspicious noise and, evidently, without waking the other prisoners. The evidence produced in investigations by Deane and by Assistant Commissioner J.H. McIllree appears in NAC, RG18, 261, 787-03.

[19] Ferguson owned the ranch at which Paddock boarded along with his hired hand and his string of horses, but Ferguson was not involved in the desertions. Indeed, he was upset with Paddock and the two policemen for taking Roske and leaving no one to mind the horses. Paddock owed Ferguson nearly $200.

Medicine Lodge detachment on the 12th. instant, and said that he had left Taschereau, Gray and Paddock at McLean's ranche on Sage Creek; that when he last saw them Gray and Taschereau were on foot and Paddock was riding, heading for Montana.

Informations were laid against these two deserters charging them with horse stealing and one against Paddock as an accessory after the fact. Sergt. Redmond with Const. Purves, team, buckboard and saddle horse, was dispatched south to trace these deserters and horse thieves. He succeeded in locating and having Gray and Taschereau arrested in Havre, Montana on the 25th. instant. Taschereau consented to return to Canada, but Gray refused, and I am now awaiting authority to extradite him. [*Gray was extradicted.*]

Paddock was seen in Havre by Sergt. Redmond, and, having expressed his desire to return to Canada, Const. Botteley was dispatched from here on the 29th. instant to receive him from Sergt. Redmond who had been carefully instructed not to arrest him prior to his arrival in Canada as his offence was not extradictable from the United States ....

On the night of the 9th instant [*a Special Constable*] was reported absent without leave. The circumstances in connection herewith have been confidentially reported.[20]

Deane, Monthly Report, May 1904 (NAC, RG18, 269, 224-04)

On the 5th. instant Const. Taschereau was brought before me on a charge of allowing prisoner Const. Gray to escape, and of desertion.

---

[20] The reason for Deane's obscure reference is that he considered the matter to be an abomination which would bring discredit upon the Mounties if it became widely known. The Special Constable had been caught in a carnal act with a dog. In order to keep things quiet, Deane let it be known that if the man were found within the country twenty-four hours hence, he would be arrested. He took advantage of the opportunity to escape and, in fact, the matter was kept under wraps. On the case, see NAC, RG18, 277, 520-04. It was not the only instance of one of Deane's men being involved in bestiality. Back in 1889, an interpreter for the police had been convicted of an "unnatural act" with a mare and had received a two year sentence (see Deane, Monthly Report, December 1889 in NAC, RG18, 30, 130-89; and Deane, Monthly Report, January, 1890 in NAC, RG18, 39, 137-90). Five years after this, Deane reported that the same man was wanted at Benton in Montana on a charge of murder (see Deane, Monthly Report, June, 1895 in NAC, RG18, 104, 131-95).

He objected to being tried on these charges, stating that he understood when he volunteered to return to Canada from Montana that he could only be tried on the charge for which he was arrested, viz: horse stealing. The hearing was adjourned pending a decision from the Commissioner on this matter.

The matter having been decided, the hearing was resumed on the 12th. instant, when, the charges being proved, he was sentenced to 1 year's imprisonment at hard labour.

Deane, Monthly Report, June 1904 (NAC, RG18, 269, 224-04)

On the 23rd. instant at Medicine Hat, Const. Taschereau, charged with horse stealing, elected to be tried by the Judge and was awarded three years in the penitentiary ....

Ex-Const. Gray on the 24th elected to be tried by a jury which, in the face of the most positive proof, acquitted him of horse stealing. That being so the Judge withdrew the case against Paddock from the jury.

In view of the fact that juries decline to assist the Police in protecting their own interests, it seems to me hardly worthwhile to keep so many men in the district. [A] jury here included four ranchers whose consciences must be most elastic, and the evil was even more pronounced at Medicine Hat. It would not be a bad plan to let them find their own Police protection, and steal from one another as they have been in the habit of doing. There are districts in this boundless country of ours where Police services are welcome and appreciated, and the district whose juries deliberately acquit criminals in the teeth of positive evidence can hardly complain if the money of the Dominion is spent in other and more profitable quarters.[21]

---

[21] Deane's outrage at the public's unwillingness to support discipline within the force was reinforced, no doubt, when he received instructions from Joseph Pope, the Under-Secretary of State, to release Taschereau after he had served a mere three months of his sentence (see Pope to Deane, 5 October 1904 in NAC, RG18, 3225, 1904 - HQ-717-K-1-Gray). Taschereau had friends in high places. His cousin was the Hon. Mr. Fitzpatrick, Minister of Justice, and his brother-in-law was Col. Fiset, presumably E.M.J. Fiset who was later knighted and served as Lieutenant Governor of Quebec from 1939-50 (see Inspector Starnes, Crime Report: Taschereau and Gray — Desertion and Horse Stealing, 11 April 1904 in NAC, RG18, 3225, 1904 - HQ-717-K-1-Gray).

V
FIVE WORLDS
CALGARY DIVISION 1906 - 1910

In 1906, Deane was moved from Division A to Division E following the resignation of Clifford Sifton and the accession of Frank Oliver as Minister of the Interior. Deane quite properly viewed this as a reprieve from the ignominious obscurity which Sifton had thrust upon him. In his new posting at Calgary a wonderful house was built for him, he was in charge of a major division, and he was in the middle of a dynamic city in a rapidly developing district. Division E stretched the full width of the new Province of Alberta from below High River to above Red Deer. The period when Deane was the C.O. of the Calgary Division from 1906 to 1914 was one of extraordinary population growth and economic development. Settlers poured in to take up farms; mining and industrial enterprises blossomed; new communities sprang up; construction was fast and furious; and Calgary boomed, its population quadrupling between 1906 and 1914 to over fifty thousand. Moving from the slow pace of life in Maple Creek to the hustle and bustle of Calgary was a major transition for Deane. On top of professional challenges came personal changes in rapid succession: his first wife died in 1906; he suffered a serious back injury in 1907; and he both re-married and reached his sixtieth birthday in 1908.

As superintendent of Division E, Deane became more of an administrator than ever. No longer was he personally involved in the apprehension of suspects or in riding the range to nab cattle thieves or in negotiating strike settlements. Because of this, because of the changed nature of the reporting system, and perhaps because of decreased interest and energy, Deane's Monthly Reports became cryptic and sterile. Mostly, they contain mere statistics on the large number of prisoners housed in the guard cells at Calgary, occasional comments on economic growth, and sometimes brief summaries of sudden-death cases. Happily, other types of Mounted Police records provide more extended insights into some of the different worlds which existed in Deane's district.

A. Death and Struggle in the Working Man's World

Police records highlight problems and difficulties. They show that while the Canadian West provided many opportunities for workers even beyond agricultural pursuits, it also presented severe challenges. Work was dangerous, and there were many ways of dying. Primary industries, manufacturing, and even white collar employment all had their casualties.

Most of the mines in the district at the time were strung along the CPR tracks near Banff. Between 1906 and 1910, deaths occurred from cave-ins, explosions of underground gas, accidents with mine rail cars, and from falls down coal chutes.

Trains also claimed numerous victims. One deaf man walking the tracks could not hear a train coming behind him and was killed. The attempt to jump on or off moving trains cost other men their lives. Being a railway worker, especially a brakeman, was a perilous occupation. Train accidents were particularly bloody affairs. Some of the body parts of one man, who had been run over while befuddled with drink, were found one hundred seventy miles from where the accident had taken place.

Modern technology, such as electricity, the wonder of the age, was yet another source of danger. But employment-related deaths were not always accidental, as shown by Document V-4. And even the work-derived animosities that underpinned much of the ethnic conflict could create life-threatening situations.

Records concerning accidental death and near-death also provide some insight into the culture of the working man. Here one finds the macho values, the drinking, the frequent threat of physical assault by other males, the alienation from larger society, the dependence upon one's mates, the struggle to provide for one's family, the hostility towards ethnic minorities, and the sickness and disability. It certainly was not an easy life. And even if a working man retained his health, his fight for survival was not secure, for there were always dreaded economic forces to contend with. Workers and employers alike confronted a risky economy, even though it was expanding. Workers faced arduous and dangerous working conditions, and often poor and unhealthy living conditions. Being lower in the pecking order, workers were more vulnerable to vagaries of the capitalist system, and in some cases they banded together to defend and promote their welfare collec-

tively. As miners seemed especially at risk, it is not surprising that they developed a strong and militant union in an attempt to protect their interests. During the many strikes of this era, of which the one at Canmore in 1909 is simply an example, tensions within the mining community often reached the breaking point. It is partly to the credit of the Mounted Police that most of these situations were resolved peaceably.

V-1 "Premature Explosion"
Deane, Monthly Report, May 1908 (NAC, RG18, 352, 129-08)

Re death of Kaliman Gyorck. This man was putting in a shot for blasting purposes at Exshaw. The explosive used is called bivite and should be tamped with a wooden tamping bar. This man was using an iron rod to tamp the shot and it is supposed that ... the iron rod striking against the rock caused a spark to fly out and ignite the charge, causing a premature explosion and a pile of rock fell on the man, crushing his legs. He was taken from under the rocks and sent to the hospital at Banff but died at Bankhead before reaching the hospital .... Mr. Bayne, Coroner, held an inquest and the jury brought in the following verdict: "That the death of the deceased, Kaliman Gyorck, was caused by accident due to a premature explosion of a composition called bivite, the explosion being due to the using of an iron rod for a tamping bar. In our opinion Mr. Sputtlework as an experienced quarry man should not have used the iron bar for a tamping bar, not knowing fully the nature of the explosive used, and on the part of the company there was a negligence in that a proper tamping bar had not been supplied to be used occasionally where the ordinary tamping bar could not be used."

V-2 "The Head Skidded Along the Rail"
Staff Sergeant J.J. Wilson, Crime Report (submitted to Deane): Death of Joseph Klosterman, 7 August 1907 (NAC, RG18, 1596, 49/199-07)

On Monday 29th Const. Drane at 5.00 a.m. went to Bankhead station, as a brakeman had been killed. On arriving at Bankhead railway station he found the body of Joseph Klosterman lying on the track with head badly smashed, evidently by wheels of car,

and both feet cut off .... Dr. Atkins arrived and examined body ....
Dr. Atkins states as follows:

" ... The body was lying crosswise between the rails. On examination I found both feet partly amputated and both legs below the knees badly torn and lacerated; his face was torn and lacerated ... on right side. The neck was fractured and appeared to me that the head skidded along the rail with body turning around causing some bruises on the shoulders, for a distance of about 12 feet ...."

W.R. Richards, Brakeman, C.P.R. says as follows:

" ... We were switching off a car about 4 a.m. at Bankhead station. It was just beginning to break day. Klosterman was on the car that we were going to cut off. I was on the ground and as soon as I uncoupled the car I gave the Engineer the signal ahead; the Engineer reversed his engine and the car broke away. I then heard a smash and looking around saw Klosterman falling between the cars he said 'Hold them'. I then signalled the Engineer ahead but before he could stop [,] the slack allowed the last car in the string [*to pass*] over his legs. There were 21 cars in the string. The train pulled up and the other car, having no brake on, came back and passed over the body .... I cannot tell what caused Klosterman to fall off. I was talking to him immediately before the accident and he was perfectly sober. I have known him about 2 years and never saw him take a drink of liquor at any time. I think he broke his neck in falling as he never seemed to move after falling and made no outcry except to say 'Hold them' when he was falling. He fell on his back with his head over one rail and his feet over the other but the wheel of the last car shoved his head off the rail and the same car coming back turned him over on his face."

Dr. H.G. [*Mackid*] says as follows:

"I have known Klosterman about 2 years. He came into my office a few days ago and complained about lumbago in his back. I advised him to lay off a few days as he had been working steady for about a year without any rest but he said 'No' his wife was about to be confined and he wanted all the money he could get. It is quite possible that he may have had a cramp in the back and caused him to fall off the car. I never knew him to drink."

V-3 Electrocution
Staff Sergeant Wilson, Crime Reports (submitted to Deane): Death of Walter Ryder, 12 and 18 October 1907 (NAC, RG18, 1596, 49/211-07)

A man named Walter Ryder was killed at the Cement works in Calgary on Thursday the 10th Oct. 07 by coming in contact with a quantity of steel lathes [*probably laths*] charged with electricity.

E.W. Davis electrical engineer at the Cement works says as follows:

"On Sunday the 6th Oct. one of the wires broke stopping the machinery. I fixed it temporarily & about 2 p.m. of the 10th Jack Lewis the timekeeper reported that while wheeling a truck past some iron lathes in the corner where the wires had been broken he had got a shock by coming into contact with one of the lathes. We were just getting ready to fix it when Ryder & Hutchinson were struck by it. Ryder was shovelling clinkers into the elevator & had no business near these lathes at all. Lew Hutchinson the man who picked Ryder up & also received a shock rendering him unconscious, was a mill hand. Hutchinson is now in hospital. These lathes were lying on top of the wires & had become charged by the breaking of the wires."

D.A. Woodlock oiler for the Cement Co. says:

"About 2 15 p.m. of the 10th I saw Walter Ryder & Lew Hutchinson go down to the end of the building where I was working. They seemed to be picking over some bags. They then came back to where the lathes were lying & Ryder took hold of one & seemed to fall forward. Then he jerked back & in doing so pulled some of the lathes with him. I ran over myself & Hutchinson took hold of Ryder. I kicked the lathes away with my foot. I then left Hutchinson holding Ryder & went to get some water. When I came back Hutchinson was lying on his back & said he had got a shock too. By this time several of the men had got there & Ryder & Hutchinson were removed. Both were unconscious then & I think Ryder was dead. I do not know how Hutchinson received his shock unless it was through holding up Ryder. I did not know the lathes were charged with electricity. I do not know how Ryder had got hold of the lathes unless Hutchinson had dared him to touch them."

... Ernest A. Lewis labourer at the Cement works says: that about 2 p.m. of the 10th Hutchinson bet him drinks that he could not touch the lathes. He did not touch them.

Dr Crawford Coroner decided to hold an inquest .... Ryder & Hutchinson both seem to have been aware that the lathes were charged as Ryder told Storey the blacksmith only a short time previous to the accident that his pincers were lying near this place. He went up & found them charged with electricity ....

E.M. James, master mechanic & ex electrical engineer of the Cement works says it is negligence on the part of the Cement works in not having these wires underground ....

Lew Hutchinson says:

"I am a mill man at the Cement Works, know where the lathes were that caused the accident. Lewis the timekeeper told me they were charged. Ryder was putting in clinkers in the elevator about 35 yards away. I told him about Lewis getting the shock. He came down that way & I came with him, didn't ask him to come."

Warned by coroner to tell the truth.

[*Hutchinson continued*] "I did ask him to come down and get a shock. I also asked another man to have a shock. I told Ryder to pick up one of the lathes knowing that he would get a shock but did not think it was so strong as it was. Don't know whether the lathes were touching the temporary wire or not ...."

The jury then brought in a verdict that deceased came to his death on the 10th day of Oct 07 at the works of the Alberta Portland Cement Works from the effects of an electric shock which was received by the said Walter Ryder through handling some metallic lathes which were highly charged with electricity & we further find that the cause of death of the said Walter Ryder was from coming in contact with the aforementioned lathes through the result of a practical joke at the instigation of one Lew Hutchinson. We are further impressed however that there was no malice on the part of the said Lew Hutchinson. But that the unfortunate occurrence was the result of what at the time was considered harmless fun.[1]

---

[1] Deane was not amused by the practical joke and, upon the advice of the office of the Alberta Attorney General, had a charge of manslaughter laid against Hutchinson before the Calgary police magistrate.

V-4 "Short in His Accounts"
Deane, Monthly Report, March 1910 (NAC, RG18, 385, 128-10)

On February 27th Charles Stanley Young, accountant &
teller of the Dominion Bank at High River was found in his
bedroom, over the Bank laying on his bed with a bullet wound on
the right side of his head, in an unconscious condition. Medical
aid was called but he died at 8 p.m. the same evening without
regaining consciousness.

Young was only seventeen years of age, had been in the
Bank for four years. He was considered a good man but erratic.
The day he took his life he was found to have been $163.00 short
in his accounts and after his death it was found that he had
neglected to credit a customer with $300.00 which he had depos-
ited on Feb. 25th.

V-5 Affray at Cochrane
Deane, Crime Report: The Cochrane Affray, 30 September,
1906 (NAC, RG18, 322, 695-06)

S/Sgt Wilson says:

"... I found that Const Gilson had 6 Italians arrested and 11
more held in a box car as witnesses.

"I found that one John Hewitt who has been working in a
saw mill and who is known as a quarrelsome man began the
trouble by pushing one or more of the Italians off the side walk.
His friends took him away from them once into a hotel, but he
went out again and resumed the making of trouble. There is
plenty of evidence to prove it. The fight then became general. 15
or 16 Italians drew their knives, and terrorized the natives."

Two of them had pistols and used them. Hewitt presently
received a bad stab in the back and was later in the night sent to
the General Hospital at Calgary. Dr. [*Mackid*] took from his
body on Sunday morning a piece of knife blade. We found the
knife from which the point had been broken, in the street. No
one has yet consented to prove the ownership of this knife, but
there are 4 witnesses who positively identify Frank Maisatio
[*actually Maisano*] as the man who stabbed Hewitt.

While this fight was going on, a harmless young rancher
named Edward Cole was walking along the sidewalk in pursuit

of his business when a man he afterwards identified as Lawrence Sarace [*actually Lorenzo Soraggie*], stabbed him in the groin, a bad wound and it is uncertain that he will live. A bystander named F.J. Cowan also identifies Sarace as the man who stabbed Cole. We found a long knife in Sarace's boot, covered with blood. This knife belonged to Sarace's brother but he says that Frank [*Deane meant Lawrence or Lorenzo*] had the knife on that date. These two cases will be sent up for trial.

There remain 10 Italians who are charged with disturbing the peace by riotous and disorderly conduct ....

The original telegrams from the source of action were misleading in that whereas there were some few shots fired, none of them took effect.[2]

V-6 Strike at Canmore
Deane, Monthly Report, May 1909 (NAC, RG18, 367, 108-09)

The strike still continues at Canmore ... An explosion occurred at the Canmore mines on Sat. 15th May. This was caused by one of the men going down into the mine to examine the pumps with an open lamp. The mine was badly wrecked but no lives were lost.

Constable R. Basil MacLarty, Crime Report (submitted to Deane): Intimidation of Mine Workers, 18 May 1909 (NAC, RG18, 374, 341-09)

Since the explosion which took place on Saturday the 15th May, the Slavs and Finns have taken a very antagonistic stand. W. McNeil, Superintendent of the mines, requested President Sherman of the Union of Mine Workers through President Fox of the local union, to allow him to give work to the various men required in cleaning the wreck etc. as only experienced men could be employed in this particular kind of work. Mr. Sherman telegraphed his sanction on Sunday night and on Monday morning the required men went to work.

---

[2] In spite of his seven knife wounds, Hewitt recovered, as did Cole. Two of those charged were fined $25, while the other eight were given a $5 fine. Maisano and Soraggie each received a three year sentence.

About 2 o'clock in the afternoon a bunch of Slavs and Finns, numbering nearly 200 or thereabouts, surrounded Fox the President of the local union and threatened to kill him if he did not at once hold a union meeting. Naturally a meeting was held, and a vote was carried to put out the men who were working, also the fire-bosses, firemen and pumpmen, men that are compelled to work in order to keep the mine clear of gas and water.

Immediately after the meeting they all went down in a body to the Prospect Mine and threatened the men who were working, and, being foreigners, they soon reached a very excitable condition. No violence was done, but if it had been offered, we should have been powerless to prevent it, as they practically comprise an army in themselves, and their actions, when aroused, are fanatical.

... People here have an uneasy feeling as they are scared the foreigners will blow up the powder house. At present Mr. McNeil does not want anything done as to swearing in Special Constable etc, as he is afraid it will work the foreigners up ....

From information received I learn that five or six foreigners left for Calgary with the intent to purchase weapons ....

Deane to Staff Sergeant Wilson, 20 May 1909 (NAC, RG18, 374, 341-09)

I note your suggestion about Mr. John T. Stirling [*who had been at the mine when the miners forced the stoppage of work*]. A Mine Inspector, and a Government official, he cannot afford to be mixed up in any way with the contending parties in a strike. I have seen him and he tells me that the mine is a total wreck, and it is his opinion, which he does not wish to obtrude, that it will take at least a month to put it in anything like working order.

... It is a pity that Mr. McNeil did not force their hands and make them go a little further. He can do it now if he chooses by informing the committee that his mine is a total wreck, that it is sinking into a worse condition with every idle day that passes, and that he intends to take repairs in hand at once.

Then, if the men choose to obstruct him, the evidence should be very carefully collected and noted.

Picqueting is unlawful and must be stopped. In stopping it, seek the line of least resistance.

If a summons to Court will answer the purpose, do not ask for a warrant and so on.

If we are to wink at an open breach of the law in one instance, to suit Mr. McNeil's ideas, and to inforce it in some other, we shall put ourselves in a most impossible position and our usefulness will be gone.

It is quite easy to make the law and yourselves respected without causing needless irritation.

Staff Sergeant Wilson, Crime Report (submitted to Deane): Strike at Canmore, 21 May 1909 (NAC, RG18, 374, 341-09)

There is no change in the situation here today, everything is quiet, no picqueting is being done by the miners.

The Secretary of the local union received a wire from Frank Sherman this morning, advising the men to go on with the repair work at the mine.

A meeting was called at 2.30 p.m. at which it was decided not to assist in the repair work.

The mine officials say that they will not go on with the repair work until the strike is finished as the delay is only hurting the miners, because when the strike is settled, it will be five or six weeks before they can mine coal. On the other hand they say the mine will not suffer by the delay of the repairs.

With regard to the intimidation charge against Mr. Fox and the three others. As you say it is a pity that [*mine manager*] Mr. Morris did not force their hands, but Morris is an old miner of 30 years standing, and understood perfectly what they meant, when they demanded that the men quit work. You will note that in his statement he says, when he asked the deputation if the men could be allowed to finish their shift, they said yes, it is only 15 minutes, showing that it was a demand and not a request, and he certainly had right to believe that they had the power and assistance to carry out their purpose.

I also find now that Chas. Johnson and Harry Evans saw the order signed.[3]

---

[3] The "order" was a statement that J.J. Morris, the mine manager, got Fox and three other representatives of the local union to sign at the time of the initial confrontation. It read as follows: "We the undersigned committee have received orders from Canmore Local No. 1387 United Mine Workers of America to stop all men from taking any active part in the repair work of this mine pending advice from Head Quarters."

... As soon as the men are back at work, we will have no difficulty in getting evidence as to threats made, as William Angel, one of the men who quit work when the deputation went to the mine, admitted today that some of the party, of which Fox was the head, said we will kill you if you do not stop work. But he is afraid to say anything in public just now.

I would like to get expert opinion on that point, viz., a demand like that above, made of men to quit work backed up by 200 men, would not that be intimidation alone without anything else said?

The mine officials see the danger in allowing this case to go by default, but do not want to do anything until the men are back at work ....

The mine officials here are very pleased that the deputation from Bankhead were not allowed to come and stir up trouble.

Deane to Staff Sergeant Wilson, 21 May 1909 (NAC, RG18, 374, 341-09)

As long as the situation at Canmore is peaceable, leave well alone. We need not stir up prosecutions unnecessarily.

There is no case to take into Court at the present time, so you may drop consideration of the milk and water notice upon which the men abandoned their work.

B. The Troubled World of Women

Women had at least as difficult a life in early Alberta as did men. For the average woman out on an isolated homestead, or even for those in a town, it was tough enough coping with the constant demands of home and family. But there were many disasters which could strike. Physical or mental illness, abandonment by or death of a husband, dangerous or undesired pregnancy, and sexual assault, were simply a few of the calamities that could befall a woman.

In some cases, women in distress were placed in the female guardroom at Calgary where they came under the care of Mrs. Stuttaford who, by all accounts, was simply wonderful. In other instances, the involvement of the Mounted Police only came after death. The suicide case reported in Document V-9 was especially poignant and caused Deane to write "Very sad reading" in the margin of the report. Given the woman's reason for killing herself, it was a macabre irony that her body was turned over to her husband.

Pregnant women faced dangers which sometimes were fatal. The woman in the case related in Document V-10 had suffered through three difficult pregnancies previously, and the doctor decided to terminate the fourth since he was sure that miscarriage was inevitable. Of course, the operation was not termed an abortion since even the attempt to acquire one was illegal. What is incidentally noteworthy about this case is the conflict-of-interest situation in which the physician who had done the operation was also the coroner who decided that an inquest was unnecessary.

V-7 The Female Prison
Deane, Annual Report for 1907 (*SP 1908,* No.28, pp.22-23)

... It is a most fortunate thing for us that she [*Mrs. Stuttaford*][4] has had a large and varied experience, extending over parts of India, South Africa and N.W. Canada, for more than 35 years ....

In one way the female prison has the worst of it, for the lunatics [*of both sexes, along with juveniles and any sick male prisoners*] are confined there and we had a terrible time with some of them.[5]

---

[4] Although Mrs. Stuttaford was in her mid-sixties, Deane persuaded her to leave Maple Creek to become the matron of the women's ward of the Calgary guard room. Deane spoke most highly of her in his *Mounted Police Life.* In April 1908, she applied for an increase in salary from $30 to $45 per month on account of her greatly increased workload. To the request Deane added: "Forwarded and strongly recommended. It is only a woman in a thousand who has the experience and general 'savoir faire' to do the work that Mrs. Stuttaford has done and is doing here." She got the raise. By 1912 Mrs. Stuttaford was in poor health, but she recovered sufficiently to establish the women's prison at its new quarters in Macleod in 1914.

[5] In his annual report for 1908, Deane noted that of the 50 persons received at the guard room on the grounds of lunacy, 17 were found not to be insane and were discharged. Deane concluded: "There must be something wrong somewhere when 17 British subjects can be deprived of their liberty on such an imputation. I do not hesitate to say that in some instances the insanity law has been abused." See *SP 1909,* No.28, p.24. One woman who suffered from epilepsy and tuberculosis was sent as a lunatic to the guard room where she died within a few days; she was buried in the potters' field (see Deane, Monthly Report, November 1908 in NAC, RG18, 352, 129-08).

Mrs. Stuttaford
GA, Gibson photograph, NA-2868-6
One senses both the strength and the compassion of the matron of the female prison in this photograph taken sometime between 1906 and 1910. Document V-7 affirms that Mrs. Stuttaford was an extraordinary person who gave prodigiously of her time and talents to the many unfortunates who came under her jurisdiction.

An old German woman, Margaret Schleiper, 75 years of age, from Olds, stayed with us from April 20 till July 22, when she was despatched to Brandon [*to enter the so-called lunatic asylum*]. Her person on arrival and her habits while here were indescribably filthy; the other female prisoners could not enter her cell without vomiting, nor could they wash her clothes for the same reason, and the matron [*Mrs. Stuttaford*] conceived it to be her duty to do it. She did it until at length her own stomach gave out, her rest at night was broken by the noises of this lunatic, extra work devolved upon her by day by reason of a sick constable with measles in the hospital ward, and she succumbed for a time ....

A Norwegian woman, Christiana Bostonstrom, who claimed to be 38 years, but who was certainly 65, stayed here for two months from January 29. On admission her hair was found not to have been combed nor her person washed since the dark ages.

It took three strong women to carry her to the bath room and the matron's ministrations had to be conducted under cover of a bottle of Florida water [*perfume*]. Before going to Brandon she became so agreeably surprised at the effect of cleanliness that she took quite a little pride in herself.

Mable McCullom, 38 years, from the city, stayed with us for almost three months after April 16. She was at first very troublesome, so violent at times that a straight jacket was required to restrain her. The matron gave her a course of iced baths and on July 10 she was handed over to her brother clothed in her right mind. It is a sad case, for she is a capable woman, but her trouble is hereditary and I hear she has relapsed and is now in Brandon.

Kate Messenger was found by the city police wandering about in Calgary with her hands badly frozen, and during the month she stayed here gave us a great deal of trouble. She had to be held by a constable and a strong half breed woman while the matron dressed her hands which were cured before she went on her way to Brandon

... Just now there is a morphine fiend from the city, sentenced to two months for theft. She has a negro husband who the other day gave her some cocaine which laid her out for several hours, and who now wonders that he is not allowed to see her.

V-8 Destitution
Constable W.V. Bruce, Report to Deane, 9 March 1910 (NAC, RG18, 1644, 127/21-10)

I saw Mrs. Carmichael on the 8th instant and obtained the following information:

The husband Alex. E. Carmichael, left his wife and family, in September 1909, in order get work in Calgary. While there he served a short time in jail for stealing a trunk, was released, and on December 18th wrote from Revelstoke B.C. saying that he was sick, and had only had 8 days' work since he left the jail, telling his wife that he was unable to send any money, and that she was to sell one of her cows in order to keep the family, until she heard from him again.

This man A.E. Carmichael, is an engineer, and is able to earn from $2.00 to $5.00 per day, but drinks heavily.

The family at present consists of Mrs. Carmichael aged 40, 7 children, (4 girls & 3 boys) the eldest 12 years old the youngest 1 year old. Mrs. Carmichael came from St. Thomas, Ontario, 2 1/2 years ago, and has lived on the homestead ... for 2 1/2 years. No improvements have been done on the land, with the exception of a small house and garden.

The stock consists of 2 cows & 2 calves (1 cow milking). There are no implements.

The neighbours have been keeping this family since last September, and all the thanks they get is abuse.

... People who have helped the family all say the same thing ... and in fact all the neighbours say that if she had seemed at all grateful for the help that has been given to her, she would have had no need to apply for assistance, and that they would have given her enough work to support herself and her family.

V-9 "A True and Faithful Wife"
Constable K.G. Murison, Crime Report (submitted to Deane): Suicide of Mrs. Mary Findlay of Kansas, 23 October 1907 (NAC, RG18, 1596, 49/186-07)

On the 14th inst I was notified that a Mrs. Findlay had been found in the yard of her house.

I notified Dr. Little & then we went there to Kansas 15 miles s.w. of Didsbury.

Mr William Findlay said as follows:

"Mary Findlay, deceased, is my wife. She is 45 years old & Irish. We have been in this country three years. My wife never spoke to me with regard to her taking her life, but she was terribly worried about the hard luck we have had in this country. We have been burned out, hailed out, & frozen out during our 3 years' residence here.

"I last saw deceased on the night of the 13th when I went to bed. She had been sleeping with the children for the last two weeks so I did not know whether she was in bed or not. I woke up about 2 a.m. & saw a light burning in the kitchen & I called to my wife to put it out but there was no answer, so I got up & looked around but could not see her. After a while I went & called my neighbour Mr. Alex Robertson & we looked together but without result. Next morning we found her dead lying just where you see her now."

Mr Alex Robertson said:

"I came over to Mr. Findlay's about 3 o'clock a.m. on the morning of the 14th inst. & helped look for Mrs. Findlay but could not find her. We found her where you see her now. No one has touched her since."

We found her body lying about 2 yds. from the water closet & in the closet I found a bottle of carbonic acid nearly empty. I also found a letter in deceased room bidding her children good bye which I enclose.

Dr Little performed a post mortem & found that she had been poisoned by carbonic acid & stated that as deceased had stated in her letter, bid good bye, & also that she would never be seen alive again, there was no doubt that she died by her own hand & therefore no inquest would be necessary.

The body was handed over to her husband. Deceased leaves 9 children, 4 of whom are under 12 years old ....

The following is a copy of the letter referred to in above report:

Sunday night, Oct. 13th 1907.

My dear dear children.

"This is likely the last words you will hear of me or from me. I have not much to say only that my life has been blighted with trouble and disappointment. I have been a true and faithful wife. Your father told me this morning to leave the place because I will not sleep with him. I love my children. God only knows how I love you all. I don't want any more children, but my heart yearns for each of your prosperity and eternal salvation. You all know that your sister Mary has gone to Heaven and [*I*] want you each one [*to*] meet her there. Jesus Christ is the way to God. I know I will lose my reward but I know in whom I have believed. If you ever get married study the matter well and never be advised by anyone unless you love the person. To you Sarah & Lizzie, Willie & John I leave to have a mother's care for the younger children. May God bless & provide for them & you all is the prayer of your own mother. Good bye till we meet again."

V-10 Miscarriage
Deane, Monthly Report, March 1909 (NAC, RG18, 367, 108-09)

Re Death of Mrs. J.A. Dangerfield of Olds: This woman who was about three months pregnant, was feeling unwell and Dr. Little was called in. He found that a miscarriage was about to occur and considered that an operation was necessary to assist nature. The operation was performed and the woman appeared to be getting along very well when she took a weak turn. The doctor was again sent for and the woman collapsed, and although everything possible was done to revive her, she died.

Dr Little held a Post Mortem the next day and found that the woman had died from heart failure and internal hemorrhage.

Dr Little who is a Coroner considered an Inquest unnecessary.

V-11 "They All Misused Me, Three Holding Me Each Time"[6]
John S. Davie, J.P., to Deane, 1 October 1906 (NAC, RG18, 314, 200-06)

A few days ago a Mr. Eakin, living a mile out of town [*Crossfield*] came to me with a complaint that his little daughter aged about 9 or 10 years old, when coming home from school,

---

[6] As this was a case involving minors born less than one hundred years ago, pseudonyms have been used.

was set upon about half way home by four boys about the same age. She was thrown down and choked until her throat was badly swollen and they went through the form of committing or trying to commit rape upon her, tearing her underclothes and using her up badly .... I am writing this to you trusting you will send a man up as soon as possible to investigate the case as the community feel that something should be done for an example to the children in the vicinity ....

Deane to Davie, 2 October 1906 (NAC, RG18, 314, 200-06)

I received your letter dated yesterday and am sending a Constable by first train to enquire into the matter which you report.

The father of the girl should lay an Information against the four boys in question. I think Common Assault would be the best charge to lay, and you can then try that yourself. If you find evidence sufficient to convict them, I would suggest for your consideration the propriety of giving the boys a good flogging.

If you order them to pay a fine their fathers' pockets will be taxed, and if you give them imprisonment up to two months which the Code allows, a prison is hardly a place for young boys, whereas you can hold imprisonment over their heads and probably induce their fathers to give them a good sound flogging, which will have more effect than anything else. You do not state the boys' ages so that I assume they are not very old.

Constable W. Gilson, Crime Report (submitted to Deane): M. Burkholder et al. Assaulting Jane Eakin, 6 October 1906 (NAC, RG18, 314, 200-06)

On Oct. 2nd acting on instructions received from Supt. R.B. Deane, I proceeded by train to Crossfield and on arriving there I saw J. Eakin who gave me the following statement:

"On Sept 25th 06 at about 4.30 p.m., I passed the Crossfield school house on my way home, and when about 100 yds s.w. of it 4 boys named M. Brickley, H. Stuart, H. & C. Wells stopped me and H. Stuart said 'If I said anything to anyone about what they were going to do, they would thrash me,' and Stuart then caught me by the neck and H. Wells caught me by the feet and together they threw me down and held me there while C. Wells and M. Brickley threw my clothes over my head and C. Wells then jumped on top of me and H. Wells then tore my clothes and all 4 of them then asked me dirty questions, after which they all misused me, three holding me each time. H. Wells then took my cap and on my asking for it, he threatened me with the same treatment again if I came back for it. I then ran home and told my parents what had happened. When H. Wells and Stuart threw me down they commenced strangling me and said if I did not quit shrieking they would hit me. My underpants were torn at the bottom holes and down the sides. I am 9 years old."

I then saw Mr. Eakin the girl's father and he said that as the boys were only youngsters none of them being 9 years old, and as they had acknowledged all to him and they had already been chastised several times both by their parents and the schoolmaster, he would be satisfied if they were flogged in public as a warning to them and a lesson to others. I then had the parents fetch the boys into the Crossfield school house where they severely flogged them in front of the other children after which I explained the seriousness of the crime.

Mr. Eakin said that as the case had not gone to court and considerable trouble had been caused, he would remit the amount of my return ticket to Crossfield viz. $2.00 which he did as per attached.

C. The Problematic World of the Nose Creek Brothels

The red light district was located about a half-mile to the east of the Mounted Police barracks in Calgary on the north side of the Bow River in the area of Nose Creek. As elsewhere, the existence of prostitution raised concerns about illicit liquor, disorder, violence, venereal and other diseases, the corruption of the morals of society, and a host of other matters. As a consequence, information about the Nose Creek brothels periodically entered Deane's reports.

The world of red lights was troubled and problematic for all concerned. For its residents it offered a livelihood, but one that resulted more often in degradation and early death than in wealth and security. However, many of those employed in brothels had little choice, especially if they were members of denigrated racial and ethnic minorities. It was also problematic for visitors to the brothels, for it was not an activity openly proclaimed as though one were going to the grocery store or hardware. Many customers felt both guilt and a sense of failure in having to resort to prostitutes. Brothels also presented a problem for civic and religious leaders and certainly for the police. All made efforts at various times to suppress the traffic, but all had to come face to face with the reality of its continued existence. With his lengthy experience as a Mounted Police officer, Deane believed that control and supervision of the brothels was all that could be achieved and, perhaps, even all that could be desired.

Nose Creek Brothels, 1911
GA, detail of photograph, NA-673-9
The large, utilitarian buildings in the photo suggest both the magnitude and the lack of elegance of the sex trade in pre-1914 Calgary. Like it or not, prostitution was an integral component of the pioneer West. In Nose Creek, as in red light districts around the world, fortunes were made and lost. Involvement in the business as client or worker or entrepreneur crossed class, ethnic, and racial barriers. Personal tragedy was no stranger to the area.

V-12 "A Necessary Evil"
Deane to Commissioner, 28 February 1907 (NAC, RG18, 1605, 133/17-07)

In reply to your letter of the 12th inst. re. Japanese houses of ill fame, I have the honour to report that this matter has been thoroughly investigated.

There are 4 Japanese houses, and a total number of 12 inmates. These women were medically examined and found to be clean, with the exception of one, who at once left town. These women are now under an obligation to obtain a clean bill of health every 9 days.

With regard to the suppression of these houses, there is a very pronounced body of opinion that these women, being a necessary evil, are well placed where they are, situated at Nose Creek. They do not obtrude themselves on anybody, and are under supervision and control.

I am informed that such people as: The Very Reverend the Dean, The Rev. Mr. Langford, License Inspector, an ex-Presbyterian Minister, and others are in favour of the present system.

If the houses in question are broken up the inmates will of course scatter, as they have done in Winnipeg, to all parts of the city, and under such conditions as to be under no control whatever.

There are also at Nose Creek some houses occupied by white women, and these are similarly under control and medical supervision.

I have just had them all examined, and one only was found to have gonorrhoea. She has left town.

V-13 Futility of Attempted Suppression
Deane, Annual Report, 1909 (*SP 1910*, No.28, p.31)

The social evil has been somewhat in evidence recently here as elsewhere. The Presbyterian and Methodist ministers of East Calgary represented to me that the existence of a colony of sporting women at Nose Creek was prejudicially affecting the morals and welfare of the community at East Calgary, and I promised to do what was possible in that connection.

In company with the Sergeant Major [*Spalding*] I visited

each one of the houses and saw the respective proprietresses and told them that they must choose some other locality to live in or they might get themselves into serious trouble. They all took the hint and departed, except one, who sent me a doctor to explain that she was not able to move just then. I found that they were paying the most extravagant rents — $100 and $150 a month in advance, and the landlords seem to be little better than sharks.

It is needless to say that every house has since been reoccupied — the landlords and their agents saw to that — and my inward conviction is that the most effective manner of dealing with this troublesome question is to make it unlawful for a person to let a house for the purposes of prostitution.

The real owners of some of these places would be ashamed to have their names known, and, to my mind, very much more effectual pressure can be applied along that line than along any other.

Deane, Annual Report, 1910 (*SP 1911*, No.28, pp.33-34)

I mentioned in my report last year that, at the request of a deputation of East Calgary residents, I had promised to do what I could to suppress the "red light" district, then situated on Nose Creek hill, which gave particular offence to the gentlemen in question.

Some of the speakers at our meeting expressed their conviction that if the keepers and inmates of these houses were, on conviction, to be punished with imprisonment instead of by fine, the evil would soon be eradicated.

Some of the women moved away to other parts, but some of the houses remained open in spite of all my efforts to induce their occupants to leave.

In some cases I awarded imprisonment on conviction, and the number of houses slowly diminished. In the case of one house which continued to remain persistently open for business, I, in conjunction with Inspector Duffus, issued a warrant to search on July 25 last. The house in question was notoriously a house of ill-fame, owned by a woman named "Diamond Dolly," who found no difficulty in renting it at $125 per month.

Corporal Ryan and Constable Rosenkrantz, men of integrity

and veracity, were detailed to execute the warrant.

I am particular in giving these minute details because the final issue of this prosecution is of interest to any and every peace officer whose duty it may be to carry out the provisions of the vagrancy section of the Criminal Code ....

Corporal Ryan and the Constable were admitted to the house by the keeper thereof at about 5 a.m. on July 26 last.[7] Corporal Ryan showed his warrant and asked if any man was in the house. She replied she did not know, gave him a lamp, and he went upstairs with the Constable. In one room he found a woman in bed alone. In another room Constable Rosenkrantz found a man and a woman in bed together. As soon as he opened the door the woman asked whom he wanted. Instead of replying to her he called Corporal Ryan, who entered the room. As he did so the woman greeted him with the remark: "This sleeper has paid me."

In the subsequent hearing at the barracks, where Ray Mason was charged with being the keeper, and Lillie Smith and Myrtle Munford with being inmates of a house of ill-fame, the man who was found in bed with the woman deposed that she was not his wife, that the house had a bad reputation, and that Ray Mason acted as mistress of the house. He said that his companion was sick and that was why he stayed with her.

The defendants were represented by counsel, who made no defence of any kind, and the keeper of the house was sentenced to three months, and the two women inmates to one month's imprisonment in Calgary guard-room.

Notice of appeal was given in the case of Ray Mason, but nothing was heard of it until the 17th September, when I received subpoenas for witnesses returnable on the 19th .... As Constable Rosenkrantz was by that time on detachment duty at Carbon, and the earliest mail could not reach him before noon of September 20, I so informed the crown prosecutor's partner.

---

[7] The hour of the raid was very strange if the police were seriously interested in discovering clear evidence of prostitution and in charging customers as well as hookers. It was only by accident that a man was actually found within the house. One suspects, therefore, that the execution of the warrant was intended, on the one hand, to be a warning to the madam to shape up, and on the other hand, to demonstrate that the police were carrying out raids supposedly in an attempt to wipe out the trade.

I heard nothing more about the matter until the afternoon of September 20, when a lawyer's clerk brought me an order from the judge of the District Court quashing the conviction.

I have vainly endeavoured to procure a copy of the judgment herein, and can only quote a newpaper report which said "Judge Winter allowed the appeal and quashed the conviction, and in his judgment stated that he found no evidence which justified the conviction having been made."

The Moral Reform League[8] must, therefore, understand that the suppression of the houses which they hold in particular abhorrence will in future be attended with more difficulty than ever; for when it becomes generally known that a man and a woman, who are not husband and wife, may with impunity meet and go to bed together in a house of assignation, so long as one poses as the patient and the other as the nurse, we may expect a widespread epidemic of a permanent nature.

V-14 Quarantine
Deane, Monthly Report, January, 1910 (NAC, RG18, 385, 128-10)

On the 2nd Jan. 1910 Professor Simpson, a piano player employed in one of the houses of ill fame at Nose Creek, kept by a woman named King, was taken sick with small-pox.

I notified Dr. Barrow of Edmonton, Provincial Health Officer & he decided to quarantine all Nose Creek, as all the women were exposed to the disease to a greater or lesser extent.

Sgt. Murison was detailed for the work. The quarantine lasted three days, during which time all the houses were fumigated & inmates vaccinated. Four women had never been vaccinated & the Health Officer decided that they be quarantined another fifteen days. The woman King evaded quarantine until the 7th instant when she was immediately confined pending

---

[8] The Moral and Social Reform Council of Canada was an outgrowth of the alliance of church and labor groups which had been successful in having the Lord's Day Act passed in 1907. Presbyterians and Methodists were the backbone of the movement. In 1913 it became the Social Service Council of Canada. See R. Allen, *The Social Passion: Religion and Social Reform in Canada 1914-28* (Toronto: University of Toronto Press, 1971), p.13.

instructions from the Medical Health Officer & was later ordered to keep in quarantine 15 days.

Whole quarantine was lifted on the 20th.

A Chinaman named Mah Gook broke quarantine and was arrested at Nanton, convicted, and fined $25.00 & costs.

V-15 Fatalities
Deane, Annual Report, 1910 (*SP 1911*, No.28, pp.32-33)

On April 15 last a tragedy occurred in the "red light" district at Nose Creek which brought that community into prominence for the time being. A man named Joe More had some time previously brought to Calgary a girl named Rose Smith who had left her husband in Brooklyn. A couple of weeks before the tragedy More had beaten the girl, who left him and took up her abode at Nose Creek. She was afraid of the man and had repeatedly refused not only to return to live with him but to see him.

On this occasion the girl said he might be admitted to the house as she wanted to speak to him. The subject matter of their conversation can only be inferred, but the inevitable inference is that he requested her to return to him, and on her refusal shot her dead and then blew his own brains out.

Obviously this might have happened in a railway station, or a hotel, or in any other place where the man could obtain access to the woman whom he was determined to kill if she would not accede to his desires, and, so far as the "red light" district was concerned, the incident had no special significance whatever.

Corpl. F.J. Basson, Report re. Guard-Room and Common Jail, in Deane, Annual Report, 1910 (*SP 1911*, pp. 34-35)

A female prisoner named Gertie Purvis died in the female jail of consumption on February 9, 1910 .... This poor woman was convicted of being an inmate of a house of ill-fame at Nose Creek and was far gone in consumption. She told the matron that she had not been sober for 14 days before coming here and, if she died in confinement, she was at least well looked after and had more comfort and better attention that she would have had if she had been left where she was.

D. The Embattled World Within the Mounted Police

*Division E was understaffed and overworked. In many loca-
tions within the vast district a single policeman had to exercise
the authority of the force on his own. In Calgary itself, the Mounties
were nearly overwhelmed by the number of prisoners lodged in
the guardroom. Deane admired the job performed and was happy
to publicize the fine work accomplished. But the inner world of
the Mounted Police was always plagued with internal disputes
and discipline problems.*

*Sometimes differences between the men themselves caused
problems. Mostly, however, they were the result of actual or
perceived dereliction of duty or breaches of the rules. In those
instances, Deane was both judge and jury. On occasion, however,
the tables were turned, and Deane himself was called on the
carpet. The dispute related in Document V-20 was not the only
time that Deane's insolent tone got him into trouble. Back in
1891, he had even been reduced two places in the seniority list of
superintendents, behind Sam Steele and A.B. Perry who became
Commissioner in 1900,[9] and there were other disputes between
Deane and his superior officers. Deane was justified both in the
pride he took in his competence as a commanding officer and in
being miffed at continually being by-passed as Commissioner or
as one of the assistant commissioners. By 1906, after all, with his
experience in the Royal Marines he had served four decades "with
the colours," as he put it, and was by far the most senior superintendent on the force. But Deane was an arrogant man who took
criticism badly. And no matter how well justified in his actions,
not even he could get away with anything that smacked of insubordination. In the final analysis, like the good soldier he was,
Deane accepted that the discipline of the force required his submission.*

---

[9] See Comptroller F. White to Commissioner L.W. Herchmer, 21 August 1891
in NAC, RG18, 2283, pp.475-476.

Calgary Mounted Police Barracks, 9 August 1912
GA, Progress Photo, NA-919-19
*Deane's house, at the left of the photograph, was completed for him in
1907 and provided the best living quarters of any Mounted Police
superintendent at the time. It offered a perfect location for watching
cricket matches, a game in which Deane had excelled but no longer
played. However, his love for cricket had limits. He had devoted
thought, time, and some money to developing the lawn and gardens
around the house. He did not mind when a stray cricket ball did minor
damage to his cucumbers or melons, but his caragana hedge was
another matter. As he put it in his book* Mounted Police Life in
Canada, *he "had sworn loudly and coherently when some maniacal
cricketer now and then had dashed through it in pursuit of his ball ...."*

V-16 Good Work
Deane, Annual Report, 1909 (*SP 1910*, No. 28, p.36)

CONDUCT AND DISCIPLINE.

Without disparaging the graceful turn of phrase which so
usefully records the "support of all ranks," I am justified in
saying of the members of "E" Division that every member thereof
has pulled his honest pound. The men on detachment have wits
and use them, and the public service duly benefits thereby.

V-17 Dunked in the Horse Trough
Evidence in Assault Case Heard by Deane as Justice of the Peace, 14 August 1907 (NAC, RG18, 342, 537-07)

Canada.
Province of Alberta.

        Rex vs John B. Dharty
        "   Ernest H. Oliver
        "   Richard B. McLarty
        "   Stuart M. Graham

Charge: Assault.
    Plea:

        John B. Dharty - Not guilty.
        Ernest H. Oliver - Not guilty.
        Richard B. McLarty - Not guilty.
        Stuart M. Graham - Not guilty.

William McCutcheon upon his oath says:

"I am a military tailor and have been in the employ of the R.N.W.M.Police at Calgary in that capacity for three months. I am a Special Constable in the Force.

"Last night about 9:15 o'clock I was going to my quarters alongside the Imperial Bank over the Bow River. When I came out of the Canteen in the Barracks I was seized by four or five men and carried bodily over to the trough at which the horses are watered. There was water in it. They put me in the trough and turned the hose on me. Const. McLarty choked me while I was in the trough. He held me by the throat. I might be mistaken. It might be someone else but I believe it was McLarty. There were four or five men. I can swear there were four. They dispersed and went away and I crawled out of the trough and reported the matter to Inspector Duffus. Then I went to my shop, put on dry clothes and went home.

"I am not certain what the man whom I believe to have been McLarty was wearing.

"I can swear to Oliver by his voice. He said 'Soak it to him'. I feel that he was one of the men who laid hands on me. I cannot swear to Graham, only what I heard this morning. It was in the dark. I heard from the cook in the kitchen that Mr. Graham was one of the parties implicated. I recognized Dharty by his height.

I positively will swear that he was one of the parties and that he laid hands on me."

Const. Dharty says: "I have no questions to ask. I know nothing whatever about the matter."

[*McCutcheon's response to questions asked by Const. Oliver:*]

"I recognised your voice at close quarters. Although it was dark it was possible to identify Dharty by his height. I am not certain where you caught hold of me. I am certain you were there. You are the man who said 'soak him'."

[*Response to*] Const. McLarty:

"You were close to me in the trough and I was pleading with you. It was not so very dark that I could not recognise you."

[*Response to*] Const. Graham:

"I am not certain about you. Until this morning I had no reason to believe you were mixed up in it."

(sd) Wm. McCutcheon.

I adjourn the hearing for a short time.

(sd) R. Burton Deane. J.P.

At 11:30 a.m., the hearing is resumed.

The four defendants now say they wish to withdraw their plea of not guilty and to substitute a plea of Guilty.

John B. Dharty says:

"I have nothing to say. I leave it to Const. Graham. I was one of the men."

Ernest H. Oliver says:

"I prefer to leave the explanation to Const. Graham as spokesman. I admit that I was there."

Richard B. McLarty says:

"I leave it to Const. Graham."

Stuart M. Graham upon his oath says:

"Ever since Special Constable McCutcheon has been in the Force he has been blackguarding the Force amongst civilians down town. He has taken away the characters of certain members of this Division. He told Const. McLarty that I was the meanest cocksucker that had ever been in the Division. Everything that occurs up here gets into the papers. It is generally believed that he does pimping for houses of ill fame. So we took the matter into our own hands.

"Civilians in town have told me what McCutcheon has said."
(sd) S.M. Graham.

I adjudge the defendants J.B. Dharty, E.H. Oliver, R.B. McLarty and S.M. Graham each to pay a fine of ten dollars and in default of payment, to be imprisoned in the Guard Room of the North West Mounted Police at Calgary for the term of one month, unless the said fine be sooner paid ....[10]
(sd) R. Burton Deane. J.P. 14th August 1907

V-18 The Unfortunate Sergeant Wilson
Deane, Monthly Report, July 1909 (NAC, RG18, 367, 108-09)

Reg. No. 3604, Sergt. H.A. Wilson of "E" Division having committed an offence in that he:

1st Charge: On and about the 10th of June 1909 at Red Deer he did through excessive drinking of intoxicants render himself unfit for duty until the 22nd June 1909.

2nd Charge: That on the 10th June 1909 he did without leave absent himself from his detachment at Red Deer.

3rd Charge: That between the 24th of May and the 10th of June 1909 he did neglect horse Reg. No. 2982 and did allow the horse to be misused by unauthorised persons.

4th Charge: That between the 21st May and the 10th June 1909 he did improperly issue three Transport Requisitions without keeping the prescribed record of the particulars of issue.

5th Charge: That on the 10th day of June his detachment stores were found to be deficient of ...[five] articles of Government property [worth $10.25] ....

6th Charge: That on or about the third day of July 1909 at Calgary he did through excessive drinking of intoxicants render himself unfit for duty until the 27th of July 1909.

---

[10] In his covering letter to the Commissioner of the same date in the same file, Deane stated that he was discharging the tailor and that if it were up to him, Dharty, McLarty, and Oliver, all of whom refused to pay the fine, would be dismissed from the Mounted Police.

Found Guilty of all six charges and reduced to the rank and pay of a Constable and to pay for the articles missing.

Deane, Monthly Report, December 1909 (NAC, RG18, 367, 108-09)

On the night of the 25th. December, 1909 Regt. No. 3604, Const. H.A. Wilson, committed suicide by shooting himself with a 45 Colt revolver. Wilson was in charge of the Innisfail detachment and had been doing good work. His wife was taken very ill. Having had a bad fall she, being four months pregnant, had to be taken to the Red Deer hospital. Before she went up Wilson sat up nursing her for several nights and being somewhat exhausted, the woman who was nursing Mrs. Wilson, or assisting, gave Const. Wilson a drink of brandy. This appears to be the starting of his drinking. On Christmas day Wilson appears to have had a number of cases to investigate in different parts of his section, and, having a horse at the detachment which was being passed on from Red Deer to the Trochu Valley detachment to break to team work, Wilson, being a good teamster, evidently decided to put in his own horse with Reg. No. 304 and make the patrol in a cutter there being good sleighing. He accordingly engaged one Byron Atkinson to make the trip with him. The latter apparently took too much liquor for his dinner, hitched up the team and they ran away, crashing into Olney Johnson's rig, that was on its way to Markerville, the pole hitting Johnson in the back, breaking his spine and throwing them out and causing such injuries to Johnson that he died the following day at the Red Deer General Hospital. Wilson, seeing Johnson's condition and [*the disposition*] of the Doctors in attendance, was positive the man could not recover; and with his wife's illness and worry over money matters, and the fear of facing another investigation, he appears to have left town sober between 4 and 5 p.m. and gone to his detachment and there taken his own life.

V-19 Mutiny
Calgary Daily News, 14 July 1910 (copied excerpt enclosed in NAC, RG18, 393, 412-10)

TEN LOCAL MOUNTED POLICEMEN GET TWO MONTHS GUARD ROOM
They went on a spree to red light district and acted mutinously.
LIABLE TO BE DISCHARGED
They thought they could have their own way as they were in the majority.

For disgracing the force by going on a spree to the houses in the red light district and mutinously refusing to return to the barracks in the morning after being out all night, ten Constables of the R.N.W.M.P. were apportioned two months each in the Calgary guard room by Supt. Deane, the commanding officer, this week.

Although the incident is being kept as quiet as possible, the story has leaked out and it is to the effect that ten members of the force went out for a "time" in the Nose Creek district on Monday night and failed to return to the barracks. In making the rounds they had gradually become imbued with a spirit of independence, bordering on the rebellious and when an officer was sent from the barracks to inveigle, cajole, persuade, threaten or otherwise induce them to return home before milking time they advised him to go away back in a quiet corner and make a little inferno all to himself. It is said that this spirit of independence was stimulated by the thought that as the entire Calgary force numbered but fifteen men, the mutineers, being the majority, would escape punishment if they maintained an organized protest. They were at length rounded up and taken to the barracks by an officer and some constables and later in the day sentenced for two months each in the guard room by Supt. Deane for insubordination. The offenders, so far as can be learned, are practically new members of the force and are a portion of a contingent recruited but a few months ago in Toronto. Several of them are said to be old soldiers who served in the South African campaign.

The mutinous constables may be discharged from the force after the expiration of their term.

Deane to Assistant Commissioner, 12 July 1910 (NAC, RG18, 393, 412-10)

I wired you today as follows:

"Am under necessity of sending to Regina ten Constables whom I have committed to imprisonment in Regina Guard Room [*for two months each*] for what practically amounts to mutiny. They will leave as soon as I can arrange transportation."

I beg to enclose herewith the charge, proceedings and sentence in each of the ten cases.

I am not able to offer any explanation of the extra-ordinary and silly conduct of these men.

... Yesterday ... I fined two prostitutes [*from the Nose Creek district*] $200.00 each for selling liquor without a license and commented upon these women living with negroes who act as pimps for them.

I am lo[a]th to accept this demonstration on the part of Constables of "E" Division as an act of sympathy with the associated black and white persons referred to, which association is universally condemned by white people on this continent, but I am unable to suggest any other reason why these men should have made such a pitiable and senseless exhibition of themselves.

If and when the Calgary people get to hear of this episode, the Mounted Police, as represented by these ten men, will surely come in for considerable opprobrium.

With my prison accom[m]odation I cannot keep the men here as there are now 75 prisoners in custody.

I understand that Const. Jones is a prime agitator in this connection; Constables Chapman, Showler and Tompkins have also been active. Const. Pearce's conduct has been very unsatisfactory during his stay here. The other men seem to have allowed themselves to be led by the agitators, and it is not easy to discriminate between them, nor to apportion the responsibility.

I have no use for old soldiers, whether of the British or any other army ....

[*The evidence was extremely brief and routine. Only Deane's conclusions were revealing.*]

FINDING

This is as near an approach to mutiny as has come under my notice during 43 years service with the colours, and I am dealing with it accordingly.

Ten Constables of "E" Division conspired together to break the disciplinary regulations of the Force, and to foregather at the most disreputable joint in the neighbourhood of Calgary, namely at a resort of white prostitutes and negro pimps.

The said men have entered into a conspiracy of silence to make no explanation of their conduct and to put in an identical defence against the very serious charge of breaking out of Barracks.

The said men have thus publicly disgraced their cloth and in my opinion are not fit to remain members of a Force which has been called the first Constabulary in the world.

Assistant Commissioner J.H. McIllree to Commissioner, 15 July 1910 (NAC, RG18, 393, 412-10)

... After inquiring into the circumstances from Supt. Deane, Sergt. Murison, Corp. Rickett and the Sergt-Major [*Spalding*] there would appear to be no doubt that the men committed a wilful act of insubordination and I think premeditated on the part of some of them. They all pleaded guilty and declined to offer any explanation as to their conduct. The men who I would say were at the bottom of it were Pearce, Showler and Tomkins. Pearce was in the American service, and the Sergt-Major states he is no good. Tompkins has knocked about a good deal and has the reputation of a barrack room lawyer, and Showler, the Sergt-Major states, is a grumbler and dissatisfied and much inclined to be cheeky. The two former have been accustomed to hold forth in the barrack rooms to the effect that men could do much better out of the Force, and Pearce and Tompkins, I am led to believe, want to get out and hope to be dismissed over this business. The Sergt-Major and Sergt. Murison are of the opinion that the men went out just to have a good time and stopping longer than was first intended, made matters worse by waiting until brought back, and Jones one of the men also says this, but it appears to me that there is something else behind the whole thing. I cannot find that there was any reason for any discontent. Pearce, Showler and Tompkins grumbled on principle and Jones had been a bit discontented for a week previous, as he had applied to go on detachment and was refused. Passes are granted lavishly here and that excuse cannot be brought up. It would appear that some at least of the men had been frequenting the houses of ill fame as Showler, Fraser and Tompkins are suffering from venereal disease. The latter was only discharged from hospital a short time ago cured.[11] Batchellor and Lawrence are according to my information the least to blame in the matter. They were weak and easily led.

I find that Chapman and Batchellor, who had been on pass, went out together. Pearce woke Lawrence up and they left together. Showler and Fraser went together, and Jones, Tompkins and Brown in another party. They all met at Nose Creek, and Green who was on pass joined them there.

An account of the affair appeared in the Daily News of yesterday evening .... The statement that they were insubordinate to the Sergt-Major is entirely false. When ordered to go to Barracks, Showler made some remark slightly cheeky but Jones said "Boys do not let us disobey orders" and they walked over quietly to Barracks.

Jones, I understand, is very penitent. Regarding the character of the men, the Sergt-Major says that Pearce, Showler and Tompkins are a bad lot. Chapman young, foolish and unreliable. Fraser, he says, is useless. Batchellor, Brown, Jones and Green good men and Lawrence well meaning but not very bright.

My opinion of the whole thing is that the breaking out was premeditated, but the stopping out not so. They apparently were having a good time and did not realise the time. When they did, they held a council and decided to wait until they were sent for. Showler was the canteen manager and the funds are found to be some $37.00 short and about which he can or will furnish no explanations ....

The whole affair is most regretable but I think the men deserved their punishments. Even when they were tried if they had behaved like men, and acknowledged they were sorry, the punishment might have been different but they simply pleaded guilty and declined to make any explanations.

---

[11] According to Mounted Police regulations, Tompkins would have been required to pay his own hospital expenses and to have had 12 1/2 cents per day deducted from his pay on the grounds that venereal disease resulted from an individual's own indiscretion (see NAC, RG18, 317, 279-06).

V-20 Deane's Insubordination
Assistant Commissioner Z.T. Wood to Deane, 26 October 1910 (NAC, RG18, 396, 563-10)

Re. Theft of Horses at Gleichen.

Referring to your letter of the 21st. October. The Commissioner is of the opinion that a special party of Police from Calgary should have been sent in pursuit, if the detachment members were otherwise employed.

Deane to Assistant Commissioner, 1 November 1910 (NAC, RG18, 396, 563-10)

Re. Theft of Horses at Gleichen.

Referring to your memo of 26th October.

I attach hereto a list of Officers, N.C. Officers, Constables and horses available for duty on the morning of the 14th October after receipt of Mr. Roueche's message that his horses had been stolen.

I am curious to know what sort of patrol the Commissioner would have selected therefrom to send to Gleichen to pick up the 3 day trail which was already lost.

Even if it had been possible, as it was not, to despatch a patrol, it would have been in my view an act of eye-service as useless as this correspondence is unnecessary.

Deane to Commissioner, 9 November 1910 (NAC, RG18, 396, 563,10)

[*The Commissioner found Deane's response impertinent and "requested" its withdrawal. When Deane was slow in answering, Perry sent a telegram "directing" him to withdraw the letter. Deane complied, but without grace.*]

In reply to your letter of the 3rd instant referring to the theft of horses at Gleichen, and to your cipher telegram of this date, I have the honour to inform that I have had under consideration whether I should withdraw my letter ... or whether I should request to have it referred to Ottawa.

I had already written prior to the receipt of your telegram to inform you that in compliance with your order I withdraw it.

Assistant Commissioner Wood to Deane, 24 October 1910 (NAC, RG18, 396, 563-10)

[*Another case at the same time compounded the dispute between Deane and the Commissioner's office.*]

Re. F. Lehrman - Theft from the person

Referring to your C.R. [*Crime Report*] of the 20th instant, the Commissioner directs me to say that he cannot understand the change in front of the Police in this matter. [*It seemed that the police were dropping the charges in a clear-cut case of theft.*]

On 10th July Insp. Duffus wrote Corpl. Tabuteau that the fact that Lehrman could not account for the money in his possession was sufficient to convict him, and the subsequent evidence forwarded by Corpl. Tabuteau on July 26th seems most conclusive.

If restitution is to be allowed to wipe out crime, it should only be with the consent of the Courts. The Commissioner cannot agree that substantial justice has been done in this case.

The mere fact that Bell asked Lehrman for the money the latter stole, and that Lehrman then gave an order for the money found in his possession, is an admission of theft.

Deane to Assistant Commissioner, 26 October 1910 (NAC, RG18, 396, 563-10)

Re. F. Lehrman - Theft from the person

The complainant herein definitely refused to lay an information against Lehrman and that charge therefore never went into Court.

The magistrate who convicted Lehrman of vagrancy awarded him 6 months imprisonment H.L. recognising the difficulty of obtaining a conviction in a charge of theft, supposing it to be made.

Lehrman therefore had a substantial dose of imprisonment, and in addition thereto gave up all but $25 of the money found on his person.

I maintain that I had a perfect right to allow the complainant and the accused to settle this matter between them if they chose, and am submitting the question to the Attorney General as to the exercise of my judgement.

Commisioner A.B. Perry to Deane, 1 November 1910 (NAC, RG18, 396, 563-10)

Am I to understand from your letter of the 26th instant, re. F. Lehrman — theft from person — that you have submitted to the Attorney General, the question as to whether you were justified in allowing the accused to settle the matter with the complainant?

Deane to Commissioner, 3 November 1910 (NAC, RG18, 396, 563-10)

re. F. Lehrman - Theft from the person.

... I did not intend to convey the impression that I was seeking justification at the hands of the Attorney General — I have no need of any such thing. My action would be endorsed not only by the Attorney General, but by the Bench of Judges.

What I do intend, as soon as my over-worked clerical staff can do the necessary, is to send a complete copy of the file in question to the Attorney General's Department for record in case of future reference and to speak to the Attorney General about it when time and opportunity permit.

Commissioner Perry to Deane, 11 November 1910 (NAC, RG18, 396, 563-10)

I have the honour to acknowledge the receipt of your letter of 9th inst., marked "confidential", in reply to my letter of the 3rd inst., informing me that in compliance with my order you withdraw your letter of 1st November, on the subject of "theft of horses at Gleichen".

On 3rd instant you addressed a letter to me on the subject "re F. Lehrman theft from the person," which was in reply to a letter from me dated 1st November.

This as well as your letter of 1st Nov., exhibits a want of deference and a contempt of my opinion, which I cannot ignore.

In the second paragraph of your letter of the third, you stated that you propose to send a complete copy of this file to the Attorney General for future reference, and to speak to the Attorney General about it, when time and opportunity permit.

I desire to explicitly instruct you, that your communications to the Attorney General of Alberta are strictly limited to the authority granted you by G.O. 2765, a copy of which I enclose.[12]

Your correspondence in future must be couched in proper and courteous language, and my opinions and criticisms received with the deference due to my position as Commissioner commanding the Force.

E. The Genteel World of the Elite

There were numerous "worlds" in southern Alberta. Of course, for hordes of newcomers in the boom years after 1905, their world was that of pioneer farming. In that world, many were successful in establishing productive, independent family enterprises, but here too the hazards and trials were frequent. Poor crops, accidental deaths and injuries, indebtedness, back-breaking labor, and depressing isolation were the lot of many.

Quite another world was that of the privileged few. These people had both money and status. They included leading entrepreneurs and public officials. Their concerns were far removed from those of ordinary folk who were attempting to scrape together a living. Their social life revolved around parties, vacations, trips, and clubs. Senior officers of the Mounted Police were members of this elite, and from time to time they were called upon to act as hosts for visiting dignitaries such as a governor general or prominent politicians. As police officers, therefore, they were in intimate, though brief, contact with the broadest possible range of humanity from drug-dealing pimps and disease-wracked vagrants to prime ministers and members of the English royal family.

In 1907 Deane was requested to organize activities for a Japanese prince during his stop-over in Calgary. Deane threw himself into the task and planned everything down to not only the minute-to-minute schedule and the menu but also to the floral arrangements and the cutlery. The mundane details presented in Document V-21 provide an insight into the lifestyle of the rich and famous. But the occasion was memorable for Deane for reasons other than having had the extraordinary responsibility of

---

[12] This was a 1907 general order restricting commanding officers from communicating directly with government officials except on routine matters. "G.O." might as well have stood for "gag order" in this instance!

entertaining Japanese royalty. In fact, during the entire visit of the prince, Deane was incapacitated and lying in bed, for he had severely injured his spine while being driven along the projected route of the prince's tour in a trial run. As his wife had died the year before, Deane had to manage affairs from his bed upstairs in the fine new commanding officer's house that had been completed just months earlier. During the dinner itself, he received breathless reports that everything was proceeding splendidly. And just as a hand injury suffered in a game of cricket many years earlier had led him to his first wife,[13] his back injury introduced him to his second. She was his nurse, and after she had concluded her treatment, he discovered that he missed her greatly. He vigorously pursued her and subsequently married her in 1908, just before his sixtieth birthday so that she might be eligible for the widow's pension provided to the police.[14]

It was some time before the newlyweds were able to have a belated honeymoon at Banff, which had already become a vacation destination for the elite. In that era, the tourist season was restricted to the summer months, but the conflict between wildlife preservation and human leisure was already evident in Mounted Police files concerning dogs running loose and the illegal shooting of game. Document V-22 reveals something of the atmosphere of Banff even though the episode was nothing more than a tiff between two branches of government service in which the simplest solution was to remove the source of the dispute.

V-21 Prince Fushimi's Visit
Deane to Commissioner Perry, 7 June 1907 (NAC, RG18, 1605, 133-07)

Can you conveniently lend us some lap robes or dust cloths for the 18th instant? I think there should be at least two to each carriage; those that we have here are a little dingy in appearance.

About waiters: I have been thinking it over. It would take one competent man to look after the wine and the icing thereof, etc, and I think it would be better for your man to undertake

---

[13] See GA, M311, "Reminiscences of a Mounted Police Officer by Captain R. Burton Deane," p.57.

[14] See Deane to Commissioner, 28 April 1908 in NAC, RG18, 3438, 0-49.

that. We shall thus require two other waiters for each table. Mrs. Gladwin tells me that there is a man named Watson in Macleod Division who waited for the Primroses when Lord Grey was there. If you can get a second man at Regina that you thought of, he and Watson would equip No.1 table. I have not yet heard about waiters here but understand that I can hire two ....

The music professor has undertaken to provide seven performers from 1 to 3 and will play some suitable music. He charges $4 for the leader and $2.50 apiece for the other artists.

The Hudson's Bay Company are so complacent that they will lend us anything we want. I have chosen the glass, etc.

Duffus offers to lend silver for the second table but if it could be avoided, with the number of strange people about, I would rather not have silver spoons and forks. There is not so much risk with electro plate, and if you can spare some electro plate from Regina, I should be obliged.

Have you any fish eaters [*servants*] that you can lend me from the Mess?

Deane, Annual Report, 1907 (*SP 1908*, No.28, pp.16-17)

In the month of June we were requested by the department to provide some sort of entertainment that would interest His Imperial Highness Prince Fushimi of Japan, who was passing through Canada on his way home from London. As he is an illustrious soldier we were naturally inclined to show him how smart an escort and equipages we could turn out, and, to that end, met him at the railway station on arrival at 10 a.m. on June 18, with a well-drilled and well-horsed escort under the command of Inspector Shaw, a smart four horse team for himself driven by Staff Sergeant [*J.J.*] Wilson and spring wagons for the rest of his party, which numbered twelve in all.

About half an hour's drive through the streets of Calgary the party was embarked in some automobiles and conveyed to Rawlinson Brothers' famous horse ranche, about eleven miles from the city. Inspector Duffus, who has an autocar of his own, drove His Imperial Highness, and other cars, sufficient for the purpose, were very kindly provided and driven by their owners, gentlemen resident in Calgary, to wit, Messrs. J.J. Young and H.L. Downey.

We had spent some little labour on the road to ensure a rapid and pleasant run and the Prince appeared to enjoy his visit, as, in the case of the well-known stallion "Commodore," he remarked, "That is the finest horse I ever saw in my life." From this ranche His Highness and suite were reconducted to Calgary to witness a game of polo, wherein they were much interested. For this event in the programme we were indebted to the Calgary Polo Club, who organized a special game for the occasion, and to the city council who very kindly had devoted some labour and money to improve the ground, which alone made the game possible.

From the polo ground the party returned to barracks, where they had luncheon with the officers. Shortly before 3 p.m. the cortege started for their car, stopping for one moment on the road to touch a button and witness the celerity with which the Central Fire Brigade could turn out to an alarm.

A corporal's guard of three men was sent to Banff to do duty at the C.P.R. Hotel during His Highness's residence there. An orderly officer in the person of Inspector Knight, was also sent thither from Regina.

The oft quoted aphorism that "The best laid plans of mice and men gang oft agley," was amusingly illustrated during His Highness's stay at Banff.

Some programme ... had been arranged for one day, but it did not meet with His Highness's approval, and he set it aside in favour of going a-fishing in a boat with Corporal Townsend, of the Bankhead detachment. The Corporal had a choice selection of flies and hooks and paraphernalia dear to the fisherman's heart, and at the first cast His Highness drew out two fish on one hook, whereat he heartily laughed. It was the first time, said his staff, that he had laughed since leaving Quebec.

V-22 The Police Team at Banff
Howard Douglas, Superintendent of the Rocky Mountain Park (Banff) to Deane, 8 February 1907 (NAC, RG18, 336, 238-07)

I regret very much having to make a complaint to you concerning the Police on detachment here with regard to the use of the Police team when not on Police duty.

Mounted Police Detachment at Banff
RCMPM, 933-10-12
*This 1897 photograph shows an earlier version of the team and waggon
that were at the centre of the dispute related in Document V-22.
Looking at the splendid horses and men, it is easy to see why one would
wish to be chauffeured about by them.*

Some 8 or 9 years ago when Insp. Harper was removed from
Banff, an order was issued that the team, when not engaged on
Police duty, was to be at the disposal of the Supt. of the Park for
taking out Govt. officials and any others who he thought it
would be in the interests of the park to entertain; or in connection with his duties as Supt., and by referring to the records kept
by the detachment here in the diary, you can satisfy yourself
that the order has not been abused in any way. During the
winter months I do not think I have used the team more than
once or twice a month and until the present man came here I
have had no cause for complaint. But for some reason unknown
to me, the man here seems to resent what has been the custom

in the past, and while I can only report one instance when they did not furnish the team when requested, I can state very many in which they would come an hour later than when I asked them, and by their actions I could judge that it was intentional. It may not seem much but it certainly is very annoying, and I do not care to have it continue, as there can be no reasonable excuse for it, and if the men can treat with contempt an order in that way, I shall in future know what course to take. I will only mention two cases, and which I can substantiate. About a month ago I saw Const. Drane in the morning and told him I would like to have the team take me down to the Buffalo about 2 o'clock, and he said all right. I waited at the house after lunch till three o'clock and then went to the Barracks, and in reply to my asking why the team did not come, Browning stated that I should have come and asked him, and also stated that the sleigh was broken, and could not go out. I merely said, out of common courtesy, that he should have advised me. However, inside of an hour the team was out with a load of dining room girls from the Sanitarium. This morning I told Drane that I had to go to the Hot Springs at one thirty, and he said all right. (Browning had not arrived from Calgary yet.) I waited in the office until 2.30 and then hired a livery and drove up, later on. Drane said that he was delayed with a sick horse; but during the interval the team was out driving Sanitarium guests until 1 o'clock; so that he really could not have got around before half past two or three.

I do not wish to dictate what the Govt. team should do here but I do not think they are kept here to daily drive the female help at the Sanitarium hotel and certain guests there, when we have to hire teams for similar drives on Govt duty.

I have not had any trouble with the men stationed here for the last ten years; in most cases they have been gentlemen, but I must say that I do not think the present men are what tourists and travellers expect to meet as representatives of the world famed R.N.W.M.P.

I would respectfully ask you to examine the records, and see how often I have had the team which has rarely been for my personal use outside of the park duty, and then advise me what to expect in the future.

As stated above, I regret very much having to trouble you in the matter; but could not avoid doing so.

Deane to Douglas, 11 February 1907 (NAC, RG18, 336, 238-07)

I have received your letter of complaint of the 8th inst and have spoken to Corporal Browning about it.

He is perfectly justified in the stand he takes which is this:

He is in charge of the detachment and is responsible for the team and the use that is made of it.

Every application for the use of the team should be made through him and he will give Constable Drane his orders. I notice that in each of the specific complaints that you make you say that you communicated with Constable Drane which in a disciplinary community is not a proper way of doing business.

As to the dining room girls from the Sanitarium riding in the vehicle, Corporal Browning denies that the team went out that day. He further says "I might say that while I have been in Banff, no dining room girl or hotel help has ridden in a police rig to my knowledge. I am not in the habit of associating with the female help from the hotel."

I am very sorry that there should be so much unnecessary friction in a simple matter of this kind, but the remedy after all is simple.

I shall be obliged if in future you will be kind enough to make your applications to Corporal Browning in writing, specifying the use that is required to be made of the team, etc. and these applications will be periodically forwarded to me with Corporal Browning's report as to what was done in each case.

I think you will find that there will be no more trouble.

Commissioner Perry to Deane, 13 February 1907 (NAC, RG18, 336, 238-07)

I have the honour to return to you, herewith, letter from Mr. Howard Douglas, Superintendant of the Rocky Mountain Park, in which he makes certain charges that the Police team and sleigh have been used in driving about female help at the Sanitarium Hotel and other guests of that Hotel.

May I request that you will proceed to Banff and hold an investigation into these charges which I consider are very serious if proven.

Deane, Report of Proceedings of Investigation, 7 March 1907 (NAC, RG18, 336, 238-07)

Mr Douglas ... said that he had no desire to press the complaint .... He expressed himself as gratified with the present arrangement whereby he will apply to Cpl. Browning in writing for use of the team when required, and said that his wish is to work in harmony with the Police ....

Reg. No. 2858, Cpl Browning says:
"... The following are the names of the only people who have driven in the Police rig at our invitation, and these drives have taken place at different times for an hour or so while exercising the horses.

Mrs. Jebb Brown. Wife of ex-Sgt Brown.

Miss Brett. Elderly lady.

Miss Boyd. Daughter of a Manitoba M.P.

Mr. and Mrs. Ham Jukes and friends.

The Matron and two of the nurses of the Sanitarium who have always been very good to our men while patients.

Mrs. Bell. Bank Manager's wife.

Mrs. Stephen. Niece of Lord MountStephen ...."

Reg. No. 4087 Const Drane says:
"... I have never driven any dining room girls from the Sanitarium or any other hotel. In any event the dining room girls of the Sanitarium are respectable girls of irreproachable character. They go to the dances in town and everybody dances with them ....

"I have never to my knowledge driven Mr. Douglas on government duty. It has always been on social business, frequently making calls, while I have had to wait the convenience of the ladies concerned in my redcoat ...."

Finding.

I find that the allegations made by Mr. Douglas the Superintendent of the Rocky Mountain Park in his letter of 8th February l[a]st, are refuted in toto.

I find that Mr. Douglas, in his dealings with the Police in connection with the use of the team, has persistently ignored

Cpl. Browning, the responsible head of the detachment, and I find that there has been considerable misconception as to the operative effect of the order which was given by the Department some years ago.

I think that the matter is now placed on a broad and intelligible basis, and that no friction need occur.

Having said this I desire to say that supposing Mr. Douglas's complaint as to the dining room girls had been verified to the letter, what would be the implication?

It would be this, that sundry females of irreproachable character and of a recognized standing in the community, whose only fault would seem to be that they are compelled to work for a living, are not considered fit and proper persons to ride in a waggon drawn by police horses. This is a suggestion so monstrous that every woman in the country would rise and protest upon the imputation upon her sex.

I should certainly agree with them.

Deane to Commissioner, 7 March 1907 (NAC, RG18, 336, 238-07)

I have the honour to forward, herewith, the report of an investigation which I held at Banff yesterday into the complaints made by Mr. Douglas ....

I was informed by a married couple who have been spending the winter at Banff, and who are intimate with the Douglas family, that in the matter of the Police team, Mrs. Douglas is the vis a tergo [*force from behind*].

She has given out that the team can only be used by visitors with Mr. Douglas' consent. Corpl. Browning says that she habitually speaks of the team as "My team" and "our team" and so on ad nauseam.

The evidence will show that the horses are used mainly for social visits by Mr. Douglas who enjoys the possession of the waggon with its red coated driver.

A knowledge of these circumstances is essential to a proper appreciation of the situation.

[*Within two months the team and waggon were removed from the Banff Detachment.*]

VI
KILLERS, FOOLS, AND PERVERTS
CALGARY DIVISION 1910 - 1914

Deane's final half-decade as a Mounted Policeman was not a happy one. He was still a competent officer, but there were indications that his enthusiasm for the job had diminished. In forwarding a 1913 report from Deane criticizing the sale of the site of the Calgary barracks to the Grand Trunk Pacific, Laurence Fortescue, the Comptroller of the Mounted Police, stated that it was "the first matter connected with the Police that Deane has taken the slightest interest in during the last 3 or 4 years ...." [1] *Perhaps the heavy work-load was just too much for a man in his seventh decade. But there were other factors.*

In the first place, his second wife fell ill in 1911, suffered from a variety of ailments, even had her foot amputated. His own health was quite adequate, but it is hardly surprising that he was not as vigorous an individual as he had been when he joined the force. The second factor was the stagnation of his career. Back in the 1880s, he had been passed over in the selection of the Commissioner. In the years that followed, he was ignored time and again. By 1913, his time was past, although Deane did not think so: "So far as the Assistant Commissionership is concerned, it is my birthright. I am by so many years the Senior Superintendent of the Force that I cannot conceive the Government passing me over or allowing strings to be pulled to my prejudice." [2] *He was*

---

[1] L. Fortescue to A.E. Blount, 22 November, 1913, in NAC, MG26 H (Robert L. Borden Papers), vol.172, p.94050. Deane considered the price to be about one-quarter of what the property was worth (see Deane, *Mounted Police Life*, pp. 126-131). While the Comptroller asserted that Deane's memorandum "shows what he can do when he tries," Fortescue undercut Deane's criticism of the sale-price by suggesting that Deane "does not want to be turned out of the very good house he now occupies." Fortescue had also been a Royal Marine and had known Deane for many years, but it cannot be assumed that his commentary on Deane was entirely objective. Perhaps he was rationalzing why the Assistant Commissionership had not been given to Deane earlier in the year.

[2] Deane to C.A. Magrath, 4 February 1913, in NAC, MG30 E82 (Charles Magrath Papers), vol. 10, file 50.

wrong; two months later, another officer received the position. In reality, however, this final humiliation from the force was of little consequence, for he wanted that post, or something similar, not because of the new challenges it would have presented, but simply because he felt it was due him and because it would have helped his pension entitlement.

In any case, at the end of 1913, with his wife in seemingly improved but still precarious health, and with no prospect of promotion, he decided to retire the following summer and leave the West "to seek out some little spot in England where the Maréchal Niel rose will grow out of doors." [3] *Unfortunately, by March 1914 his wife had been diagnosed with tuberculosis and so they stayed in Calgary. She died on 22 July, 1914. Her headstone read, "with loved ones far away," for Deane remained determined to leave Canada.*

No doubt, Deane's troubled personal life contributed to his disillusion with the development of the West. True, southern Alberta was mightily transformed. No longer was it the wide-open range where Deane could ride his horse for miles without encountering another human. On the contrary, his wonderful house was in the very heart of a burgeoning urban centre. No more was there the same spirit of adventure that united the nineteenth century white pioneers of Alberta. At last, Deane understood the feelings expressed by his first boss in the Mounted Police, Commissioner A.G. Irvine. In Irvine's journal entry for 16 November 1883, he noted that Deane's family was sharing his household in Regina until they were able to settle in their own home:

> *It seemed odd to me in this far west to see a lady sitting at the head of my table pouring out tea, & a lot of cheery little faces round my table .... The* whole country *is* too civilized *for* me now. *It was twice as jolly in the old days of Indians & Buffalo.* [4]

Thirty years later, Deane felt the same way; the changes were too great and too rapid — in spite of the fact that the fundamental purpose of the police had always been to promote that transformation. To Deane, the West seemed to be heading in the same

---

[3] Deane, *Mounted Police Life*, p.130.
[4] RCMPM, 75-54-1 (Col. A. Irvine, Journal), p.55.

direction as most other societies, that is, on a downward spiral. Deane now emphasized the negative aspects of western Canadian society: its venality, its degradation, its barbarity. By the time he left the West, largely unheralded and unappreciated,[5] Deane was happy to shake its dust from his feet. He departed Calgary on 30 September 1914. While it seems that he never returned to Canada, not even to visit his children and grandchildren, he did enjoy more than a decade of retirement tending his beloved roses and marrying for a third time.

The positive element, the bright side of the pre-1914 years, was the fact that Deane himself remained committed to values of substance. Amidst the crass materialism, killing, debauchery, and outright stupidity around him, he retained high personal standards, urged an elevated moral tone for the Prairies, and worked for the achievement of a better society. In a sense, therefore, his disillusionment with what he saw as the decline of the West, reflected standards he had espoused from the very beginning of his career as a Mounted Police officer.

A. Characteristics of Growth

Good economic times continued unabated after 1909. Prosperity both encouraged and was promoted by a massive influx of agricultural settlers and business expansion including the discovery of oil. The optimism and achievements of these years were celebrated on such occasions as the Calgary rodeo in which the native people played an important role. But nothing lasts forever, and by 1913 the signs of economic stagnation were multiplying, only to be confirmed by the experience of 1914. The flow of immigrants dried up, business slackened, and public works projects began to be shelved. Of course, even the advances of the boom years were not entirely positive as, for example, automobiles clashed with horses, and, as seen in Document VI-4, the production of electricity threatened to infringe upon land rights of natives.

---

[5] An exception was the biographical sketch that appeared in the *Calgary News Telegram,* 18 July, 1914.

VI-1 Good Times to Bad
Deane, Annual Report, 1911 (*SP 1912*, No.28, p.32)

Settlers from all quarters are coming into the country in great numbers.

We have had a very extraordinary season, such as I have never seen during my 28 summers in the Northwest.

The unprecedented rainfall has had the effect of stocking our Barrack garden so plentifully that we have more produce than we know what to do with.

Deane, Monthly Report, May 1912 (NAC, RG18, 420, 113-12)

The stock in this district is in very good condition and the crops never looked better at this time of the year.

There is a large amount of breaking being done with steam plows which will be seeded later to fall wheat.

Deane, Annual Report, 1912 (*SP 1913*, No.28, p.39)

Settlers continue to pour into the country and demands for new detachments are numerous.

Deane, Monthly Report, October 1913 (NAC, RG18, 438, 135-13)

Oil was struck in the vicinity of Okotoks which has created considerable excitement in Calgary and the surrounding country. From all accounts it is of a very high grade and has been used in automobiles. Whether it is in commercial quantities is a question.

Deane, Monthly Report, April 1913 (NAC, RG18, 438, 135-13)

Business throughout the district has been quiet.

Deane, Monthly Report, December 1913 (NAC, RG18, 438, 135-13)

There are a very large number of unemployed in the vicinity. Provision is being made for them as much as is possible.

VI-2 The Stampede
Deane, Monthly Report, September 1912 (NAC, RG18, 420, 113-12)

The Stampede was held in Calgary during the first week of September. It was very largely attended by people from all parts of Western Canada and the United States.

Deane, Annual Report, 1912 (*SP 1913*, No.28, p.49)

The Indians made a brave showing at the "stampede" which was held here .... I should judge there were some twelve hundred of them in the procession which passed through Calgary streets on the opening day, and the fact of there having been so few found intoxicated during the week's visit induces the reflection that, after all, it does no harm to let the Indian have a little holiday and to let him see what is going on in the world ....

"Tom Threepersons," a Blood Indian young man, covered himself with glory by riding a celebrated bucking horse, called "Cyclone," and by thus, carrying off a thousand dollar prize and the championship belt offered at the "stampede."

VI-3 Horses vs. The Auto
Proceedings of Board of Officers (consisting of Deane and Insp. A.W. Duffus), 12 December 1911 (NAC, RG18, 422, 160-12)

Thomas R. Usher states:
"... On Saturday evening Nov. 18th about 8.30 p.m., I was driving west on Ninth Avenue approaching 1st East in Mr. R.H. Emmett's motor-car. I was driving the car and sitting in the front seat with Mr. Emmett.

"We were going about eight miles per hour, and just before we reached First Street East, a hotel bus came in the opposite direction at a walking pace. The bus was about the centre of the road, we were on the right hand side. All of a sudden a Police rig going East on Ninth Avenue appeared from behind the bus and came right on top of our car. I didn't see the rig until it appeared from behind the bus and was on top of us. As soon as I saw it I put on the brakes and stopped the car. The horses straddled the

Bronc Riding Champion of the Stampede, September 1912
GA, NA-584-1
Tom Three Persons, a Blood Indian cowboy, is shown on the occasion of his victory at the inaugural Calgary Stampede, as reported in Document VI-2. He was obviously a hero to the youth at his side.

hood of the motor and the pole came through the wind shield
between Mr. Emmett and myself. There may have been a rig
between the bus and our left hand side of the road but I did not
see it that I remember. If there had not been one the Police rig
could have passed between the bus and the inside of the road
and not have swerved around on our side. The Police horses
were travelling about fifteen or eighteen miles per hour at the
least. The pavement was very slippery and it was hard to pull
up. We were under the electric light and could not see very
plainly for any distance. Ninth Avenue is poorly lighted .... The
car was badly damaged. The radiator, fan, fenders, head lamp,
one side lamp and wind shield were all broken and the car
scratched up, several of the rods etc were bent."

Reg. No. 4749 Constable Frodsham, H.R.S., states:

"On Saturday November 18th 1911, I was returning to the
Barracks from the C.P.R. station, coming east on Ninth Avenue
at 8.30 p.m. with Constable Todd and three prisoners, driving
team Reg. No. 152 and 436. Just as I was approaching First
Street East, driving on my right hand side of the road, I overtook
a hotel bus. In order to pass the bus which was in the middle of
the road, I pulled to the left. The reason I did not pass on the
right hand side of the bus was that there was a dray coming up
First Street East and turning into Ninth Avenue going west.
The bus was a canvas covered one and you could not see through
it.

"As I passed the bus I saw ahead of me the lights of an auto
coming west on Ninth Avenue. I tried to pull over to the right
hand side of the road, but I could not get Horse Reg. No. 436 to
answer to the line quickly enough, so I started to pull back to the
left of the street and collided with the car. The horses straddled
the motor of the car, the pole going through the wind shield. I
know I damaged the lamps, hood and wind shield.

"Had I continued my original intention of crossing over to
the right I should have struck the car at an angle with both
horses. By pulling to the left I only struck the car with my off
horse. The horses or rig were not hurt. When the collision occurred my off horse and half the rig were in the centre of the car
tracks or in other words I was straddling the left hand side rail
going east. As the rails on Ninth Avenue are not in the centre of

the street, but slightly on the north side of it, my horse would have been about twelve feet from the curb. I claim the motor car was in the centre of the road and not on the left hand side [*as Frodsham approached*]. Had he been I could have avoided the accident.

"I was travelling about eight or nine miles per hour. The horses were travelling at their usual pace. Had I been travelling fifteen miles per hour my horses with the heavy load behind them would have piled on the car. When I pulled round the bus and first saw the car I was only about thirty feet from it. I don't know how fast they were travelling. There was considerable slush that night on Ninth Avenue which made the pavement very slippery. My horses were sharp shod.

"The cause of the whole trouble was the heavy dray turning the corner from First Street East, west into Ninth Avenue. This dray should have kept well to the right on First Street East until it was nearly across Ninth Avenue and then turned west. Instead of that it turned west into Ninth Avenue on the left hand side, which is against the City by-laws. I have been unable to find out who the owner of the dray is."

OPINION [*of Deane and Duffus*]:

Having heard the ... evidence the Board are of opinion that the damage to the motor car ... was the result of an accident wherein a Mounted Police team ... collided with the car aforesaid and inflicted damage thereupon to the extent of one hundred and sixty dollars and five cents.

The paved streets at this time were very slippery and the grade of the street was rather steep from the apex to the curb.

It is a fact within the knowledge of the Board that on account of this pitch heavy teams are in the habit of monopolizing the centre of the roads, and the rule of the road is not properly observed except where a policeman is stationed at a dangerous corner.

Constable Todd's evidence that on the following day he saw fragments of glass from the windshield in the middle of the road at the spot where the accident had taken place on the previous evening goes to show that the driver of the motor was not as far over on his own side of the road as he might and should have been.

The occupants of the car say that the horses were travelling at from 15 to 18 miles per hour. This is an excessive rate at which the horses in question are not capable of trotting. Their utmost limit would not exceed 12 miles per hour, and Constables Frodsham and Todd say that the team was travelling at its natural gait, which would certainly not exceed 10 miles per hour.

It is clear from statements on both sides that Constable Frodsham was obeying the rule of the road, and that he was right in attempting to pass the obstructing wagon of the left hand side ....

The Board is of opinion that the owner of the car should look to the driver thereof for re-imbursement as to one-half of the value of the damage done, and to Constable Frodsham, as to the value of the other half.[6]

VI-4 Calgary Power vs. Stony Indians
Const. A.J. Barber, Crime Report (submitted to Deane), 1 July 1913 (NAC, RG18, 448, 455-13)

I have the honour to report that Mr. Waddy, Indian Agent [*at Morley*] has forwarded me the attached report.

Sir:

"For your information I want to say that it is probable the Stony Indians will attempt to damage the property of the Power Company this week. I do not yet know where the trouble will start but understand the Indians have the idea of burning up some of the power line for a start. I have advised the power company to put on a few watchmen at the works but do not know if they have done so as they might think it a bluff on the part of the Indians ...."

Deane to Const. Barber, 3 July 1913 (NAC, RG18, 448, 455-13)

What is the trouble between the Stony Indians and the Power Company? You had better go and see the Manager of the Power Company and ascertain what steps he is taking to protect his own interests.

---

[6] A more detailed account of the expense involved in fixing the vehicle, a Mitchell car, set the figure at $207.73. Some five months after the accident, the federal Deputy Minister of Justice disavowed any liability of the Crown and doubted that Frodsham could successfully be sued for damages (see E.L. Newcombe to Comptroller, 15 April 1912 in NAC, RG18, 422, 160-12).

* * *
POLICE WORK

"I've been blackjacked and robbed sir."

"Don't bother me, I'm timing an automobile."

Police Work, 1911
GA, NA-789-18
Although the source of this cartoon is unclear, it may well be lampooning the Mounted Police investigation of the accident reported in Document VI-3, and the policeman depicted may have been Deane himself. In any event, it illustrates that new police activities brought about by the advent of the automobile did not sit well with some observers.

Const. Barber, Crime Report (submitted to Deane), 3 July 1913 (NAC, RG18, 448, 455-13)

I understand that the Calgary Power Company are building a dam on the property of the Stony Indian Reserve at Morley and that there has been no agreement signed as to the land. Mr. Moore, Manager of the Power Company held a meeting with the Indians in April last, where the Power Company was to give each Indian twenty-five ($25) dollars, the money to be paid within two weeks of the meeting. The Indians have not received this money yet nor have they received any satisfaction from the Indian Department. By Mr. Waddy's report sent to me on the 30th instant stating that the Indians are going to do damage to the Power Company's property this week, is the first I have heard of the matter.

Deane to Commissioner, 4 July 1913 (NAC, RG18, 448, 445-13)

... It will be seen from [*Const. Barber's*] report that this trouble has been brewing for some time, but this is the first I have ever heard of any arrangement between the Calgary Power Company and these Indians.

I presume the Indian Department has cognizance of the matter.

Inspector Worsley is now inspecting the western detachments, and will probably be at Morley on Sunday. I have instructed him to enquire into the matter.

Insp. G.S. Worsley to Deane. 6 July 1913 (NAC, RG18, 448, 445-13)

While at Morley I interviewed the Indian Agent Mr. Waddy.

The trouble is that the Power Company have established their plant without any previous definite arrangement with the Indians or the Indian Dept.

The Indians want $25.00 per head for the privilege of putting the dam on the Reserve. The dam is altogether on the Reserve, the Reserve being on either side of the river where the dam is.

The Indians are now waiting till Mr. Glen Campbell comes before taking any steps. Mr. Campbell [*Inspector of Indian Agencies*] will be at Morley on Tuesday next.

The Indians own all the land and water rights on the Reserve.

It is supposed that storekeepers are pushing the Indians to claim this money. It would in all amount to $16,500.00. The agent considers the claim of the Indians just.

Work was started by the Power Company without the Indian Department having any knowledge of their intentions.[7]

---

[7] On 7 July Deane forwarded a copy of Worsley's report to the Commissioner with the comment: "The Indian Department seem to have a funny way of doing business." Evidently, the conflict came to an amicable conclusion.

B. Violent Crime

One negative feature of growth was the increase in crime. Annual statistics fluctuated, but there was no doubt about the upward trend. Already by 1911, there were 1,051 cases entered which resulted in 940 convictions of which 487 people were sentenced to jail or penitentiary. In 1913, the numbers had escalated to alarming proportions: 1,808 cases entered with 1,598 convictions, 527 of which resulted in jail or penitentiary sentences. While all types of criminal cases were on the increase, the amount of violent crime was noteworthy. The statistics culled from the annual reports of 1911 and 1913 and presented in Document VI-5 concern offences against the person. They are not the only types of violent crime, but they are indicative of the changed scale of Mounted Police duties since Deane's days in Lethbridge. In the Calgary Division, for example, Deane had more murders to deal with than during his entire career until then. But while statistics provide a revealing insight into violent crime, each case has its own tale, and Documents VI-6 to VI-9 tell a few of them.

VI-5 Offences Against the Person, 1911 and 1913
Deane, Annual Report, 1911 (*SP 1912*, No. 28, p.33)

Offences	Cases Entered	Convictions	Dismissals	Withdrawn	For Trial
Assault, common	77	58	11	8	—
Assault, causing bodily harm	4	1	—	1	2
Assault, aggravated	1	1	—	—	—
Attempted suicide	1	—	1	—	—
Attempted murder	2	1	—	—	1
Murder	3	2	1	—	—
Carnal knowledge	1	1	—	—	—
Rape and attempted rape	1	1	—	—	—
Criminal libel	1	—	—	—	1
Administering noxious drugs	2	—	—	—	2
[TOTALS	93	65	13	9	6]

Deane, Annual Report, 1913 (*SP 1914*, No.28, p.48)

Offences	Cases Entered	Convictions	Discharged	Withdrawn	For Trial
Assault, common	132	113	18	1	—
Assault, indecent	3	1	2	—	—
Assault, causing bodily harm	7	6	—	—	1
Threatening to do bodily harm	1	1	—	—	—
Murder	10	3	4	—	3
Murder, attempted	6	3	3	—	—
Murder, aiding and abetting	1	1	—	—	—
Rape	3	—	1	1	1
Rape, attempted	2	—	1	—	1
Manslaughter	3	—	3	—	—
Intimidation	1	1	—	—	—
Carnal knowledge	3	—	3	—	—
Carnal knowledge, attempted	2	—	—	—	2
Neglect of child	4	4	—	—	—
Shooting with intent	1	—	1	—	—
Seduction	1	—	—	1	—
Suicide, attempted	2	1	—	—	1
Unlawfully retaining children	2	—	2	—	—
[TOTALS	184	134	38	3	9]

VI-6 A Fight Over Chickens
Deane, Annual Report, 1913 (*SP 1914*, No.28, pp.56-57)

Assault upon Jim Lee, Chinaman, at Bowden: On the 20th February last at Bowden an old woman named Elizabeth Wilkinson, about 70 years of age, rather weak-minded, and with a violent temper, having an old husband to look after who is said to be approaching the century mark, got into an altercation with a Chinaman about some chickens which both claimed. At all events the Chinaman went into the old woman's yard, and the village constable of Bowden said: "I hurried towards Mrs. Wilkinson's yard where the row was taking place and, when some distance away, I saw Mr. and Mrs. Wilkinson in the yard making some threatening gestures at the Chinaman. The woman hit the Chinaman with a stick and he grabbed the stick from her, and pushed her over a snow-bank and threw the stick away. The old man then made a hit at the Chinaman who also pushed him over. The woman then got another stick and came at the Chinaman again. He got this stick from her and threw that away too. She then went off a few feet and grabbed what I then thought to be another stick, and struck the Chinaman over the head with this. He fell down and when he was staggering back on to his knees she hit him again and he went down and lay there. She then raised the weapon to hit him again but I had by this time got to the spot and grabbed it out of her hand. I found the weapon was an iron sleigh shoe about 4 feet in length."

The Chinaman's head was badly hurt and he was in very critical condition for some time.

The old woman was arrested and released on bail in charge of her married daughter. The preliminary hearing was held at Bowden by a local Justice of the Peace on the 3rd March, counsel appearing for both sides and a great number of witnesses were examined. Finally the case was dismissed.

VI-7 Boxing Fatality
Deane, Annual Report, 1913 (*SP 1914*, No.28, pp.59-60)

Boxing Contests: In the course of last year, as he was unable to obtain from the city authorities permission to hold boxing contests in the city of Calgary, Mr. Tommy Burns, the heavy-weight ex-champion of the world, constructed an arena a short distance outside the city limits and the following contests have been held therein:

On the 28th October, 1912, Hyland met Bayley in a fifteen-round bout, which was an exhibition of good clean boxing, the result being a draw.

On the 30th November following, Hyland met Thompson in what was intended to be a fifteen-round contest; no exception could be taken to the boxing but, in the thirteenth round, Thompson had received as much punishment as he was able to stand in the opinion of Sergeant Major Vickery, who stopped the fight. His action in so doing was generally approved of by the public.

On the 25th December, Hyland was, for the second time, defeated by Brown in a fair and square boxing bout.

The Pelkey-McCarty Fight
GA, W.J. Oliver photograph, NA-1912-1
Less than two minutes after this photograph was taken, the handsome
boxer on the right, Luther McCarty, lay unconscious. He died three
hours later. As Document VI-7 relates, Tommy Burns, the only world
heavyweight champion Canada has ever produced, had trained Pelkey
and had organized the bout.

On the 3rd April a six-round no-decision contest took place
between Burns and Pelkey which passed off without any unusual incident.

On the 2nd May last, in a Pelkey-Morris contest, Mr. Burns,
the referee, stopped the fight in order to save Morris from being
knocked out.

On the 24th May, Victoria Day, Luther McCarty was imported from the United States to try conclusions with Arthur
Pelkey in a no-decision bout of ten rounds. The contract called
for eight-ounce gloves, which McCarty's supporters considered
rather extreme. The referee was Mr. Edward Smith, the sporting editor of the *Chicago American*. Pelkey had been trained by
Mr. T. Burns.

The first round had lasted one minute and forty-five seconds when McCarty was unconscious, counted out, and, to all intents and purposes, a dead man, for he never spoke again although he did not cease to breathe until some three hours later. The only two noticeable blows that were struck by Pelkey in the minute and a half of actual boxing were a left punch to the jaw and a right jab to the heart, and the result, in my opinion at least, shows that the punch to the jaw was a harder blow than it seemed to be. Dr. Mosher, who made the autopsy, testified to the coroner's jury that death was caused by a subluxation of the fourth cervical vertebra which resulted in the formation of a blood clot in the brain. A slight bruise on the right angle of the jaw showed where Pelkey's left punch had gone home.

Dr. Stewart, who was called by a juryman, disagreed with Dr. Mosher's opinion, and told the jury that in his opinion McCarty's neck was dislocated before he went into the ring, and that he did not believe that Pelkey did it.

The coroner's jury exonerated Pelkey, who was then charged with manslaughter and found not guilty, albeit the jury found that the contest in question was a prize fight.

There had been some controversy as to the legality of these contests — one reverend gentleman called them "commercialized sport," the man in the street called them "a money-making scheme," but that did not necessarily make them unlawful. According to the law, as it existed ... it was impossible to be wise until after the event.

Crankshaw, quoting the decision in Rex. vs. Orton, says: "A mere exhibition of skill in sparring has been held not to be illegal; but if parties meet together to fight until one gives in from exhaustion or from injury received, it is a prize fight, and it is illegal whether the combatants fight in gloves or not."

VI-8 Killed By Her Husband
Deane, Annual Report, 1913 (*SP 1914*, No.28, p.51)

The Anderson murder and attempted suicide: The following statement was given to Constable E.G. Baker, of Youngstown Detachment [*east of Hanna*], by Peter G. Dahl, a brother-in-law of the accused man, and an eye-witness of the tragedy:

"On July 3, at about 8.30 a.m., I was in a wagon in the yard taking out water for the horses, when I saw Axel Anderson and his wife watering some plants in the garden. They then went to the back of the barn and I saw them carrying straw to the pig pen. I was busy at my work and was not paying any particular attention to Mr. and Mrs. Anderson, when I heard Mrs. Anderson exclaim in a loud voice, 'Axel,' 'Axel.' This caused me to look in that direction and I saw Anderson and his wife standing near the pig pen. I saw Anderson strike his wife with a hay fork — he held the fork by the handle with both hands, and struck her several times about the head with the fork. I run over at once and took the fork away from Anderson, who offered no resistance.

"Mrs. Anderson was lying on the ground bleeding from the face and head. She drew a few long breaths and I think she died immediately. I took Anderson by the arm and led him over to the wagon where we met my wife (Louisa Dahl); we stood there just a moment and Anderson ran into his house. I followed him and when I reached the house Anderson was in the next room standing with his back towards me, and I saw him pass his hand across his throat, after which he turned round, came towards me, and went out through the door into the yard holding his hand to his throat. Blood was running from his throat and dripping to the floor. He went about two rods from the house and lay down on the grass .... I ran and got a towel and put it round his neck. I then got a horse and went to summons the neighbours for help .... As soon as I made the nearest neighbour hear my shouts, I returned and found that my wife had dressed Anderson's neck. I then went ... to see Mrs. Anderson and found her in the same position as she had fallen, and was quite dead ....

"Whilst Anderson was striking his wife, I heard him say in Swedish, 'You won't fool me any more now.' When I got close to Anderson, he said to me in Swedish, 'She fooled me in Minnesota, and expected to fool me now'."

An inquest was held and the following verdict returned: "Anna Axel Anderson came to her death at the hands of her husband; cause of death, fractured skull."

The accused was committed for trial at Youngstown, and on the 17th July, arrived at Calgary, where his condition was such that he was sent to the General hospital.

Having cut into his gullet the food and drink given him came through the wound, which had had twelve stitches put into it on the spot by Dr. Naysmith. The patient made such progress that he was able to be discharged from the hospital on the 16th July. He is now in the guard-room here awaiting trial.

Insp. Worsley, Annual Report, 1914 (*SP 1915*, No.28, p.156)

This case was tried in the Supreme Court at Medicine Hat, and Anderson was sentenced to death, 14th November [*1913*]. He was granted a new trial, and the jury brought in a verdict that Anderson was insane, and not fit to stand trial. He was sent to the Ponoka asylum.

VI-9 Murder of Old Tucker
Deane, Annual Report, 1911 (*SP 1912*, No.28, pp.35-42)

This was a case which taxed our resources to the utmost. I have never been connected with a case in which it was so difficult to procure evidence, as the sequel will show.

The murdered man himself wrapped up his business in impenetrable mystery. He was known to have a large sum of money — how much no one knew, but it consisted of a large roll of bills. He was scrupulously honest in his dealings and was well liked by his neighbours, who, however, knew very little about him. He was the personification of eccentricity. He would not entrust his money to a Bank, and no one knew where he kept it. I was able to find only one man who ever saw him with a roll of bills in his hand, and that on one occasion ... where he was making some small payment .... He was known to have at least one sister in England, but, after weeks of correspondence with English authorities, I failed to find her. He himself led his neighbours to believe that he was in process of selling his ranch and its belongings to a young Scotchman, and when he disappeared without having gone to bid his old-time neighbours good-bye, they thought it strange and unneighbourly, but put the omission down to eccentricity, and nothing was ever said to the Police about it.

His real name was A.J. Tucker Peach, but he was generally known as "Old Tucker" and comparatively few people knew that his name was Peach at all. The Postmaster at Gladys and John Fisk were two of the few.

On June 29, 1910, the headless trunk of a man was found in the Bow river where it had been washed by the current against a fallen tree. Part of the body which was out of the water was very much discoloured, and the whole of it was decomposed. A shirt and undershirt were on it, but these gave no clue to its identity. No one was known to be missing and Dr. Nyblett, Coroner, of Macleod, who was called to the spot issued his order for burial. The remains were buried on the river bank by two settlers.

In the month of November following a skull was found under the fallen tree previously mentioned, and near it, half buried in the sand and frozen stiff were a blanket, a cowhide and a piece of rope. The skull had a small clean hole in the centre of the forehead; a few iron grey hairs attached to it; a piece of cotton batting in one of the ears, and a slight dent, apparently the mark of an injury received many years previously during life time, which extended both ways across the forehead from the centre; some few teeth were also missing.

A few of the settlers in that neighbourhood, on being shown the skull, said from the first that it "looked like Old Tucker."

One settler remembered that some 25 years previously "Old Tucker" had been kicked in the forehead by a horse, and he had bound up his head for him. Another recalled that "Old Tucker" always wore cotton batting in one or both ears. A third judged from the shape of the skull and the iron grey hairs that it was "Old Tucker's" cranium that was presented to him.

The skull was sent for examination to Dr. Revell, Provincial Bacteriologist, at Edmonton. An inquest was called for November 29, at Okotoks, and the previously buried body was exhumed.

In the interim we searched high and low for Tucker Peach, of whose disappearance we now learnt for the first time.

A young man was then living on his ranch as caretaker for the young Scotchman who was said to have bought it, Thomas Mitchell Robertson. This latter young man was working as a brakesman on the C.P.R. between Medicine Hat and Calgary.

Robertson had left word with the Postmaster at Gladys to forward any mail matter for Tucker Peach to his Calgary address. On being served with a summons to attend the inquest at

Okotoks, Robertson told us that he had bought the Peach ranch of 160 acres for $26 per acre — half down — half payable in 12 months. He told us also that Peach went first to Carstairs and from there to England, whence he had written about his money. We had Robertson interviewed at various times and places, and on each occasion he told a somewhat different story to what he had previously told. We investigated each story as we received it, to find that it was founded on fiction, but we never said a word to let him think that we regarded him with suspicion.

On the day before the inquest Robertson left Calgary for the South, having stolen $90 from a fellow boarder, but, instead of leaving the train at Okotoks, he went on to Macleod, where he spent the afternoon in dissipation at a house of ill-fame. Towards evening he became the worse for liquor and said that he had stolen $75,000 in Alaska, that the police were after him, and that he wanted to catch the Spokane flier that night. The woman of the house communicated with the officer commanding the Mounted Police, and Robertson was taken into custody.[8] The summons to the inquest being found upon him, the Coroner was appealed to, and he issued a warrant under which Robertson was conducted to Okotoks next day.

The first witnesses called established the identity of the dead man to the satisfaction of the jury, and Dr. Revell, who had made a masterly examination of the skull, showed clearly the course which the bullet must have taken after entering the forehead to find an exit at the inner corner of the left eye. Dr. Revell repeated his story to two other juries, who unreservedly accepted his able exposition.

In the afternoon Robertson underwent a lengthy examination and his story then differed from any of his previous stories. He swore that he had bought two quarter sections from Tucker Peach, being 320 acres at $26 per acre, which price included 21 horses on the place. The purchase money to the extent of $5,000, had come to him by bank draft from Scotland to the Bank of

---

[8] Behind this sentence lay a serious rift that had taken place between Deane and his son-in-law, P.C.H. Primrose, the Commanding Officer of the Macleod Division. Deane was outraged that, according to him, Primrose failed to inform him about a pertinent piece of evidence in relation to the case. Correspondence on this matter and the case as a whole is contained in a massive file in NAC, RG18, 3238, HQ-681-K-3.

Montreal at Calgary, where he cashed it for notes and gold. He did not remember the respective amounts of each, and so the silly story went on until at last he was informed that Bank of Montreal officials could, and would, be called to contradict his statements in detail, and he was then asked by Inspector Duffus if he had any explanation to offer as to the conflict of evidence between himself and them. His reply was "Well I guess this isn't the place to say it. I do not wish to say anything further."

Inspector Duffus who was watching the case for the Mounted Police, and who did it very judgmatically, saw that the psychological moment had arrived — obtained the Coroner's permission to speak to the witness — asked Robertson if he had anything he would like to say to him privately, and, on an affirmative gesture, took him to another part of the house. There, in the presence of witnesses, having given the witness the full caution laid down in the Criminal Code, he wrote down Robertson's confession and asked him to sign it, which he did. The confession briefly set forth that ... Robertson and one John Fisk had murdered Tucker Peach in his own shack; that they had wrapped the body in the dead man's blanket and cowhide, and with his own horses and wagon, had driven it into the middle of the Bow river, and there dumped it into the stream.

It was after 10 o'clock that evening before I read and digested the reports made by Inspector Duffus, and there was no time to lose. John Fisk had recently left the Gladys district and gone to Carbon to the north-east of Calgary, where he had bought a livery stable. We had a detachment at Carbon, but for some reason or other the wires were down and we could not communicate with them quickly enough.

Soon after midnight on November 29, therefore, the most powerful motor that I could hire in Calgary, containing two non-commissioned officers, crept quietly out of the city on its 75 mile run to Carbon.

The men had positive orders to wait for the opening up of the stable in the morning, and to take Fisk while he was engaged in his daily routine, for he was well known to be a desperate man. The arrest was effected without difficulty, and the motor discharged its three passengers into Calgary Barracks by 1 p.m. of November 30. Five dollars per hour for thirteen hours paid the motorman's account.

Now that the two perpetrators of the murder were secured, there was obviously only one course to pursue to convict both men, namely: to use Robertson's evidence against Fisk, and Robertson's confession against himself.

Robertson never weakened in the stand he had taken. It was such a relief to him to have disburdened his guilty conscience that he became cheerful, and was not only willing but anxious to give us every assistance in his power.

Inspector Duffus, having been the recipient of his first confidence, was the only person allowed to talk to him, and any conversations were reduced to writing, and taken in the presence of the Provost, for my information.

After I had heard by wire from Sergt. Tucker[9] at Irricana that Fisk was in custody on November 30, Inspector Duffus had an interview with Robertson and the following is what he said — I give it in extenso in order to show how completely a man of weak mind may be dominated by a stronger will.

Thomas Mitchell Robertson states as follows: "The latter end of January, 1910, I was working down at Bob Begg's at the corner of the Bow and High [*presumably the river now called the Highwood*] rivers. One day — I don't remember the date or month — I think it was February last, Jack Fisk drove down with a team and box sleigh to Begg's place.

"Mrs. Begg, the two children and I were the only ones there. He sold her a washing machine and a couple of patent fasteners for horse collars he had with him. This was the first time I met Jack Fisk.

"About two or three weeks after this Old Man Tucker came down to the river at Mrs. Begg's for water. He said that Jack Fisk's pigs disturbed the water on the top of the hill and he couldn't drink it. He took a barrel of water with him with a team and wagon he had with him.

"I rode the range for Begg for about a month looking after his cattle and one day I rode over to Begg's gate at the north-east corner of his place, where I met Jack Fisk chasing his milk cows into Begg's place. I had some conversation with him about some horses. It was then that he told me that Old Man Tucker was

---

[9] It was a curious coincidence that Sgt. R.R. *Tucker* was involved in the investigation of the murder of *Tucker* Peach.

getting after him about some horses he (Tucker) had lost. He said Tucker was going to have him run in for stealing them. He said 'I'm scared the old man will get me into trouble' and as he (Tucker) had no friends and no relations and no one to take care of him, he thought it would be a good thing to get him out of the way. I said, 'if you have got his horses the old man is right and you should get into trouble.' He then said to me 'if you will help me get Peach out of the way you can have his land and I will take the horses as I want 'em.' I didn't say anything to this as I was scared. He then threatened me and said 'if you say anything about this I will put a shot into you.' I said nothing to nobody and rode home to Begg's, and he went on rolling his fall wheat. I used to meet him nearly every morning after this when I was riding. He would ask me what I thought of it, and if I had said anything to anyone. We discussed the thing on and off for about two months, until the last Saturday in April, 1910. I think it was Saturday when I came to Calgary about my job on the C.P.R. I stayed at the King Edward while at Calgary. Begg was in town and stopped at the Dominion I think. The two of us went home on Monday — this would be the beginning of May.

"That afternoon the team I was working got up in a bunch and got away from me. Mrs. Begg sent me on the top to look for them. While I was up on the hill I met Fisk when he began talking about getting rid of old Peach, and said then if I helped I could have the land and he would take the horses. He was to take them at any time he wanted them. I then agreed to help him.

"Two weeks after this I went into Calgary and started working on the C.P.R. as brakesman. I made a couple of trips and went out to Fisk's place the following Wednesday. Before going out to Fisk's I hired a rig from Frank Pashak, who runs a store at DeWinton. I told Pashak that I was going to drive to Tucker Peach's. When I got to Fisk's place he sent me to Tucker's shack about three or four hundred yards away. This was Thursday afternoon. I helped to clean his grain that afternoon and talked to him about selling his place and horses. He made out a memorandum on a sheet of paper, which is now at Medicine Hat in my box. The memorandum showed what he wanted for the horses, land, &c. I went back to Fisk's that night and slept there. Fisk and I agreed that night that we would kill Tucker Peach the next morning. He was to fire the first shot and I was to fire the second.

"He wanted me to fire the first one but I wouldn't.

"The next morning, Friday, the day of King Edward's funeral, about 6 o'clock, Fisk and I went to Peach's shack and tried to look in the window. We couldn't see anything as it was covered over with a tent. I knocked at his door and the old man called 'who is there' I said I was there, telling him my name. He opened the door. He had his drawers and shirt on, he sat down on his bed, which was on the floor and started to put on his trousers. Fisk then fired a shot at Peach with a revolver. Blood started to trickle down his face, at the same time he fell back. Fisk handed the revolver to me and told me to do the same. I took the revolver, pointed it at Peach and fired. I don't know whether I hit him or not, I was so excited, but I guess I did. Peach never spoke. He was dead after the shots. We both came out of the shack and looked around to see if anyone was there. There was no one in sight. We then hitched up Tucker's team and drove up to the door, rolled the body in some blankets and drove it down to the Bow river to Tucker's lower place. We drove into the river along the west fence or west side of his property and dumped the body into it. The blankets and cow robe which we rolled him into were tied around him.The river at this point runs east.

"From what I heard the body was found about a quarter of a mile from where we dumped it.

"After this I came into town but stayed at the Dunbow School Saturday night. I told some of them there that I had bought the place. The team I took in were Peach's. I sold them to the Alberta barn for $200 and put the money in the savings Bank of Montreal. I was to give Fisk any money that he needed. I gave him two payments, one of $50 and one of $30. The amounts show in my pass book in Medicine Hat.

"I went back to the ranch in about two weeks. I saw Earny Adams there and he told me that Fisk had been looking after the horses, and that four two year old horses were missing. Adams told me he thought Fisk had stolen them. I didn't say anything. Shortly after this the body was found. Fisk I think was living on his place, but shortly after this left for Carbon. Shortly before the body was found I brought one of Peach's horses to town and traded it for one belonging to Mr. Gilmore, the plumber, of 827, 5th Avenue, west. I sold the horse I got from him to a grocer, who has a store east of the post office, for $18; the grocer is just east of the Queen's Hotel. I gave him a bill of sale. I sold a stud about two weeks ago. My cousin sold it for me. My cousin is E. Davis and is looking after the place for me. He knows nothing about this affair.

"Fisk threw the revolver we shot Peach with into the middle of the river. When I speak of Tucker I mean Tucker Peach."

... Our next steps were to obtain some corroboration of Robertson's story.

I sent him with Inspector Duffus and others in a motor to try to find the revolver with which the murder had been committed. The days were short, and the distance from here was about 25 miles, and nothing but a motor could cover the ground. Slush ice was found to be running down the river, the water was up to a man's middle and cold, Robertson could not tell within a hundred yards where the pistol had been thrown into the river, and the party returned to Calgary, without having accomplished anything in the way of corroboration.

It was, of course, incumbent upon us to corroborate Robertson's story ... so far as we could, but for the information of my confrères, who may be confronted with similar cases, I think it worth while to reproduce for their benefit the dictum of the Lord Chief Justice of England upon this matter. It formed the subject of a conversation between the President of the Parnell Commission and Sir Henry James on November 13, 1889, and I quote the conversation as reported in the *Weekly Times* of November 14, 1889; I cut out this extract at the time it appeared and pasted it in my Text book.[10] It read as follows:

---

[10] While this text has not come to light, the reference demonstrates the interest and care that Deane took in legal matters. The expertise he developed enabled him to prepare a constables' manual for the Mounties in the 1880s (see NAC, RG18, 32, 217-89), but it also made him rather opinionated about judicial decisions. Even within the force, his knowledge of English military and legal practices and precedents was not always well-received. In reprimanding Deane in January 1910, the Comptroller ordered the Commissioner to "call Supt. Deane's attention to the fact that the R.N.W. Mounted Police Force is not governed by Imperial Regulations — either Naval or Military ...." (see White to Perry, 5 January 1910, in NAC, RG18, 390, 238-10).

Sir HENRY JAMES: "I submit to you that even if there were no corroboration of Manion's testimony his evidence should not be struck out on the ground that this principle of law which requires corroboration of the evidence of an accomplice does not apply in this case."

The PRESIDENT: "I rather regard it as a doctrine of expediency and prudence than a principle of law. Juries are strongly recommended not to act upon the uncorroborated evidence of an accomplice, but it has never been a rule of law. I may add that the corroboration required is only of the surrounding circumstances so as to lead up to a general presumption as to the truth of the evidence. *It would be an absurdity* [*Deane's emphasis*] to say ... that no evidence of an accomplice can be received unless corroborated by other independent testimony, because then there would be no need of an accomplice's evidence."

In order to test the accuracy of Robertson's statement the services of Dr. Revell were again called in.

He spent several hours with the evil-smelling corpse and the thoroughness of his examination was manifested when he reported: "In the left side of the body about midway between the front and the back, and just over the 8th rib, there was a 32 calibre bullet embedded. In the shirts that were on the body when found there are holes corresponding in situation to the situation of the bullet." Adhering to the bullet he found minute particles of the underclothing through which it had passed, and a single red fibre from the blanket where it had passed through a stripe. From the position of the bullet the doctor was inclined to think that it was a ricochet, and a visit was paid to the Tucker Peach shack for further examination. We had already examined this shack once and found that it had been thoroughly ransacked, evidently in search for the money (variously estimated at from $1,200 to $1,500), which the dead man was known to have possessed. On this second visit, Dr. Revell and his associate non-commissioned officer found an indentation in the floor close under the bed which accounted for the upward turn of the bullet. The bed itself consisted of nothing more than a few gunny sacks filled with hay. We tried in vain to account for the dead man's money — the person who should have told us about it rigidly held his peace until after John Fisk had been convicted.

He then permitted himself to say that on August 25, 1910, he had met Fisk at DeWinton, and had had supper with him at the Minto House. He saw Fisk pay for a twenty-five cent supper with a ten dollar bill, which he drew from a large roll of bills which he had in his hand. He was surprised to see so much money as Fisk was generally impecunious. This information did not come to my knowledge until last April, and was given in evidence against Robertson, as it was advisable that the Department of Justice should know it.

That incident is a fair sample of the difficulty we experienced in collecting evidence. John Fisk seemed to have terrorized the entire neighbourhood. It was no uncommon thing to hear a witness say "If Fisk gets off I shall have to quit the country."

It was some time before I could obtain corroboration of Robertson's story as to the conveying of the body to the river, but it presently transpired that a settler named Robert Jones, who lived between Tucker Peach and the river, with an Indian boy, was working at a fence on his quarter section when the funeral procession passed. Both he and the boy recognized the Tucker Peach team and wagon, saw John Fisk, in a Khaki coloured shirt, driving on the front seat, with a person whom they took to be Robertson in the rear part of the wagon.

A bitter controversy raged over this testimony and desperate attempts were made by the defence to shake it. One witness went the length of deposing on oath that, on a particular Sunday after Church service, he had a conversation with Robert Jones who told him that he had not seen the team and wagon on the road to the river.

This evidence was offset by Constable Crane who swore that on the Sunday in question he spent the forenoon with Robert Jones and that Jones did not go to church at all. It came out later, after Fisk had been hanged, that another settler and his daughter saw the team and wagon as described by Jones and the Indian boy but refrained from saying a word about it for fear of Fisk's vengeance. Both father and daughter had given valuable testimony but suppressed this important little item. After sentence of death had been carried out, as I have said, the father met a juryman at High River and said "Your conscience may be quite clear about the verdict you gave — John Fisk was guilty all right." He then in the roundabout way affected by the denizens of the Western States intimated that he and his daughter had seen the outfit, and what Jones and the boy had said was true.

Robertson was mistaken in telling us that the murder was committed on the day of the late King's funeral.

It doubtless would have taken place on that day but for the circumstance that, when Fisk looked round in the morning, he saw Ernest Adams, Tucker Peach's nearest neighbour, moving about on a hill which commanded a view of Peach's house, and his attention would doubtless have been attracted by any shots fired then.

That afternoon Robertson spent with Tucker Peach, at Fisk's suggestion. He helped him fan some barley which he had contracted to sell for seed, and to fan which the old man had borrowed Adam's fanning mill. In the course of the afternoon a hired man arrived with team and wagon to fetch the barley for the purchaser, and waited while the fanning was completed by Peach and Robertson. Adams had deposed that his fanning mill was returned to him by Peach at dinner time, (mid-day). Whereas Robertson had said that it was not returned until the evening. The advent of the teamster in the afternoon settled this question in Robertson's favour. He also learnt from Tucker Peach himself that he was making arrangements to sell his place to the young man who was then helping him.

The trial of John Fisk beginning on February 21, lasted for 10 days, and 41 witnesses were examined.

The verdict was "Guilty — with a recommendation to mercy." This was to solve the susceptibilities of a juryman who was not in favour of capital punishment, and who required that concession. Fisk was executed in the prison yard here on June 27 last.

Robertson's trial began on May 16 and continued for 4 days — 43 witnesses being examined for the Crown and 6 for the defence. He was found guilty with a strong recommendation to mercy, and personally I was glad when his death sentence was commuted to life imprisonment. He is certainly not a desirable young man to have at large.

C. Decline of the West

Mounting levels of crime prompted Deane's conviction that the Canadian West was a society in decline, if not hurtling into the abyss. In part, this reflected Deane's personal disillusionment as he suffered one slight after another within the force itself. On top of that, his second wife, whom he had wooed with such ardor and determination, was dying. But Deane would hardly have thought that his perspective on western Canada was a mere figment of his cynicism and anxiety. To Deane the evidence of the degradation of society was all around, from the success of demagoguery in the 1911 election which resulted in the defeat of Charles Magrath, his old Conservative friend from Lethbridge days, to the "sweetheart" sale of the Calgary barracks to railway interests by the new Tory Government, to an increase of juvenile delinquency, to abominable assaults on children. Settlement may have brought a measure of prosperity, but, as far as Deane could see, it also brought in hordes of undesirables who were neither Anglo-Canadians nor British. Deane had always been a British imperialist; a belief in the racial superiority of Anglos was an object of faith for him. But like many other Anglos both within and outside Canada in the years just before the First World War, he feared race degeneration. Moreover, he believed that many of the social problems that had emerged could be attributed to the increasingly weakened grip that Anglos held on society. Certainly, he saw the decline of western Canada as part of this process. While Deane was entitled to his political views and his concerns about law enforcement, he was incorrect if he thought that white anglophones no longer dominated western Canada, and his memory was faulty if he believed that depravity and brutality, even towards children, had not existed earlier in his career as an officer. Be that as it may, Deane was outraged by what he saw occurring about him.

VI-10 "Abominable Fools"
Deane to C. Magrath, 30 September 1911 (NAC, Charles Magrath Papers, MG30 E82, 4, 11)

I have been wondering where a letter would find you and have recently seen in some papers that you have left Medicine Hat for Ottawa.

Three Staunch Conservatives: Borden, Bennett, and Deane
NAC, detail of C38719

In all likelihood, this photograph was taken on 26 July 1911 during the Calgary stop of Robert Borden's pre-election tour of the Prairies. The balding Bennett was an MLA at the time but became the victorious Tory candidate for Calgary East in the federal election later that year and, of course, also became a Prime Minister of Canada. As for Deane, he asserted that he was an ardent Conservative. But the Conservative meeting which drew some five thousand persons demonstrated that his loyalty to the party had definite limits. The problem was the proposed sale of the Calgary barracks. Grand Trunk Pacific authorities were surprised that Laurier had been unwilling to turn over the thirty-five acres on which the barracks were situated for a pittance and had set the selling price at one million dollars. Deane concurred with this valuation if, indeed, it made sense to part with the land at all. At the political gathering of 1911, however, the sitting member for Calgary, a Conservative, took the partisan anti-Government position that the asking price was highway robbery and suggested the property was worth about $150 thousand. At this point, Deane and his wife became so disgusted that they abandoned their seats on the platform, no less, and went home. But, within three years, the railway syndicate took over the property for $250 thousand, and Deane and his ailing wife had to leave their spendid house behind. He gained a small measure of revenge by digging up his prize caragana hedge and giving it to a friend. This action left the solicitor for the railway spluttering in impotent protest.

I am very, very sorry for the unfortunate result of your election contest. I was loath to believe that intelligent people could be such abominable fools as to swallow the rubbish that the reciprocity agents told them. For one thing, I confidently looked forward to seeing you Minister of the Interior, and was thus disappointed as well as disgusted. However, I hope yet to see you in the Office Chair. What a terrible district you had to cover — I did not realize it until I asked my man at Carbon, who happened to be in here temporarily, who the conservative candidate was.

The result in Alberta and Saskatchewan just shows what a miserable class of American immigrant we are getting. Mr. Wm. Taft's ears must be tingling still!

With kind regards to Mrs. Magrath and deepseated hope for better luck next time.

VI-11 Boys In Trouble[11]
Deane, Annual Report, 1911 (*SP 1912*, No.28, pp.44-45)

Boy, Norman Rivers was sentenced to two years at Portage la Prairie Industrial School by Judge Carpenter on January 27, 1911, for housebreaking and theft.

Boy, George Pruitt, who escaped from the Children's Shelter at Edmonton was taken to the Portage la Prairie Industrial School on February 27, 1911, by order of R.B. Chadwick, superintendent of neglected children.

Boy, Leighton Rollinson, who escaped from the Children's Aid Society's Home in Calgary, was taken to Portage la Prairie Industrial School by order of R.B. Chadwick ....

Boy, Leonard McIntosh, was sent to Portage la Prairie Industrial School for an indefinite term by R.B. Chadwick ....

Boy, Earl Russell, was taken to Portage la Prairie Industrial School on August 3, 1911, having been sentenced to three years by Judge Winter at Calgary.

---

[11] As in Document V-11, pseudonyms have been provided for these cases involving youth offenders who were born after 1893.

VI-12 Child Molestation
Deane, "Tampering with young children," [c.1914] (GA, M6017)

At the Assizes for the Calgary Judicial District which opened at Calgary on the 21st October, 1913, there was set down for trial an unusually long docket comprising 41 cases, and of these no less than 11 involved carnal knowledge of young children. At the opening of the Court the presiding Judge commented upon this extraordinary circumstance. Large as was the number of cases for trial, it did not cover all the complaints of a like nature which had been made since the previous Assizes, for I investigated at least two others, besides a third very bad instance of juvenile depravity which would have gone into Court had not the girl's mother, whose own chastity was said to be questionable, carried her daughter off into the United States and remained there, so that it was impossible for us to put the girl in the witness box.

This is a very real danger with which Western Canada is confronted, and the indications are that it is likely to grow worse instead of better.

I am moved to these reflections by the following clippings from the Calgary *Daily Herald* ... which may speak for themselves:[12]

[Herald] 30th October, 1913.
"MARTIN IS FOUND GUILTY ON CHARGE"
Jury brings in recommendation of Leniency on behalf of Moral Reprobate

"Lewis V. Martin was found guilty in the criminal assize court yesterday afternoon of committing an indecent assault upon two little girls, aged ten and twelve respectively, with a rider, 'with a recommendation to leniency.'

"Mr. Justice Walsh seemed evidently surprised when the foreman added the recommendation to the verdict, and there

---

[12] The original reports in the *Herald* are quoted throughout Document VI-12, rather than the abbreviated versions, in which names were deleted that appeared in Deane's manuscript. A report in the *Herald* of 29 October gave a summary report of the case, but had been so vague on details that one does not know what transpired.

were murmurs of surprise and disapprobation when the foreman made this announcement.

"'Upon what grounds is your recommendation based?' asked
Mr. Justice Walsh.

"'Oh!' casually replied E.D. Benson, the foreman, 'on the
grounds of former good character.'"

Judge Postpones Sentence

"After this bombshell had exploded in the Courtroom, his
lordship gave the matter a few moments' thought, and said that,
owing to the recommendation of the jury, he would postpone
sentence.

"The accused was then removed to the Barracks, and will
come up for sentence at some future date.

"The following composed the jury: E.D. Benson, foreman; T.
Vanderlinden, Fred Gee, Alf. J. Bartle, T.W. Gravelle, and
Thomas Copeland.

"Mr. Justice Walsh charged strongly against the accused,
who was ably defended by J. McKinley Cameron."

[Herald] 31st October, 1913.

"Lewis V. Martin, who yesterday afternoon had been found
guilty of committing an indecent assault upon two little girls,
aged 10 and 12 years respectively, was sentenced to two months
in the guardroom at the R.N.W.M.P. barracks.

"When Martin stood up in the dock, James Short, K.C.,
crown prosecutor said that the family of the accused was emi-
nently respectable and he had known the accused himself for
some time, and therefore felt more pity and sympathy for him
than he might otherwise have done. The crown prosecutor thought
that a short sentence would do the prisoner as much good as a
long sentence and would give him an opportunity to lead a good
life and become a useful citizen."

Martin Sent Down

"Mr. Justice Walsh, addressing the prisoner remarked that
the jury had recommended him to leniency for the reason that
he had always borne a good character and a man's good character should always stand him in good stead in his hour of trouble.
His lordship believed the prisoner had no other intention but to
have a game with the two little girls and although he had it in
his power to seriously injure the two girls he had not thus

injured them though what he had done was very wrong.

"'I take into consideration,' said Mr. Justice Walsh, 'the fact that you have already been in jail for two months awaiting your trial and I have been told that you are not a strong man physically and have a mother entirely dependent upon you for her support.'

"'I fear,' said his lordship, 'that the public, who do not understand all the facts of the case, will think it an insufficient punishment for the crime which you have committed. People who do not fully understand ... all the circumstances of a case are too ready to criticize the verdict or the sentence and I endeavor to do my duty to the public and to the state.'

"Martin was then sentenced to two months confinement in the guardroom at the mounted police barracks.

"'I am sure that this will be a lesson to you for the rest of your life,' remarked Mr. Justice Walsh, as the prisoner was removed from the dock."

It is devoutly to be hoped that the Judge's pious wish with regard to the prisoner may be realized, as it may also be charitable to assume that the recommendation to mercy of the jury and the Crown Prosecutor was justified by the circumstances of the case. The chief consideration was that the prisoner was the sole support of an aged mother.

But what about the little girls? Who can tell what effect the experience which they went through may have upon their future lives? Their innate sense of modesty must at least have received a rude shock from the bare necessity of having to go into Court and to tell their story before a Court composed exclusively of men. What may have been "a game" to the man was not a proper "game" for little girls to play.

I turn now to ... [*the Dionne*] case which had been previously tried at the selfsame Assizes; it was a case wherein a man of French Canadian extraction was tried for the murder of a little girl between five and six years of age on the 5th May, 1913, in his shack at Riverside, one of the many suburbs of Calgary.

After murdering the child by almost severing the head from her body, he threw the corpse into the cellar. In the meantime, the mother had missed the little girl and was looking for her. As she approached the murderer's shack the man ran out; the woman noticed blood on his hands, and gave the alarm. A crowd soon collected, and he was taken into custody. He was brought up for trial on the 22nd June and, at the request of his Counsel, the trial was postponed until the October Session of the Court.

I merely mention these dates to show that we had this man in custody and under close supervision for more than five months. If any symptoms of insanity had manifested themselves during that time, is it probable that they would have escaped the observation of the Guard Room staff and the visiting Surgeon? I trow [*think*] not.

The trial opened on the 21st October, and, on the following day, the Defence placed in the witness box a medical man who was Inspector of Prisons and Asylums in Ontario. This gentleman had had only two conversations with the prisoner, (the latter during the luncheon hour adjournment of the second day) and swore that he had examined the prisoner[,] that he found him to be a sadist, that is a "sexual pervert," and that, at the time he committed the crime, he was not responsible for his act.

In rebuttal of this evidence the Crown called two Calgary doctors, both of whom, in the capacity of gaol surgeon, had had the prisoner under observation, and each of them swore that he had found no symptoms of insanity about the man. The prison officials could have given details of the prisoner's daily life for five months if they had been placed in the witness box, which they were not.

After a retirement of three hours, the jury brought in a verdict of "Not guilty, owing to Insanity," and the Judge remanded the prisoner to custody in the Guard Room to await the pleasure of the Lieutenant Governor.

A few days later I required the cell, which had been occupied by this innocent man, for the accommodation of another murderer who was condemned, and had a telephonic conversation thereanent with the Deputy Attorney General at Edmonton.

He began by suggesting that proceedings should be initiated under the Provincial Insanity Act with a view to having the so-called lunatic committed to the Asylum, but I replied to this effect: "I do not know of anybody here who will swear that this man is insane — the doctors will not — the Guard Room officials will not — and if, after one tribunal has declared the man to be insane, another should find him to be in full possession of his senses, won't you be in rather an awkward predicament?" He admitted that it would be so, and added, "If that jury had only found him guilty of manslaughter, we could have sent him to the Penitentiary, which we cannot do now." I re-iterated "If I were you, I should take no chances with the Insanity Act." "All right" he replied "If you will send him to the Asylum I will give orders there for his admission."

So it was, and, after this long preamble, I come now to the burden of my song.

For some time past gradually, but very surely, the conviction has been growing in my mind that the law should make some special provision for the class of offence which is comprehended in this chapter. For instance, the so-called insanity expert told the jury that the murderer's sexual perversion had been brought about by a long course of self-abuse, and that, in consequence of this self-inflicted infirmity, he was not responsible for his crime.

If that be so I held that, in the interests of society, no less than in the interests of the individual himself, the law should provide that where a male person has been convicted of such a crime as debauching girls of tender age, he should be for ever after rendered incapable of repeating the offence. Two snicks of the surgeon's knife under a local anaesthetic will sever the spermatic cord, leave no disfigurement behind, give the Criminal a chance of repairing the damage he has done to himself, and effectually protect the female section of society at large.[13] The infliction of this penalty should be made obligatory on conviction, and should not be left to the discretion of a Court, whether or not any other punishment be inflicted ....

I had written this much when, on the 11th November, 1913, the following letter appeared in the Calgary *Daily Herald* ....

"REPLY TO 'COSMOPOLITE'"

Editor, The Herald: "I am sorry to have kept my friend "Cosmopolite" waiting so long for an answer to his letter of the 28th ult. Being a woman, I like to have the proverbial last word, and, as the delay was quite unavoidable, I hope it will be pardoned.

---

[13] Deane was talking about what would now be called a vasectomy. His belief that the operation would prevent violence against women and children shows a misunderstanding of sexual assault. But he was not unusual in his thinking. Many physicians, perhaps even Deane's son, held the same view.

"In the first place I want to make myself a little clearer. I am not criticising any special court, judge nor jury, nor have I any personal prejudice whatever against any criminal in particular.

"My complaint is that while a man who steals a horse, a purse, or an overcoat is dealt a sharp, clear sentence, a man who commits an unspeakable offence against some little girl receives clemency.

"About a year ago a country school teacher, in Manitoba, was fined some three hundred dollars for assaulting several of his little girl pupils, all under fourteen years of age. His fine made an average of thirty dollars apiece for the little girls in question.

"What mother ever lived who valued her little girl's virtue at thirty dollars?

"You and I, no matter who we are, have no reason to believe that our little girls are safe, simply because they are ours.

"Money is powerful, but it is an uncertain commodity — here to-day and gone to-morrow. And none of us have any guarantee that we will live to protect our children until they reach years of discretion.

"We are told that 'women receive fair treatment in the criminal code.' That sounds good, but we, who are mere onlookers, read reports of a youth who stole thirty dollars receiving a six months' sentence, while a man who assaulted two little girls, twelve and fourteen years of age, received two months in the Barracks guard-room.

"A man who stole a ring, a mere glittering bauble, receives three years' hard labour, while a man who treated his own daughter, just sixteen years of age, in an unthinkable manner, is allowed to go free, with the threat that, 'if he does not behave himself he will probably (please note that word probably) spend the next two years in jail.'

"Two men who stole twenty-eight dollars from a friend were sentenced to two years in the penitentiary, while a Chinaman, accused of assaulting a little girl fourteen years old, was dismissed because 'the evidence was not of a very convincing order.' One wonders just how convincing evidence must be. Certainly no man is going to call in witnesses when he commits such a dastardly deed.

"I quote these cases because they are all fresh in the public mind, and they make us wonder why this deranged sense of values.

"Yet, if we criticize the verdicts, we are told that we do not understand the case.

"I, for one, frankly confess that I do not understand.

"Mercy?

"Yes. But there is a time when mercy ceases to be a virtue ....

"In closing, I want to make an appeal to you good men of Canada. You do not want us to follow the example of the women in the mother land, and start throwing bricks through your office windows, do you?

"Well, we don't want to do it. But we do want justice and protection for our children. It is 'up to you'."

ELIZABETH FORDMAN

"(Note: 'The Herald has already announced that it would print no more letters on the Dionne case. As the writer of the above communication started the correspondence, The Herald thought it was only fair that she should be allowed to conclude it, so that her letter will be absolutely the last on the subject to find its way into the columns of this paper. In order to further clear the matter up and to prevent any misconceptions, The Herald would point out that Dionne's victim was not outraged before being murdered. The case was purely one of murder, as the little girl was not assaulted in any manner.' — Editor, The Herald.)"

The Editor was strictly correct in saying that the "victim was not outraged before being murdered," but the expert who procured the murderer's acquittal told the Court that the murderer had told him that he had lured the child into his shack for the express purpose of violating her, but that she had made such an outcry that he savagely cut her throat with a razor, and threw the body into his cellar through a trapdoor.

That seems to have been the one solitary act which constituted his insanity, for his neighbours, among whom he had lived for some time, say to-day that they had never observed any symptoms to lead them to think that he was not as sane as the best of them.

The author of the foregoing letter says "It is up to you, men, to provide justice and protection for our children," and unquestionably so it should have been, but the men have failed to make adequate provision to protect the purity of the future mothers of the race, and now it is "up to" the women to see to the matter themselves.

They should agitate for the vote and get it, and when they have got it, they should use it.

They should insist upon the law being amended to the extent even of providing that in such cases as are now under discussion, half of the jury should be composed of women.

They will then be able to off-set this foreign vote from the cock-pit of Europe which is flooding the prairie provinces. It was in the month of November, 1913, that the City of Calgary Police Magistrate said to a witness in his Court: "Do you mean to tell me that you have been in this country for three years, and have not learned to understand and speak our language?"

That man, notwithstanding that he will know nothing of the points at issue, will nevertheless cast his vote at future elections at the behest of whichever political party happens to have control of him.

On Sunday the 28th December, 1913, the Reverend Doctor Kirby, preaching in the Wesley Methodist Church at Calgary, told his congregation that there were then "two thousand Ruthenians [*Ukrainians*] in Calgary whose religion was marked by deep superstition, and who were a menace to the city until such time as they were shown the error of their ways." He contended that the Ruthenians should not be allowed to come into Canada until they could qualify as good citizens.

"Do you know" he asked (*The Western Standard* - 28 Dec. 1913) "that there is a greater immigration into Canada of foreigners in proportion to the population than there is into the United States? The republic to the south has been experiencing trouble, serious trouble, because it has permitted the entry of these foreigners, and it is putting up the bars. But we have to face the problem as it exists in Calgary, and I must tell you that it is serious."

This doctrine that I am inculcating is no new thing in the Western Hemisphere. It is been openly discussed in the United States press with a view to placing some restriction upon the prop[a]gation of undesirable citizens in the criminal and degenerate classes. I am not disposed to go as far as some of the propositions which I have seen in print but I have very strongly the conviction that a man who is proved to have defiled one little girl should by process of law be incapacitated from ever defiling another.

The following clipping which I take from the *Morning Albertan*, of Calgary, of the 10th January, 1914, goes to show that the punishment does not always fit the crime even when a conviction is obtained:

"WHITE SLAVERS GET SHORT SENTENCE IN THIS CITY"

"On the charge of procuring a 14 year old girl for immoral purposes, Charles Pace and Sam Ouiche were sentenced to a year's imprisonment at the city police court yesterday afternoon. They induced the girl to run away from the Social Service home last Sunday night. They were also fined $20 and costs for an infraction of the children's protective act in connection with the same occurrence.

"Pace was released a short time ago from the barracks where he served three months for conducting a disorderly house."

D. Absurdities of the Moral Reformers

While Deane worried about the decline of western Canadian society, he placed little faith in the efforts of the moral reformers. They were just too foolish and hypocritical to suit the old officer who thought he had seen and heard everything and still considered that he knew everything. As ever, Deane was particularly critical of those crusading ministers who implied that the Mounties winked at violations of laws relating to morality. From Deane's perspective, not only did those clergymen fail to understand the impossibility of changing human nature and the difficulty of getting convictions on morals cases that were brought before the judiciary, but also they were frequently mere do-gooders and busy-bodies whose clerical garb was simply a disguise for intolerance and ignorance. Whether in responding to the interfering Presbyterian missionary John Templeton, or in discussing the operation of the Lord's Day Act, or in recounting the story of a woman who starved herself after hearing the order of God, Deane was barely able to avoid expressing his contempt for the views of the ultra-Christians. But it was not just the ministers who needed educating. Before anyone embarked on wild schemes to reform society, such as the prohibition of alcohol, the voice of experience

— the voice of a Mounted Police officer of three decades' standing, for instance — needed to be heard.

VI-13 Complaint About Liquor Offences and Sunday Baseball
The Rev. John Templeton to Deane, 27 July 1911 (NAC, RG18, 1663, 131/7-11)

I am writing you desirous of your help in a matter that your officers in this district seem to ignore.

On 1st July, celebrations were held at Steveville on the Red Deer River, where intoxicating liquors were sold, (as far as I know there was no license). The Officers were not present but the knowledge of this liquor selling is common property and as yet they are making no movement to secure punishment for the offending parties.

I have also to complain of gross slackness in the Brooks district where it is customary for the Brooks Baseball Team to play ball on Sabbaths. I am sure that the "Lord's Day Act" gives no liberty for such proceedings and I wish you to use your influence and have this sort of thing stopped. One of my members of my congregation told me that this has gone on for several months and he himself has seen it on several occasions when staying over week-ends at Brooks.

I know that your men are kept busy but such gross contempt of law cannot be tolerated and I am determined that if this note does not secure your prompt attention to this matter that I will carry the matter to the Supreme Officer in Charge before I am finished with it.

I am confident that this will not be necessary and I thank you in anticipation for your consideration and help.

Deane to Templeton, 7 August 1911 (NAC, RG18, 1663, 131/7-11)

I beg to acknowledge the receipt of your letter of the 27th July last, this date received, and to say that the Mounted Police have nothing to do with the enforcement of the Liquor License Law. You should apply to the Chief License Inspector, Edmonton.

With regard to the playing of baseball at Brooks on Sundays, there is nothing in the Lord's Day Act to forbid such playing, unless the game is played for gain, or a prize, or for reward.

I am forwarding a copy of this correspondence to the Office of the Commissioner, R.N.W.M.P., Regina, Sask., and to the Deputy Attorney General, Edmonton, so that those Departments may be prepared for any representations that you may wish to make to them.

VI-14 The Lord's Day Act and the "Fancy Religions"
Deane, "A Hallowe'en Prank," [c.1914] (GA, M313, pp.6-9)

It happened ... [*in autumn 1912*] that we found ourselves between the devil and the deep sea. The Lord's Day Act had been placed in the Statute Book through the efforts of the Moral and Reform League .... The most active, in fact, so far as my experience went, the only active members of this league were the ministers of the various fancy religions. Perhaps I had better explain that term. In the early days at Regina we had a sergeant major, who had been trained in the 12th Royal Lancers, and in superintending the falling in of the Church Parade (if we had any), he used to command "Church of England on the right" - "Roman Catholics on the left" - "Fancy religions in the centre". The "Fancy Religions" included Presbyterians, Baptists, Unitarians, Methodists, Mormons, Seventh Day Adventists, Congregationalists, *et hoc genus omne* [*all persons of that classification*]. It happened that near a place called Strathmore Sunday threshing had been the rule rather than the exception. One very prominent offender used to plough also. Some of the "Fancy Religion" ministers wanted to have this stopped and instead of communicating with the Attorney General, or even with me, they worried a young constable, who was there stationed, until he went out and told one of the farmers to stop working. He had no right to do this, and should have applied to me for instructions.[14] The farmer in question enlisted the sympathies of a

---

[14] Deane held that no Mounted Policeman could order anyone to stop threshing on a Sunday and that offenders could not even be prosecuted without the consent of the Attorney General, to whom all the circumstances had to be reported before any action could be taken (see Deane to Const. Todd, 21 November 1912, one of the numerous items related to the case filed in NAC, RG18, 430, 539-12).

Calgary newspaper, which printed a paragraph to the effect that the Mounted Police were forbidding Sunday threshing. This paragraph was repeated all over the country, and I was called upon from Ottawa for a telegraphic report on the subject. I simply replied that I had no knowledge of any of the circumstances referred to.

Some few days later the constable in question reported what he had done, and why .... Just then the Field Secretary of the Moral and Reform League wrote to ask what instructions had been given to detachments with regard to the enforcement of this Act. I replied that the language of the Act was so plain that no special instructions were given or required. He then wanted to know whether constables had been instructed not to lay complaints themselves, but to wait for others to do it. I said "No" — they had been given no orders on the subject. So far as my division was concerned, I expected every man to give himself and his horse a rest, and to go to church on the Sabbath Day. I added that a constable was under no necessity to ride about the country on that day prying into his neighbours' affairs, as it was open to anyone whose conscience might be offended by a neighbour's disregard of the Sabbath, to bring the matter to the notice of the Attorney General.

I did recommend that the principal offender at Strathmore, who had defied the law in such a high-handed manner, should be prosecuted, but the Liberal Government of the Province was in too unstable a position to warrant the possible alienation of any votes, and I never received even the passing civility of a reply.

For all practical purposes the "Lord's Day Act" might as well be repealed. I remember one occasion on which a curate of the Church of England transmitted to me a complaint made to him by a female parishioner that a neighbour of hers would persist in working on Sunday. I enquired into the complaint, and found that the offender was a Seventh Day Adventist, who religiously observed his own Sabbath Day, but contended that he was entitled to work for six days out of the seven, and that as long as the railways were permitted to run on Sundays he intended to continue working. I submitted all the facts to the Attorney General, who said he would issue a fiat if I would ask for it. I replied that I had formed the impression that the man was being persecuted by a quarrelsome neighbour, who had not sufficient business of her own to mind, and I thought prosecution was quite unnecessary. In addition to that I quite agreed with the farmer about the Railways. The Police Barracks at Calgary were situated on a plot of about 35 acres within about 300 yards of the Canadian Pacific yards, and their engines made day and night hideous with the unnecessary noises they used to make. No one in the City suffered from the annoyance as we did. The "Lord's Day Act" came into force on the 1st March 1907, and, for a time, the railway people were very quiet on Sundays. They did not quite know what to expect — it remained to be seen whether or not the Mounted Police would take notes and numbers of their engines working, or whether the Reform League would have something to say. So far as the latter was concerned the Railway authorities always selected as General Superintendent of the Western Division a Methodist of the most pronounced type, and with him the League took good care not to quarrel. As time went on and no question was raised Sunday in the Canadian Pacific yards became just as busy a day as any other day of the week.

VI-15 Fasting to Death
Deane, Annual Report, 1913 (*SP 1914*, No.28, pp.52-53)

Rex vs. A.H. Irvine - Manslaughter. - We had rather an extraordinary experience last December of a faith of which I then heard for the first time called the Apostolic or Pentecostal faith. Divine healing is one of the articles of this faith, which is not to be confounded with Christian Science.

Dr. Costello, coroner, informed us on the 12th December that some suspicious circumstances in connection with the death of two persons in the family of one Irvine, living some ten miles north of Calgary, required investigation, and Sergeant Major Vickery accompanied the doctor to the house in question.

There were two rooms upstairs: on a bed in one of them lay the dead body of Mrs. Irvine, fully dressed, and on the bed in the other room, wrapped in a sheet, lay the dead body of a child, badly decomposed. Irvine and his sister-in-law and two young children, 3 and 4 years old respectively, were the other occupants of the house, and must have shared these beds between them.

At the inquest, the doctor who examined the body said that death was due to starvation.

The deceased woman's husband said that the child died on the 15th October, and that his wife believed that the Lord had told her to sanctify a fast. It seems that the child was born in the middle of August. The father said: "The child was dead five or six weeks before my wife received instructions to fast right steady, but she fasted a little before that; dropped a meal or so at a time .... I did not report the death as we expected the child to be raised, and spent the time praying. It never struck me that it was against the law to keep a body so long without reporting .... I did not think anything about it .... I cannot tell how the Lord communicated with my wife."

The dead woman's sister said that for the last two weeks they went without food or drink and she did not break her fast until after her sister had died. She testified that she had heard Mr. Irvine at times protest against the fasting. She told the coroner's jury that the child was a very strong boy and was sick for only one day before he died. He had diarrhoea. They did not think of getting a doctor as they believed in Divine healing and prayed over him. They did not bury the body as they believed that the Lord was going to raise him.

The jury found that the woman died as a result of voluntary starvation, and that her husband was guilty of negligence in permitting his wife to conceal the death of his son, and in permitting her to inflict upon herself such privations as would, by the law of nature, cause death.

A charge of manslaughter against the husband was heard before the Hon. Mr. Justice Stuart on the 26th February last and a verdict of not guilty was returned. The evidence had shown that, while the man had tolerated his wife's conduct, he had not encouraged it. From the religious standpoint he considered himself the weaker vessel, and was not in the same class as the two prospective saints, namely, his wife and her sister.

The judge advised the man to get someone to teach him a little common sense and to forget his pronounced religious views.

VI-16 Abolish the Bar, Madame Alberta
Deane, Untitled Manuscript [c.1914] (GA, M6017)

At about the dawn of the year 1914 an agitation was set on foot with the ultimate object of abolishing the bar-room or saloon.

In January of that year a deputation, with identical views, interviewed the Premier of the Province of Manitoba [*Sir Rodmond Roblin*], but he distinctly disagreed with them as to the advisability of the proposed step. He said "If you propose to abolish liquor altogether I am with you heart and soul, but, if you do no more than abolish the bar-room, you will simply drive the liquor into the blacksmith's shop, the carpenter's shop and places like that."

With all respect to the Honorable gentleman I am unable to concur with him. He has not had the advantage of thirty-one years service as a Police Officer, nor has he ever had my active experience in enforcing a prohibitory law.

He does not know that the crimes such as theft, perjury and the general lowering of the moral sense begotten by a prohibitory law are ten times worse than the drink habit which it is intended to suppress. Do we not see day by day that a prohibitory law is absolutely unworkable! It is a punishable offence under the Indian Act for an Indian to have liquor and for any person to supply him with it.

Police records are surely sufficient to show that an Indian who wants liquor can always get it, notwithstanding that imprisonment is usually the punishment inflicted for supplying it.

After a drunken Indian shot Const. Davies, R.N.W.M.P. dead on the trail near Brooks in 1912,[15] the Attorney General [*C.W. Cross*], in a circular to Justices of the Peace, suggested that imprisonment rather than a fine was the more appropriate punishment for this offence [*drunkenness*].[16]

In the year ending the 30th September, 1913, there were 19 convictions under this head in the Calgary District alone, and sentences aggregating 62 months imprisonment were imposed.

---

[15] On the killing of Davies see Deane, Annual Report, 1912 in *SP 1913*, No.28, pp. 42-44; and Deane, Annual Report, 1913 in *SP 1914*, No.28, p.50.

[16] When handing out sentences to Indians found guilty of being drunk, Deane himself had long followed the practice of time in jail rather than a fine.

The point that I am getting at is this — if an Indian can obtain liquor with such facility, in spite of the attendant penalties, is it to be supposed that a whiteman is going to permit himself to be deprived of the same privilege?

The history of the early days in the West is a sufficient comment upon any supposition of the kind.

Here is where the woman of Alberta with her vote comes in, and I propose to address myself to her for a short space and give her the benefit, if she will accept it, of my experience of thirty years in North West Canada. I desire to preface my remarks by saying that the woman of the West has always had my heartfelt sympathy, for I know the work she has had to do, the children she has borne, the hardships she has undergone, and the few thanks that she has in many cases received. Some of the stories that I have heard of insane female patients who have passed through my Guard room in Calgary were enough to make one's heart bleed. One poor woman in the north who committed suicide left a letter for her husband and children saying that she simply could not stand the racket any longer — the demands made upon her as wife and mother, combined with the never ending drudgery of daily toil, had broken her spirit and made life unendurable. Thus she ended it.

Now, it is to this over-worked woman that I say "Agitate for the vote, and when you get it, abolish the bar," for thereinto goes a great deal of the money that should contribute to the welfare and comfort of yourself and your children.

I take upon myself to describe how the bar operates against a family's well-being.

My experience is taken from an American bar for the reason that I have nothing to do with bars in Western Canada. I have always throughout my service, held very strongly the belief that it was little short of criminal for a man to frequent illicit drinking places, or bars, etc., during illicit hours, when he might, in the course of his judicial duty, be called upon to sit in judgment upon a vendor who had previously supplied liquor illicitly or unlawfully to himself. There was far too much of that practice in the early days in the West and I always considered it so reprehensible that I would not participate in it.

That, Madame, is the reason why I have to go to Montana for the story I am now going to tell you, but the practice in Alberta differs little from that in Montana.

I was in Great Falls on duty in 1901, in connection with a horse stealing case, and, in the course of one evening while I was practically waiting in the hotel for bed-time to come, the son of the house accosted me and asked if I would have a drink at his expense. Without giving offence I could not very well say "no" and we went towards the bar together. On the way my host met a couple of men whom he invited to join us saying "I want you to know Captain Deane of the Canadian Mounted Police." While we were giving our orders at the bar another man looked in. "Come in George" said our host, "shake hands with Captain Deane" and so on.

This tactical move on the part of our host had secured a few rounds of drinks for the good of the house, the bar not having done much business that evening, and I very readily assimilated the fact.

The next round of drinks was of course at my expense and then there were at least three more rounds to follow mine, but as more men dropped in from time to time the circle became gradually enlarged until it was possible for me to slip away to bed. The bar-room was fairly full when I left it and considerable business was being done.

That, Madame Alberta, is how a great deal of your money goes, for the practice is universal. Can I not persuade you to agree with me that it would be very much better for a man to drink what he wants to drink in his own home, and give his wife a chance to have a sip if she wants to? He would be better off physically and financially if he were to take his beer with his dinner, instead of filling himself up with fluid beforehand in the same way that a horse is watered before he is fed his oats.

Now, Madame, I will give you another reason why bar-room drinking is to be deprecated. The cheapest drink that a man can buy at a bar costs him fifteen cents, that is, seven pence half-penny in English money. Think of it! When a glass of lager beer, which costs something less than ten cents a gallon to brew, costs a thirsty man fifteen cents, and a glass of whiskey and aerated water costs the same money, is it not extremely likely that the customer will think he is getting better value for his money if he chooses the whiskey instead of the beer.

The Calgary Brewing and Malting Company, in which, to my sorrow, I have not a penny of interest, and which is one of the

Superintendent R. Burton Deane, c. 1913
GA, NA-2172-12

In his mid-sixties, Deane remained a striking and formidable figure as this photograph demonstrates. He had always had a good horse and jealously guarded its use by others. The fine house in the background was used for a variety of purposes and actually was moved a couple of times in the years after the sale of the barracks. It is now the historic site known, appropriately, as Deane House. For this final picture as a Mounted Policeman Deane wore what was known as the Officer's Review Order uniform. By this time, even the superintendent's jacket was scarlet but with blue collar and epaulettes. Blue pants with gold stripe, white forage cap with dark leather headpiece and gold band on the peak, brown gloves, belts and boots, and ceremonial sword completed the outfit. However, the article of wear he seemed to like best was hidden from view — underwear. For some of the men the scratchy underclothing was torture, but even ten years after his retirement he was getting a supply from the quartermaster stores of the Calgary Division through the intercession of his son. It is fitting that, however far away from southern Alberta he may have been, to the end of his life, a piece of the Mounted Police uniform remained next to Deane's skin.

best paying propositions in the world, brews a lager beer which will bear favorable comparison with any other lager that is brewed. The manager of this Company proposed to the hotel keepers that if they would sell it across their bars at five cents per glass he would give it to them at a price which would enable the bars to make a handsome profit. What do you suppose was the reply of the bar-keepers? They absolutely refused to reduce the price below fifteen cents, and said they would boycott him if he made any such move.

If, Madame Alberta, you have been following me attentively, you would probably now be disposed to agree with me when I say that you and your husband can each have a pint bottle of excellent lager beer for dinner for less money than your man used to pay for his one drink at the bar.

Is that, do you think, one valid reason why you should help to put out of business an institution which has done its best to keep you poor?

Now, Madame, if you concede this much, you give the proverbial inch, and I propose to take the proverbial ell.[17] In short, I am going to tender to you some advice, which of course you will please yourself about accepting.

It is this: Do not be too hard upon your menkind in the matter of drink. I may tell you a case wherein a wife had a great trouble in that respect.

It happened after the Territorial Liquor License Law had superseded the Dominion Prohibitory Statute in 1892. An English lady and gentleman were ranching in the West — just where they were settled does not matter, but not within the limits of my district. They were very nice people and were doing fairly well but the husband became too fond of liquor, so much so that the family interests were endangered. The local ordinance provided that a justice of the peace might in such a case, upon complaint duly made and established, make an order forbidding every licensee in the Territories to sell the accused person any liquor for the space of one year. A complaint under this section entailed a hearing before a justice and a certain amount of publicity, which the wife under consideration was anxious to

---

[17] This was an earlier and less absurd form of the current saying "give him an inch and he'll take a mile." An ell was a measure of length used mainly for measuring cloth. In England an ell was forty-five inches.

avoid. The same ordinance contained a provision that "Any husband or wife whose wife or husband has contracted the habit of drinking intoxicating liquors to excess may require the license inspector for the district to give notice in writing to every licensee in the license district that he is not to sell or deliver any liquor to the person named."

In order to avoid all possible publicity, the poor lady betook herself to the License Inspector, who issued the requisite notices, and the husband was duly interdicted.

After a time the man grew restive under this prohibition and wanted to have it removed, but he and his wife found to their mutual astonishment that the law had set no limit to the prohibition of a license inspector, and, in her distress, the lady came to me, probably because I was not officially concerned with the police district in which she lived.

The husband submitted to the interdiction for a time but as under the wording of the ordinance, it was interminable, he became very hostile and his wife told me that she was afraid to live with him. I could but advise her that the only lawful way out of the difficulty was to have the law amended at the next session of the Legislature, and this was done in the year 1900 when the License Inspector's interdiction was limited to one year. "But in the meanwhile," queried the unhappy lady, "what am I to do?"

I replied that I knew of a case in Lethbridge where the wife kept some liquor in the house, and gave her husband as much as she thought good for him, and that he was glad to get it on those terms. I never saw the lady afterwards, so do not know how the difficulty settled itself.

Another case that I have in my mind's eye is that of a prominent official who has been married for more than thirty years and who has led his wife to believe during all that time that he does not touch a drop of intoxicating liquor.

When he is away from home he drinks like a fish, but when he is at home he never takes a drop.

He has a son of whom the late Paddy Nolan, K.C. told me the last time I saw him — "The boy is a chip of the old block" said he — "He and Papa were in the Club last night, and as long as Papa was there he would not take anything stronger than ginger beer. But after Papa had kissed us all goodnight and gone off to catch his train, somebody asked the boy if he wouldn't change his mind and have a little scotch and soda, and he did change his mind, and afterwards took whatever was going."

Now, Madame Alberta, a man who can successfully deceive his family for more than thirty years must be saturated with hypocrisy and deceit. Can you accept his unsupported word in the everyday transactions of life wherein his interests happen to conflict with yours? I have abundant proof that you cannot. Is it worth while for the sake of a little liquor to drive men into lifelong deceit?

If I may take the liberty, I would advise you to have nothing to do with what is called across the border a "Dry State." In the early days of the Canadian West, rich and influential persons in the East used to send their sons into the Mounted Police believing that they could not in the West obtain the liquors to which they had become addicted.

No greater mistake was every made in this world. In the East, the boys drank too much, but, if they got drunk, they got drunk on good honest liquor, whereas in the prohibitory days of the West they became crazed on the vile decotions that were purchasable at a very high figure. History will repeat itself, and inferior liquors will be smuggled into the country if any prohibitory law should be enacted.

Index